AF115587

Pharo 9 by Example

Stéphane Ducasse and Gordana Rakic with Sebastijan Kaplar and Quentin Ducasse

March 26, 2022

Copyright 2021 by Stéphane Ducasse and Gordana Rakic with Sebastijan Kaplar and Quentin Ducasse.

The contents of this book are protected under the Creative Commons Attribution-ShareAlike 3.0 Unported license.

You are **free**:

- to **Share**: to copy, distribute and transmit the work,
- to **Remix**: to adapt the work,

Under the following conditions:

Attribution. You must attribute the work in the manner specified by the author or licensor (but not in any way that suggests that they endorse you or your use of the work).

Share Alike. If you alter, transform, or build upon this work, you may distribute the resulting work only under the same, similar or a compatible license.

For any reuse or distribution, you must make clear to others the license terms of this work. The best way to do this is with a link to this web page:
http://creativecommons.org/licenses/by-sa/3.0/

Any of the above conditions can be waived if you get permission from the copyright holder. Nothing in this license impairs or restricts the author's moral rights.

Your fair dealing and other rights are in no way affected by the above. This is a human-readable summary of the Legal Code (the full license):
http://creativecommons.org/licenses/by-sa/3.0/legalcode

Keepers of the lighthouse
Édition: BoD – Books on Demand, info@bod.fr
Impression : BoD – Books on Demand, In de Tarpen 42,
Norderstedt (Allemagne)
Impression à la demande
ISBN: 9782322394104
Dépôt légal: Mai 2022
Layout and typography based on the sbabook LaTeX class by Damien Pollet. Layout and typography based on the sbabook LaTeX class by Damien Pollet.
Cover photo by Joseph Guégan

Contents

Illustrations — viii

1 About this book — 1
1.1 What is Pharo? — 2
1.2 Who should read this book? — 3
1.3 A word of advice — 4
1.4 An open book — 4
1.5 The Pharo community — 5
1.6 Examples and exercises — 5
1.7 Typographic conventions — 6
1.8 Acknowledgments — 6
1.9 Hyper special acknowledgments — 7

2 Getting Started with Pharo — 9
2.1 Installing Pharo — 9
2.2 File components — 10
2.3 Launching Pharo with the Pharo Launcher — 11
2.4 Launching Pharo via the command line — 12
2.5 Saving, quitting and restarting a Pharo session — 14
2.6 For the fast and furious — 15
2.7 Chapter summary — 16

3 A quick tour of Pharo — 17
3.1 The World Menu — 17
3.2 Interacting with Pharo — 18
3.3 Playgrounds and Transcripts — 20
3.4 Keyboard shortcuts — 21
3.5 Doing vs. printing — 21
3.6 Inspect — 22
3.7 Other operations — 23
3.8 Calypso: the System Browser — 24
3.9 Chapter summary — 26

4	**Finding information in Pharo**	**27**
4.1	Navigating using the System Browser	27
4.2	Finding classes	28
4.3	Finding methods	30
4.4	Finding Methods using Examples	32
4.5	Conclusion	33

5	**A first tutorial: Developing a simple counter**	**35**
5.1	Our use case	36
5.2	Create a package and class	36
5.3	Defining protocols and methods	38
5.4	Create a method	39
5.5	Adding a setter method	41
5.6	Define a Test Class	41
5.7	Saving your code as a git repository with Iceberg	43
5.8	Adding more messages	47
5.9	Instance initialization method	47
5.10	Define an initialize method	48
5.11	Define a new instance creation method	49
5.12	Better object description	50
5.13	Saving your code on a remote server	51
5.14	Conclusion	53

6	**Building a little game**	**55**
6.1	The Lights Out game	56
6.2	Creating a new package	56
6.3	Defining the class `LOCell`	56
6.4	Creating a new class	57
6.5	About comments	58
6.6	Adding methods to a class	59
6.7	Inspecting an object	61
6.8	Defining the class `LOGame`	64
6.9	Initializing our game	64
6.10	Taking advantage of the Debugger	65
6.11	Studying the initialize method	67
6.12	Organizing methods into protocols	69
6.13	Finishing the game	69
6.14	Final `LOCell` methods	71
6.15	Using the Debugger	72
6.16	And if all else fails...	74
6.17	Saving and sharing Pharo code	75
6.18	Saving code in a file	75
6.19	Accessor conventions	75
6.20	Chapter summary	77

Contents

7	**Publishing and packaging your first Pharo project**	**79**
7.1	For the impatient	79
7.2	Basic architecture	80
7.3	Iceberg repositories browser	82
7.4	Add a new project to Iceberg	83
7.5	Add and commit your package using the 'Working copy' browser	87
7.6	What if I did not create a remote repository?	90
7.7	Configuring your project	92
7.8	Loading from an existing repository	93
7.9	Stepping back...	94
7.10	Conclusion	95

8	**Syntax in a nutshell**	**97**
8.1	Syntactic elements	97
8.2	Pseudo-variables	101
8.3	Messages and message sends	101
8.4	Sequences and cascades	102
8.5	Method syntax	103
8.6	Block syntax	104
8.7	Conditionals and loops	105
8.8	Method annotations: Primitives and pragmas	107
8.9	Chapter summary	108

9	**Understanding message syntax**	**111**
9.1	Identifying messages	111
9.2	Three kinds of messages	113
9.3	Message composition	116
9.4	Hints for identifying keyword messages	122
9.5	Expression sequences	124
9.6	Cascaded messages	124
9.7	Chapter summary	125

10	**The Pharo object model**	**127**
10.1	The rules of the core model	127
10.2	Everything is an Object	128
10.3	Every object is an instance of a class	129
10.4	Instance structure and behavior	129
10.5	Every class has a superclass	131
10.6	Everything happens by sending messages	132
10.7	Sending a message: a two-step process	134
10.8	Method lookup follows the inheritance chain	135
10.9	Method execution	135
10.10	Message not understood	137
10.11	About returning self	138

10.12	Overriding and extension	138
10.13	Self and super sends	139
10.14	Stepping back	141
10.15	The instance and class sides	142
10.16	Class methods	144
10.17	Class instance variables	145
10.18	Example: Class instance variables and subclasses	145
10.19	Stepping back	147
10.20	Example: Defining a Singleton	147
10.21	A note on lazy initialization	149
10.22	Shared variables	149
10.23	Class variables: Shared variables	151
10.24	Pool variables	153
10.25	Abstract methods and abstract classes	154
10.26	Example: the abstract class `Magnitude`	154
10.27	Chapter summary	155
11	**Traits: reusable class fragments**	**157**
11.1	A simple trait	157
11.2	Using a required method	158
11.3	Self in a trait is the message receiver	159
11.4	Trait state	159
11.5	A class can use two traits	160
11.6	Overriding method takes precedence over trait methods	161
11.7	Accessing overridden trait methods	162
11.8	Handling conflict	162
11.9	Conflict resolution: excluding a method	163
11.10	Conflict resolution: redefining the method	164
11.11	Conclusion	164
12	**SUnit: Tests in Pharo**	**165**
12.1	Introduction	165
12.2	Why testing is important	166
12.3	What makes a good test?	167
12.4	SUnit step by step	167
12.5	Step 1: Create the test class	168
12.6	Step 2: Initialize the test context	168
12.7	Step 3: Write some test methods	168
12.8	Step 4: Run the tests	169
12.9	Step 5: Interpret the results	170
12.10	Using `assert:equals:`	171
12.11	Skipping a test	171
12.12	Asserting exceptions	172
12.13	Programmatically running tests	172

| 12.14 | Conclusion | 173 |

13 Basic classes — 175

13.1	Object	175
13.2	Object printing	176
13.3	Representation and self-evaluating representation	177
13.4	Identity and equality	179
13.5	Class membership	180
13.6	About `isKindOf:` and `respondTo:`	181
13.7	Shallow copying objects	181
13.8	Deep copying objects	181
13.9	Debugging	182
13.10	Error handling	183
13.11	Testing	185
13.12	Initialize	185
13.13	Numbers	186
13.14	Magnitude	187
13.15	Numbers	187
13.16	Floats	188
13.17	Fractions	189
13.18	Integers	189
13.19	Characters	190
13.20	Strings	191
13.21	Booleans	193
13.22	Chapter summary	194

14 Collections — 197

14.1	High-order functions	198
14.2	The varieties of collections	199
14.3	Collection implementations	200
14.4	Examples of key classes	201
14.5	Common creation protocol	202
14.6	Array	203
14.7	`OrderedCollection`	205
14.8	`Interval`	206
14.9	`Dictionary`	206
14.10	`IdentityDictionary`	207
14.11	`Set`	208
14.12	`SortedCollection`	209
14.13	`Strings`	210
14.14	Collection iterators	215
14.15	Collecting results (`collect:`)	216
14.16	Selecting and rejecting elements	218
14.17	Other high-order messages	219

14.18	A common mistake: using `add: result`	219
14.19	A common mistake: Removing an element while iterating	220
14.20	A common mitaske: Redefining = but not `hash`	220
14.21	Chapter summary	221

15 Streams — 223

15.1	Two sequences of elements	223
15.2	Streams vs. collections	224
15.3	Reading collections	225
15.4	Peek	226
15.5	Positioning to an index	227
15.6	Skipping elements	227
15.7	Predicates	228
15.8	Writing to collections	229
15.9	About string concatenation	230
15.10	About printString	231
15.11	Reading and writing at the same time	233
15.12	Chapter summary	236

16 Morphic — 237

16.1	The history of Morphic	237
16.2	Morphs	238
16.3	Manipulating morphs	240
16.4	Composing morphs	241
16.5	Creating and drawing your own morphs	242
16.6	Mouse events for interaction	246
16.7	Keyboard events	247
16.8	Morphic animations	248
16.9	Interactors	249
16.10	Drag-and-drop	250
16.11	A complete example	253
16.12	More about the canvas	257
16.13	Chapter summary	258

17 Classes and metaclasses — 259

17.1	Rules for classes	259
17.2	Metaclasses	260
17.3	Revisiting the Pharo object model	260
17.4	Every class is an instance of a metaclass	261
17.5	Querying Metaclasses	263
17.6	The metaclass hierarchy parallels the class hierarchy	263
17.7	Uniformity between Classes and Objects	264
17.8	Inspecting objects and classes	266
17.9	Every metaclass inherits from `Class` and `Behavior`	266

17.10	Responsibilities of `Behavior`, `ClassDescription`, and `Class`	268
17.11	Every metaclass is an instance of `Metaclass`	269
17.12	The metaclass of `Metaclass` is an instance of `Metaclass`	269
17.13	Chapter summary	271

18 Reflection — 273

18.1	Reflection in a nutshell	273
18.2	Introspection	274
18.3	Accessing instance variables	275
18.4	About reflective behavior	276
18.5	About primitives	277
18.6	Querying classes and interfaces	277
18.7	Simple code metrics	278
18.8	Browsing instances	279
18.9	From methods to instance variables	280
18.10	About SystemNavigation	281
18.11	Classes, method dictionaries, and methods	282
18.12	Browsing environments	285
18.13	Pragmas: method annotation	286
18.14	Accessing the run-time context	288
18.15	Intelligent contextual breakpoints	289
18.16	Intercepting not understood messages	291
18.17	Lightweight proxies	291
18.18	Generating missing methods	294
18.19	Objects as method wrappers	296
18.20	Chapter summary	297

Illustrations

1-1	Small example.	6
2-1	Pharo Launcher - the easy way to manage your Pharo images.	12
2-2	When Pharo opens you should see the following.	13
2-3	Executing an expression is simple with the **Do it** menu item.	15
2-4	ProfStef is a simple interactive tutorial to learn about Pharo syntax.	16
3-1	World menu (left click) brings the world menu.	18
3-2	Action Click (right click) brings the contextual menu.	19
3-3	Meta-Clicking on a window opens the Halos.	19
3-4	Executing an expression: displaying a string in the Transcript.	21
3-5	Inspecting a simple number using `Inspect`.	22
3-6	Inspecting a Morph using `Inspect`.	23
3-7	The System Browser shows the `slowFactorial` method of the class `Integer`.	24
3-8	The System Browser showing the `printString` method of class `Object`.	25
4-1	Using Spotter `Shift-Enter` to browse the class `Point`.	29
4-2	Looking for implementors matching `printString`.	30
4-3	The Finder tool	31
4-4	Looking for a method that given the string `'eureka'` returns the string `'EUREKA'`.	32
5-1	Package created and class creation template.	37
5-2	Class created: It inherits from `Object` class and has one instance variable named `count`.	38
5-3	Counter class has now a comment! Well done.	39
5-4	The method editor selected and ready to define a method.	40
5-5	The method `count` defined in the protocol *accessing*.	41
5-6	A first test is defined and it passes.	42
5-7	Iceberg *Repositories* browser on a fresh image indicates that if you want to version modifications to Pharo itself you will have to tell Iceberg where the Pharo clone is located. But you do not care.	44
5-8	Add and create a project named MyCounter and with the `src` subdirectory.	44
5-9	Selecting the Add package iconic button, add your package MyCounter to your project.	45

5-10	Now Iceberg shows you that you did not commit your code.	46
5-11	Iceberg shows you the changes about to be committed.	46
5-12	Once you save your change, Iceberg shows you that.	47
5-13	Class with more green tests.	48
5-14	Counter instance better description.	50
5-15	A *Repository* browser opened on your project.	51
5-16	GitHub HTTPS address our our project.	52
5-17	Using the GitHub HTTPS address.	52
5-18	Commits sent to the remote repository.	53
6-1	The Lights Out game board.	55
6-2	Create a Package and class template.	56
6-3	Filtering our package to work more efficiently.	57
6-4	LOCell class definition	57
6-5	The newly-created class LOCell.	58
6-6	Initializing instance of LOCell	59
6-7	The newly-created method `initialize`.	60
6-8	The inspector used to examine a LOCell object.	62
6-9	When we click on an instance variable, we inspect its value (another object).	62
6-10	A LOCell opened in the **World**.	63
6-11	Defining the LOGame class	64
6-12	Initialize the game	64
6-13	Declaring `cells` as a new instance variable.	65
6-14	Pharo detecting an unknown selector.	65
6-15	The system created a new method with a body to be defined.	66
6-16	Defining `cellsPerSide` in the debugger.	67
6-17	Initialize the game	67
6-18	The callback method	70
6-19	Drag a method to a protocol.	71
6-20	A typical setter method	71
6-21	An event handler	71
6-22	The Debugger, with the method `toggleNeighboursOfCell:at:` selected.	73
6-23	Fixing the bug.	73
6-24	Overriding mouse move actions	74
6-25	File out the `PBE-LightsOut` package.	76
6-26	Import your code with the file browser.	76
7-1	Git: A distributed versioning system.	80
7-2	Create a new project on GitHub.	81
7-3	Use Custom SSH keys settings.	81
7-4	Iceberg *Repositories* browser on a fresh image indicates that if you want to version modifications to Pharo itself you will have to tell Iceberg where the Pharo clone is located. But you do not care.	82
7-5	Cloning a project hosted on GitHub via SSH.	83

7-6	Cloning a project hosted on GitHub via HTTPS.	83
7-7	Just after cloning an empty project, Iceberg reports that the project is missing information.	84
7-8	Adding a project with some contents shows that the project is not loaded - not that it is not found.	84
7-9	Create project metadata action and explanation.	85
7-10	Showing where the metadata will be saved and the file encoding.	86
7-11	Adding a src repository for code storage.	86
7-12	Resulting situation with a src folder: Pay attention to select it.	87
7-13	Details of metadata commit.	87
7-14	Adding a package to your project using the *Working copy* browser.	88
7-15	Iceberg indicates that your project has unsaved changes – indeed you just added your package.	88
7-16	When you commit changes, Iceberg shows you the code about to be committed and you can chose the code entities that will effectively be saved.	89
7-17	Once changes committed, Iceberg reflects that your project is in sync with the code in your local repository.	89
7-18	Publishing your committed changes.	89
7-19	Creating a local repository without pre-existing remote repository.	90
7-20	Opening the repository browser let you add and browse branches as well as remote repositories.	91
7-21	Adding a remote using the *Repository* browser of your project (SSH version).	91
7-22	Adding a remote using the *Repository* browser of your project (HTTP version).	91
7-23	Once you pushed you changes to the remote repository.	92
7-24	Added the baseline package to your project using the *Working copy* browser.	93
9-1	Two message sends composed of a receiver, a method selector, and a set of arguments.	112
9-2	Two messages: `Color yellow` and `aMorph color: Color yellow`.	112
9-3	Unary messages are sent first so Color yellow is sent. This returns a color object which is passed as argument of the message aPen color:.	116
9-4	Binary messages are sent before keyword messages.	118
9-5	Decomposing Pen new go: 100 + 20.	118
9-6	Decomposing Pen new down.	120
9-7	Default execution order.	121
9-8	Changing default execution order using parentheses.	122
9-9	Equivalent messages using parentheses.	122
9-10	Equivalent messages using parentheses.	122
10-1	Sending `+ 4` to 3 yields the object 7.	128
10-2	Sending `factorial` to 20 yields a large number.	128
10-3	Sending `today` to class `Date` yields the current date	128
10-4	Sending `allInstVarNames` to class `Date` returns the instance variables	129
10-5	Distance between two points.	130

10-6	The definition of the class `Point`.	132
10-7	Sending message + with argument 4 to integer 3.	132
10-8	Sending message + with argument 4 to point (1@2).	133
10-9	A locally implemented method.	135
10-10	An inherited method.	135
10-11	Method lookup follows the inheritance hierarchy.	136
10-12	Another locally implemented method.	136
10-13	Message `foo` is not understood.	137
10-14	Explicitly returning `self`.	138
10-15	Super initialize.	139
10-16	A `self` send.	140
10-17	A `self` send.	140
10-18	Combining `super` and `self` sends.	140
10-19	`self` and `super` sends.	141
10-20	Browsing a class and its metaclass.	143
10-21	The class method `blue` (defined on the class-side).	144
10-22	Using the accessor method `red` (defined on the instance-side).	144
10-23	Using the accessor method `blue` (defined on the instance-side).	144
10-24	Dog class definition.	145
10-25	Adding a class instance variable.	145
10-26	Hyena class definition.	146
10-27	Initialize the count of dogs.	146
10-28	Keeping count of new dogs.	146
10-29	Accessing to count.	146
10-30	.	147
10-31	New state for classes.	148
10-32	Class-side accessor method `uniqueInstance`.	148
10-33	Instance and class methods accessing different variables.	151
10-34	Color and its class variables.	152
10-35	Using Lazy initialization.	152
10-36	Initializing the `Color` class.	153
10-37	Pool dictionaries in the `Text` class.	153
10-38	`Text>>testCR`.	153
10-39	`Magnitude>> <`.	155
10-40	`Magnitude>> >=`.	155
10-41	`Character>> <=`.	155
11-1	A simple trait.	158
12-1	An Example Set Test class	168
12-2	Running SUnit tests from the System Browser.	170
12-3	Testing error raising	172

13-1	printOn: redefinition.	177
13-2	Self-evaluation of `Point`	178
13-3	Self-evaluation of `Interval`	179
13-4	Object equality.	179
13-5	Copying objects as a template method	182
13-6	Checking a pre-condition	183
13-7	Signaling that a method is abstract	184
13-8	`initialize` as an empty hook method	185
13-9	new as a class-side template method	186
13-10	The number hierarchy.	186
13-11	Abstract comparison methods	187
13-12	The String Hierarchy.	191
13-13	The Boolean Hierarchy.	193
13-14	Implementations of `ifTrue:ifFalse:`	193
13-15	Implementing negation	194
14-1	Some of the key collection classes in Pharo.	198
14-2	Some collection classes categorized by implementation technique.	201
14-3	Redefining = and `hash`.	221
15-1	A stream positioned at its beginning.	223
15-2	The same stream after the execution of the method `next`: the character a is *in the past* whereas b, c, d and e are *in the future*.	224
15-3	The same stream after having written an x.	224
15-4	A stream at position 2.	227
15-5	A new history is empty. Nothing is displayed in the web browser.	233
15-6	The user opens to page 1.	233
15-7	The user clicks on a link to page 2.	233
15-8	The user clicks on a link to page 3.	233
15-9	The user clicks on the Back button. They are now viewing page 2 again.	234
15-10	The user clicks again the back button. Page 1 is now displayed.	234
15-11	From page 1, the user clicks on a link to page 4. The history forgets pages 2 and 3.	234
16-1	Detaching a morph, here the `Playground` menu item, to make it an independent button.	238
16-2	Dropping the menu item on the desktop, here the `Playground` menu item is now an independent button.	238
16-3	Creation of a String Morph	239
16-4	`(Morph new color: Color orange) openInWorld.`	239
16-5	Bill and Joe after 10 moves.	241
16-6	Bill follows Joe.	242
16-7	The balloon is contained inside joe, the translucent orange morph.	242
16-8	A `CrossMorph` with its halo; you can resize it as you wish.	243

16-9	The center of the cross is filled twice with the color.	245
16-10	The cross-shaped morph, showing a row of unfilled pixels.	245
16-11	An input dialog.	250
16-12	Pop-up menu.	250
16-13	A `ReceiverMorph` and an `EllipseMorph`.	252
16-14	Creation of `DroppedMorph` and `ReceiverMorph`.	253
16-15	The die in Morphic.	253
16-16	Create a Die 6	256
16-17	A new die 6 with `(DieMorph faces: 6) openInWorld`	256
16-18	Result of `(DieMorph faces: 6) openInWorld; dieValue: 5`.	257
16-19	The die displayed with alpha-transparency	258
17-1	Sending the message `class` to a sorted collection	261
17-2	The metaclasses of `SortedCollection` and its superclasses (elided).	262
17-3	The metaclass hierarchy parallels the class hierarchy (elided).	263
17-4	Message lookup for classes is the same as for ordinary objects.	264
17-5	Classes are objects too.	265
17-6	Metaclasses inherit from `Class` and `Behavior`.	267
17-7	`new` is an ordinary message looked up in the metaclass chain.	268
17-8	Every metaclass is a `Metaclass`.	270
17-9	All metaclasses are instances of the class `Metaclass`, even the metaclass of `Metaclass`.	270
18-1	Reification and reflection.	274
18-2	Inspecting a `StPlayground`.	275
18-3	Browse all implementations of `ifTrue:`.	282
18-4	Inspector on class `Point` and the bytecode of its `#*` method.	283
18-5	Classes, method dictionaries, and compiled methods	283
18-6	Finding methods that send a different super message.	286
18-7	Inspecting `thisContext`.	289
18-8	Dynamically creating accessors.	295

CHAPTER 1

About this book

This version of the book is based on the previous version authored by Andrew P. Black, Stéphane Ducasse, Oscar Nierstrasz, Damien Pollet, Damien Cassou and Marcus Denker called, *Pharo by Example*. It also builds on the version that was issued for Pharo 50, *Updated Pharo by Example*, authored by Stéphane Ducasse and edited by Dmitri Zagidulin, Nicolai Hess, and Dimitris Chloupis.

Many aspects of Pharo's tooling have changed since the last edition, and we have worked hard to cover these changes:

- We have reorganized the beginning of the book to get shorter chapters.
- We have introduced a new 'first contact' chapter with a simple counter example. This lets the reader see the most important operations to define a class, its tests, and save its code.
- We briefly cover the new system browser, Calypso, as well as the Pharo Launcher.
- We have introduced a new chapter covering Iceberg and package management. A larger book on Pharo and git is available at http://books.pharo.org.
- We added a new chapter on Traits.
- We have simplified the SUnit chapter, since a companion book is now available at http://books.pharo.org/
- We have revised parts of the book that were wrong in previous editions, such as the Morphic chapter; the current version is a considerable improvement over *Pharo by Example 5*.

Pharo by Example has received many edits, modifications and updates to bring it into line with the current version of Pharo. It does not magically update itself; improvements are the result of many people's hard work; one does not simply change a '5.0' to a '9'. This is why I decided, as one of the original and main authors of the book over the years, to invite Sebastijan, Gordana and Quentin to be listed as authors of *Pharo by Example 9*.

1.1 What is Pharo?

Pharo is a modern, open-source, dynamically-typed language that supports live coding and is inspired by Smalltalk. Pharo and its ecosystem are composed of six fundamental elements:

- A dynamically-typed language with a minimalist syntax, similar to natural language writing, that can fit on a postcard and be read by people who are unfamiliar with it.
- A live coding environment that allows the programmer to seamlessly modify their code as it executes.
- A powerful IDE providing tools to help manage complex code and promote good design.
- A rich library that creates an environment so powerful that it can be viewed as a virtual OS, including a very fast JITing VM and full access to OS libraries and features via its FFI.
- A culture where changes and improvements are encouraged and highly valued.
- A community that welcomes coders from any corner of the world, of any skill level or experience, in any programming language.

Pharo strives to offer a lean, open platform for professional software development, as well as a robust and stable platform for research and development into dynamic languages and environments. Pharo serves as the reference implementation for the Seaside web development framework, available at http://www.seaside.st.

Pharo's core contains only code that has been contributed under the MIT license. The Pharo project started in March 2008 as a fork of Squeak (a modern implementation of Smalltalk-80), and the first 1.0 beta version was released on July 31, 2009. Since then, Pharo has reached a new version every year or year and a half. The current version is Pharo 9.0, released in July 2021.

Pharo is highly portable. Pharo can run on OS X, Windows, Linux, Android, iOS, and Raspberry Pi. Its virtual machine is written entirely in a subset of Pharo, making it easy to simulate, debug, analyze, and change from within

Pharo itself. Pharo is the vehicle for a wide range of innovative projects, from multimedia applications and educational platforms to commercial web development environments.

There is an important principle behind Pharo: Pharo does not just copy the past, it *reinvents* the essence of Smalltalk. However, we realize that Big Bang style approaches that start from scratch rarely succeed. Pharo instead favors evolutionary and incremental changes. Rather than leaping for the perfect solution in one big step, a multitude of small changes keeps even the bleeding edge relatively stable while allowing us to experiment with important new features and libraries. This facilitates contributions and rapid feedback from the community, which Pharo relies on for its success. Finally, Pharo is not read-only: changes from the community are integrated daily. Pharo has around 100 contributors, based all over the world. You can have an impact on Pharo too! Just take a look at http://github.com/pharo-project/pharo.

1.2 Who should read this book?

This book will not teach you how to program. The reader should have some familiarity with programming languages. Some background in object-oriented programming would also be helpful.

The current book will introduce the Pharo programming environment, the language, and the associated tools. You will be exposed to common idioms and practices, but the focus is on the technology, not on object-oriented design. We will show you good, illustrative examples as often as possible.

The Pharo MOOC

An excellent MOOC (Massive open online course) for Pharo is freely available at http://mooc.pharo.org. The MOOC makes for a good introduction to Pharo and object-oriented programming, and complements this book well.

Further reading

This book will not teach you everything you need, or want, to learn about Pharo. Here is a short commented list of other books that you can find at http://books.pharo.org:

- *Learning Object-Oriented Programming, Design and TDD with Pharo.* This book teaches the key aspects of object-oriented design and test-driven development. A good book to learn about object-oriented programming.

- *Pharo with Style.* This book is a must read. It discusses how to write good and readable Pharo code. In just one hour, you will boost the standard of your code.
- *The Spec UI framework.* This book will show you how to develop standard user interface applications in Pharo.

More technical books are:

- *Managing your code with Iceberg.* This book covers how to manage your code with git in further detail.
- *Enterprise Pharo.* This book contains different chapters relating to the web, converters, reporting, and documentation that you need for delivering applications.
- *Deep into Pharo.* This book covers more advanced topics than *Pharo by Example*.

And there are also books to expand your mind:

- *A simple reflective object kernel* revisits all the fundamental points of "objects all the way down" by taking you on a little journey to build a reflective language core. It is truly excellent.

In addition, there are numerous other books on Smalltalk freely available at http://stephane.ducasse.free.fr/FreeBooks.html.

1.3 A word of advice

Do not be frustrated by parts of Pharo that you do not immediately understand: *You do not have to know everything.* Alan Knight expresses this as follows:

Try not to care. Beginning Pharo programmers often have trouble because they think they need to understand all the details of how a thing works before they can use it. This means it takes quite a while before they can master `Transcript show: 'Hello World'`. One of the great leaps in OO [object-oriented programming] is to be able to answer the question "How does this work?" with "I don't care".

When you do not understand something, simple or complex, do not hesitate to ask us on our mailing lists (pharo-users@lists.pharo.org or pharo-dev@lists.pharo.org), IRC and Discord. We love questions and we welcome people of any skill.

1.4 An open book

This book is an open book in the following senses:

- The content of this book is released under the Creative Commons Attribution-ShareAlike (by-sa) license. In short, you are allowed to freely share and adapt this book, as long as you respect the conditions of the license available at the following URL http://creativecommons.org/licenses/by-sa/3.0/.

- This book just describes the core of Pharo. We encourage others to contribute chapters on the parts of Pharo that we have not described. If you would like to participate in this effort, please contact us. We would like to see more books about Pharo!

- It is also possible to contribute directly to this book via GitHub. Just follow the instructions there and ask any questions you have on the mailing list, IRC or Discord. You can find the GitHub repo at https://github.com/SquareBracketAssociates/PharoByExample90

1.5 The Pharo community

The Pharo community is friendly and active. Here is a short list of resources that you may find useful:

- http://www.pharo.org is the main web site of Pharo.

- http://www.github.com/pharo-project/pharo is the main GitHub account for Pharo.

- Pharo has an active on Discord server - a platform for chat based on IRC, just ask for an invitation on Pharo's website http://pharo.org/community, in the Discord section. Everybody is welcome.

- Pharoers started a wiki on Pharo: https://github.com/pharo-open-documentation/pharo-wiki

- An Awesome catalog is maintained with projects: https://github.com/pharo-open-documentation/awesome-pharo

- If you hear about SmalltalkHub, http://www.smalltalkhub.com/ was the equivalent of SourceForge/GitHub for Pharo projects for about 10 years. Many extra packages and projects for Pharo lived there. Now the community is mainly using git repositories such as GitHub, GitLab, and Bitbucket.

1.6 Examples and exercises

We have tried to provide as many examples as possible. In particular, there are examples that show a fragment of code which can be evaluated. We use a

Listing 1-1 Small example
```
3 + 4
>>> 7   "if you select 3+4 and 'print it', you will see 7"
```

long arrow to indicate the result you obtain when you select an expression and from its context menu and choose **print it**:

In case you want to play with these code snippets in Pharo, you can download a plain text file with all the example code from the Resources sidebar of the original book's web site: http://books.pharo.org/pharo-by-example.

1.7 Typographic conventions

We always prefix method source code with the class of the method. This way you can also know of which class the method is.

For example, the book shows a method as:

```
MyExampleSetTest >> testIncludes
    | full empty |
    full := Set with: 5 with: 6.
    empty := Set new.
    self assert: (full includes: 5).
    self assert: (full includes: 6).
    self assert: (empty includes: 5) not
```

And if you want to type it into Pharo you should type the following in the corresponding class.

```
testIncludes
    | full empty |
    full := Set with: 5 with: 6.
    empty := Set new.
    self assert: (full includes: 5).
    self assert: (full includes: 6).
    self assert: (empty includes: 5) not
```

1.8 Acknowledgments

We would like to thank Alan Kay, Dan Ingalls and their team for making Squeak, an amazing Smalltalk development environment, that became the open-source project from which Pharo took root. Pharo also would not be possible without the incredible work of the Squeak developers.

We would also like to thank Hilaire Fernandes and Serge Stinckwich who allowed us to translate parts of their columns on Smalltalk, and Damien Cassou for contributing the chapter on Streams. We especially thank Alexandre Bergel, Orla Greevy, Fabrizio Perin, Lukas Renggli, Jorge Ressia and Erwann Wernli for their detailed reviews. We thank the University of Bern, Switzerland, for graciously supporting this open-source project and for hosting the web site of this book for some years.

We also thank the Pharo community for their enthusiastic support of this book project, as well as for all the translations of the first edition of *Pharo by Example*.

1.9 Hyper special acknowledgments

We want to thank the original authors of this book! Without the initial version it would have been difficult to make this one. *Pharo by Example* is a central book for Pharo to welcome newcomers, it has immense value.

Special thank to David Wickes for his massive copy-edit pass.

Thanks to Adrian Sampaleanu, Manfred Kröhnert, Markus Schlager, Werner Kassens, Michael OKeefe, Aryeh Hoffman, Paul MacIntosh, Gaurav Singh, Jigyasa Grover, Craig Allen, Serge Stinckwich, avh-on1, Yuriy Timchuk, ziopietro, Vivien Moreau, Liwei Chou for the typos and feedback. Special thanks to Damien Cassou and Cyril Ferlicot for their great help in the book update.

Finally we want to thank Inria for its steady and important financial support, and the RMoD team members for the constant energy pushing Pharo forward. We want to thank also the Pharo consortium members.

Super special thanks to Damien Pollet for this great book template and Joseph Guégan for giving us the right to use his great picture of the Eckmuhl lighthouse' staircase.

S. Ducasse, S. Kaplar, Gordana Rakic, and Q. Ducasse

CHAPTER 2

Getting Started with Pharo

In this chapter, you will learn how to start Pharo and the different files that make up a Pharo system and the roles they perform, learn about the different ways of interacting with the system, and discover some of the basic tools. You will also learn how to define a new method, create an object, and send it messages. The chapter shows (1) how to install Pharo and (2) how to launch Pharo.

2.1 Installing Pharo

Pharo does not need to install anything in your system, as it's perfectly capable of running standalone. As will be explained later, Pharo consists of a virtual machine (VM), an image, a set of changes and a set of sources. There are a number of different ways of getting these installed and set up on your system.

The Pharo Launcher

Pharo Launcher is a cross-platform application that facilitates the management of multiple Pharo images and VMs. It is available as a free download from http://pharo.org/download. Click the button for your operating system to download the appropriate Pharo Launcher; it contains everything you need to run Pharo.

Zeroconf scripts

Alternatively, https://get.pharo.org/ offers a collection of scripts to download specific versions of Pharo. This is really handy for automating the installation of Pharo, or if you prefer to work using your operating system's command line interface.

To download the latest Pharo 9.0 full system, use the following snippet:

```
wget -O- get.pharo.org/90+vm | bash
```

Then you can execute the following to start the image:

```
./pharo-ui Pharo.image
```

At present these scripts will only work on a a macOS or Linux system.

2.2 File components

Pharo consists of four main component files. Although you do not need to deal with them directly for the purposes of this book, it is useful to understand the role that they each play.

1. The **virtual machine** (VM) is the only component that is different for each operating system. The VM is the execution engine (similar to the Java Virtual Machine). It takes Pharo bytecode that is generated each time a user compiles a piece of code, converts it to machine code, and then executes it. Pharo comes with the Cog VM, a very fast JITing VM.

The VM executable is named:

- `Pharo.exe` for Windows,
- `pharo` for Linux, and
- `Pharo` for macOS (inside a package also named `Pharo.app`).

The other components listed below are portable across operating systems, and can be copied and run on any appropriate virtual machine.

2. The **image** file provides a snapshot of a running Pharo system. It's a cross-platform format: an image file on one operating system can be used on any other operating system with a compatible VM. An image file contains all the objects of a running system and their state at a given point in time, including all the classes and the compiled methods (since they are objects too). An image is basically a virtual object container.

The image file is named for the release (so `Pharo9.0.image` for a Pharo 9.0 image) and it is synced with the **changes** file.

3. The **changes** file logs of all source code modifications (such as the changes you make while programming in Pharo) made to the Pharo system. Each release provides a nearly empty file named for the release, for example `Pharo9.0.changes` This file supports a per-method history which can be used for showing diffs or

reverting changes. It means that even if you did not manage to save the image file before a crash (or you just forgot), you can still recover your changes from this file. A changes file is always coupled with an image file. They work as a pair. Do not mess with it. Even if Pharo can run without it, you could lose all of your work if haven't saved it with git.

4. The **sources** file contains the source code for parts of Pharo that do not change frequently. This file is important because the image file format stores only objects including compiled methods and their bytecode and not their source code. Typically a new **sources** file is generated once per major release of Pharo. For Pharo 9.0, this file is named `PharoV90.sources`.

Image/Changes pair

The `.image` and `.changes` files provided by a Pharo release are the starting point for a live environment that you will adapt to suit your needs. These files are modified as you work with Pharo, so you need to make sure that they are writable. It's also a good idea to stop your anti-virus software from scanning these files. The `.image` and `.changes` files are intimately linked and should always be kept together, with matching base filenames. *Never* edit them directly with a text editor, as `.image` holds your live object runtime memory, which indexes into the `.changes` files for the source. It is a good idea to keep a backup copy of the downloaded `.image` and `.changes` files so you can always start from a fresh image and reload your code. However, the most efficient way to back up code is to use Iceberg with git (a version control system), provides an easy and powerful way to both back up and track your changes.

Common setup

The four main component files above can be placed in the same directory, but it's a common practice to put the virtual machine and sources file in a separate directory where everyone has read-only access to them.

Do whatever works best for your style of working and your operating system. If you're just starting out with Pharo it's better to use the Pharo Launcher, since it will manage everything for you.

2.3 Launching Pharo with the Pharo Launcher

Pharo Launcher is a tool that helps you download and manage Pharo images. It is very useful for getting new versions of Pharo (as well as updates to the existing versions that contain important bug fixes). It also gives you access to images preloaded with specific libraries that make it very easy to use those tools without having to manually install and configure them.

Getting Started with Pharo

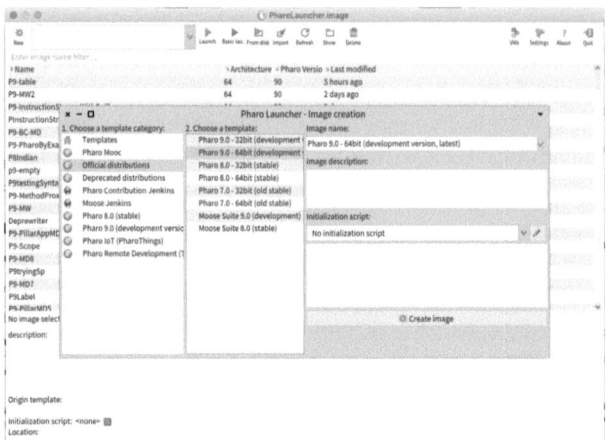

Figure 2-1 Pharo Launcher - the easy way to manage your Pharo images.

Pharo Launcher can be found at https://pharo.org/download together with installation instructions and download links depending on your platform.

After installing Pharo Launcher and opening it (like you would do for any Pharo image), you should get a GUI similar to Figure 2-1. Here we clicked on the top left **New** icon to download a new Pharo image from the server.

The back column lists images that live locally on your machine (usually in a shared system folder). You can launch any local image directly (either by double-clicking, or by selecting it and pressing the **Launch** button). A right-click context menu provides several useful functions like copying and renaming your images, as well as locating them on the file system.

You can use your own local images with Pharo Launcher, in addition to working with the images you downloaded. To do so, simply import your `.image` and its associated `.changes` files using the launcher.

2.4 Launching Pharo via the command line

If you are using standalone version do whatever your operating system expects: drag the `.image` file onto the icon of the virtual machine, or double-click on the `.image` file, or at the command line type the name of the virtual machine followed by the path to the `.image` file.

- On **macOS,** double click the `Pharo9.0.app` bundle in the unzipped download.

2.4 Launching Pharo via the command line

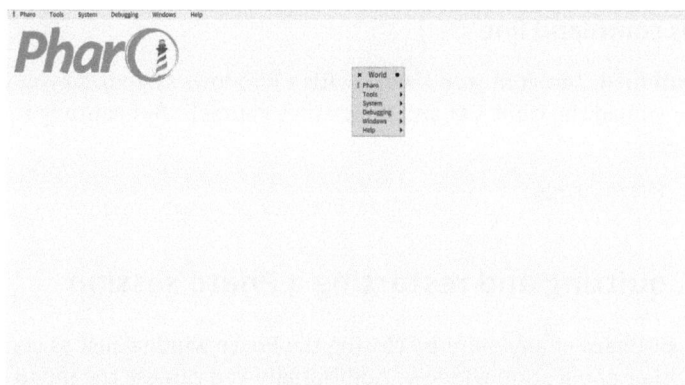

Figure 2-2 When Pharo opens you should see the following.

- On **Linux**, double click (or invoke from the command line) the `pharo` executable `Bash` script from the unzipped Pharo folder.
- On **Windows**, enter the unzipped Pharo folder and double click `Pharo.exe`.

In general, Pharo tries to "do the right thing". If you double click on the VM, it looks for an image file in the default location. If you double click on an `.image` file, it tries to find the nearest VM to launch it with.

If you have multiple VMs installed on your machine, the operating system may no longer be able to guess the right one. In this case, it is safer to specify exactly which ones you meant to launch, either by dragging and dropping the image file onto the VM, or specifying the image on the command line (see the next section).

The general pattern for launching Pharo from the command line is:

```
<Pharo executable> <path to Pharo image>
```

Linux command line

Assuming you're in the directory where the Zeroconf script downloaded the required files:

```
./pharo Pharo.image
```

macOS command line

Again, assuming you downloaded Pharo using Zeroconf:

```
./pharo Pharo.image
```

Windows command line

As we mentioned, Zeroconf won't work with a Windows system, so you will have to download the right VM and image files yourself. But running it should be just as easy:

```
Pharo.exe Pharo.image
```

2.5 Saving, quitting and restarting a Pharo session

You can exit Pharo at any point by closing the Pharo window just as you do with any other application window. Additionally you can use the menu bar, or the World Menu, and select either **Save and quit** or **Quit**.

In either case, Pharo will display a prompt to ask you about saving your image. If you do save your image and reopen it, you will see that things are *exactly* as you left them: the running programs, the open windows, the *positions* of the open windows. This happens because the image file stores *all* the objects (the edited text, the added methods, the window positions... because they are *all* objects) that Pharo has loaded into your memory so that *nothing* is lost on exit.

When you start Pharo for the first time, the Pharo virtual machine loads the image file that you specified. This file contains a snapshot of a large number of objects, including a vast amount of pre-existing code and programming tools (all of which are also, you guessed it, objects). As you work with Pharo, you will send messages to these objects, you will create new objects (by sending messages to objects!), and some of these objects will 'die' and their memory will be reclaimed (garbage collected).

When you quit Pharo, you will normally save a snapshot that contains all of your objects. If you save normally, you will overwrite your old image file with the new snapshot. Alternatively, you may save the image under a new name.

When you save your image the `.image` file is updated with the snapshot of your running Pharo system. The `.changes` file will also be updated: it will have a log of all the changes you've made to the image since the last update appended to it. As we've seen above, the `.changes` file can be very useful for recovering from errors, or replaying lost changes. More about this later!

It may seem like the image file should be the key mechanism for storing and managing software projects, but in practice that is not the case at all. There are much better tools for managing code and sharing software that is developed in a team. Images are useful, but you should be very cavalier about creating and throwing away images. Versioning tools such as Iceberg offer us a much better way to manage and share code. In addition, if you need to persist objects, you can use a package such as Fuel (a fast object binary serializer) or STON (a textual object serializer), or even use a database.

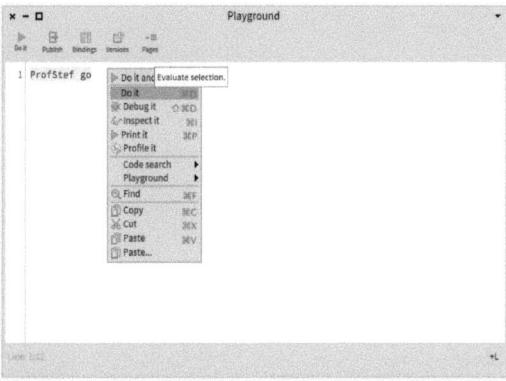

Figure 2-3 Executing an expression is simple with the **Do it** menu item.

2.6 For the fast and furious

Sometimes reading long chapters about a system that's as full of features as Pharo can be, well, *boring*. If you've already got a working Pharo system installed on your computer, and you know a little bit about how everything works, you might want to learn the basics by using ProfStef and then skip forward to the next chapter: a tutorial to define a simple counter and its associated tests. You can also watch the corresponding video available at http://mooc.pharo.org.

To launch ProfStef type the following expression:

```
ProfStef go
```

in a **Playground**, and then execute it by performing a **Do it**, as shown in Figure 2-3.

If all of that means nothing to you, then don't worry: it will soon enough. Just read on...

This expression will trigger the **ProfStef** tutorial (as shown in Figure 2-4), which is a great place to start to get a feel for Pharo syntax.

Congratulations! You have just sent your first message! Pharo is based on the concept of sending messages to objects. The Pharo objects are like your soldiers, just waiting for you to send them a message they can understand. We will see exactly how an object understands a message later on.

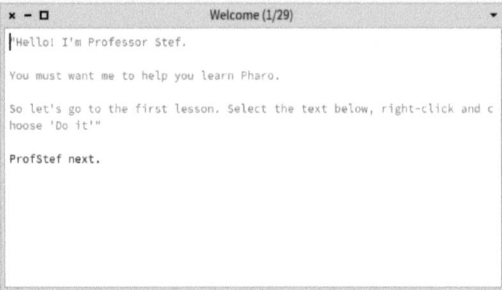

Figure 2-4 ProfStef is a simple interactive tutorial to learn about Pharo syntax.

2.7 Chapter summary

- Pharo systems can be managed on your computer using the Pharo Launcher. Alternatively, you can download Pharo using the Zeroconf scripts.
- A running Pharo system consists of a **virtual machine**, a **source file** (.sources), an **image file** (.image) and a **changes file** (.changes). Only these last two change, as they record the latest snapshot of your running system.
- When you open a Pharo image, you will find yourself in exactly the same state (i.e., with exactly the same running objects) that you had when you last saved that image.

CHAPTER 3

A quick tour of Pharo

This chapter will take you on a high level tour of Pharo, to help you get comfortable with the environment. There will be plenty of opportunities to try things out, so it would be a good idea to have a computer handy when you read this chapter.

In particular, you will learn about the different ways of interacting with the system, and discover some of the basic tools. You will also learn how to define a new method, create an object, and send it messages.

Try to remember that this is a *quick* tour of Pharo, a taster of the environment. Don't become stuck when you don't understand something, it will almost certainly be covered in more detail in the next few chapters. *You do not have to know everything*, or at least, you don't have to know everything right away anyway. Make a note of what confuses or intrigues you and keep just keep going; it will all become clearer the further you read on.

Note: Most of the introductory material in this book will work with any Pharo version, so if you already have one installed, you may as well continue to use it. However, since this book is written for Pharo 90, if you notice differences between the appearance or behavior of your system and what is described here, do not be surprised.

3.1 The World Menu

Once Pharo is running, you should see a single large window, possibly containing some open playground windows (see Figure 3-1). You might notice a menu bar, but Pharo also makes use of context-dependent pop-up menus.

A quick tour of Pharo

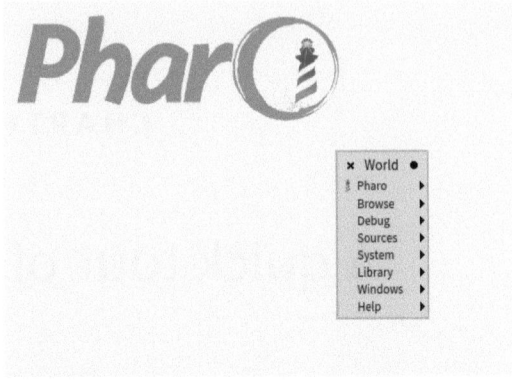

Figure 3-1 World menu (left click) brings the world menu.

Clicking anywhere on the background of the Pharo window will display the **World Menu**, which contains many of the Pharo tools, utilities, and settings.

Take a minute to explore the World Menu. You will see a list containing many of Pharo's core tools, including the System Browser, the Playground, the package manager Iceberg, and many others. We will discuss them all in more detail in the coming chapters.

3.2 Interacting with Pharo

Pharo offers three ways to interact with the system using a mouse or other pointing device.

click (or left-click): this is the most commonly used mouse button, and is normally equivalent to left-clicking (or clicking a single mouse button without any modifier key). For example, click on the background of the Pharo window to bring up the World Menu (Figure 3-1).

action-click (or right-click): this is the next most used button. It is used to bring up a contextual menu that offers different sets of actions depending on where the mouse is pointing (see Figure 3-2). If you do not have a multi-button mouse, then normally you would configure action-click to be performed when clicking the mouse button and holding down the control modifier.

meta-click: Finally, you may meta-click on any object displayed in the image to activate the "Morphic halo", an array of handles that are used to perform operations on the on-screen objects themselves, such as inspecting or resizing them (see Figure 3-3). If you let the mouse linger over a handle, a help balloon will explain its function. In Pharo, how you meta-click depends on your oper-

3.2 Interacting with Pharo

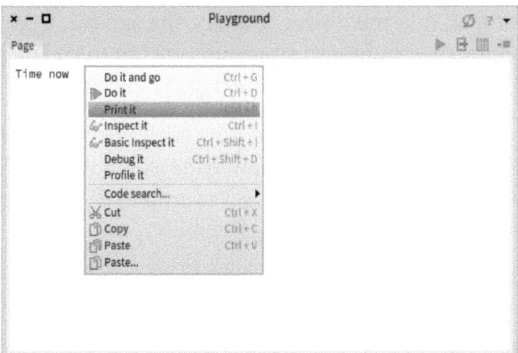

Figure 3-2 Action Click (right click) brings the contextual menu.

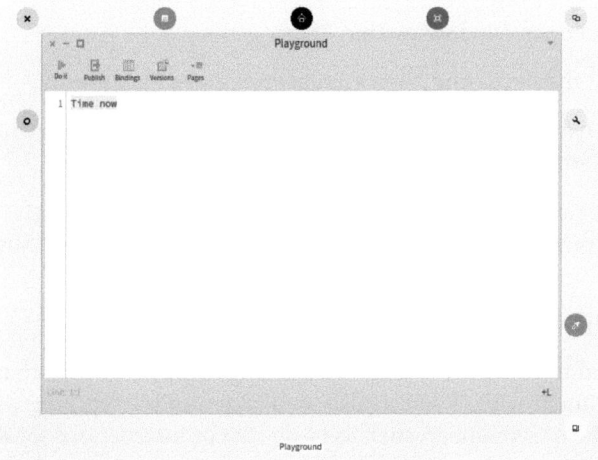

Figure 3-3 Meta-Clicking on a window opens the Halos.

ating system: either you must hold `Ctrl-Shift` or `Alt-Shift` (on Windows or Linux) or `Option-Shift` (on macOS) while clicking.

About vocabulary

If you talk to Pharoers for a while, you will notice that they generally do not use phrases like *call an operation* or *invoke a method*, which you might hear in other programming languages. Instead, they will say *send a message*. This reflects the idea that objects are responsible for their own actions and that the method associated with the message is looked up dynamically. When sending a message to an object, it is the object, and not the sender, that selects the appropriate method for responding to your message. In most (but not all) cases, the method with the same name as the message is executed.

As a user, you do not need to understand how each message works, the only thing you need to know is what the available messages are for the objects that interest you. This way, an object can hide its complexity, and coding can be kept as simple as possible without losing flexibility.

How to find the available messages for each object is something we will explore later on.

3.3 Playgrounds and Transcripts

Let's do some simple exercises to get comfortable in our new environment:

1. Close all open windows within Pharo.
2. Look in the menu and open a Transcript and a Playground.
3. Position and resize the transcript and playground windows so that the Playground just overlaps the Transcript (see Figure 3-4).

You can resize windows by dragging one of the corners. At any given time only one window is active; it is the one in front and has its border highlighted.

About Playground

A **Playground** is useful for typing and running snippets of code that you would like to experiment with. You can also use Playgrounds for typing *any* text that you would like to remember, such as to-do lists or instructions for anyone who will use your image.

Type the following text into the Playground:

```
Transcript show: 'hello world'; cr.
```

Try double-clicking at various points on the text you have just typed. Notice how an entire word, an entire line, or all of the text is selected, depending on whether you click within a word, at the end of a line, or at the end of the entire expression. In particular, if you place the cursor before the first character or after the last character and double-click, you select the entire paragraph.

Select the text you have typed, right click and select **Do it**. Notice how the text hello world appears in the Transcript window (See Figure 3-4). Do it again!

3.4 Keyboard shortcuts

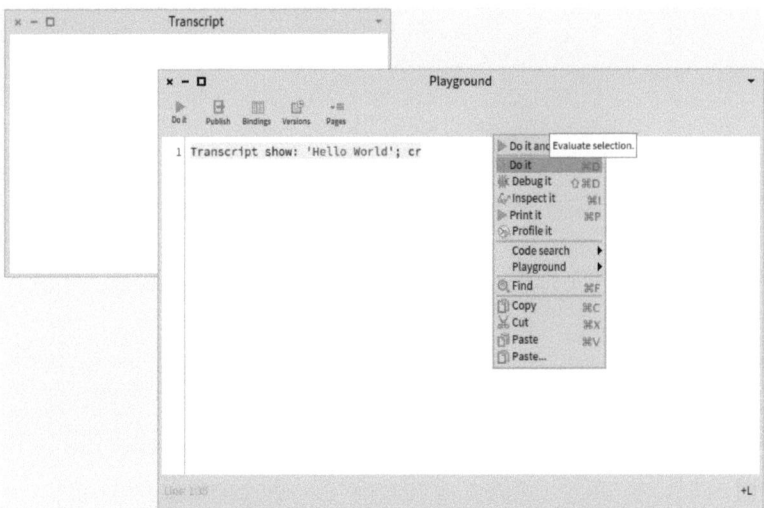

Figure 3-4 Executing an expression: displaying a string in the Transcript.

3.4 Keyboard shortcuts

If you want to evaluate an expression, you do not always have to right click. Instead, you can use the keyboard shortcuts that are shown next to each menu item. Even though Pharo may seem like a mouse driven environment, it contains over 200 shortcuts for all of its different tools, as well as the facility to assign a keyboard shortcut to *any* of the 143 000 methods contained in the Pharo image.

Depending on your platform, you may have to press one of the modifier keys, which are Control, Alt, and Command. We will use Cmd in the rest of the book, so each time you see something like Cmd-D, just replace it with the appropriate modifier key depending on your operating system. The corresponding modifier key in Windows is Ctrl, and in Linux it is either Alt or Ctrl.

In addition to **Do it**, you might have noticed **Do it and go**, **Print it**, **Inspect it** and several other options in the context menu. Let's have a quick look at each of these.

3.5 Doing vs. printing

Type the expression 3 + 4 into the playground. Now **Do it** with the keyboard shortcut Cmd-D.

A quick tour of Pharo

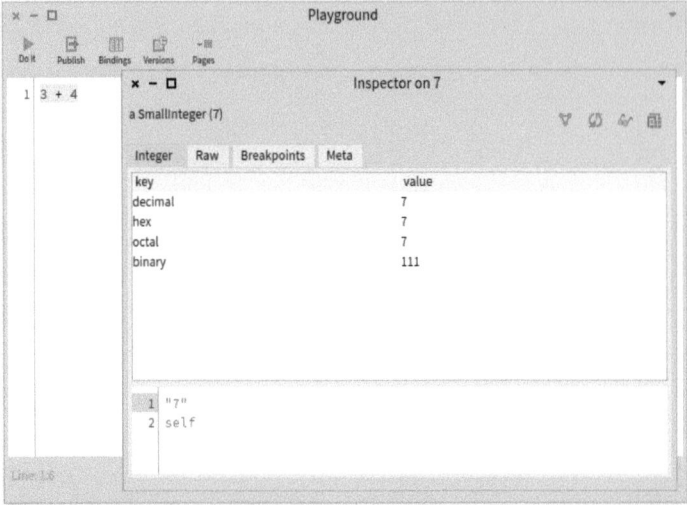

Figure 3-5 Inspecting a simple number using `Inspect`.

Don't be surprised if nothing happened! What you just did is send the message + with argument 4 to the number 3. Normally, the resulting 7 would have been computed and returned to you, but since the playground did not know what to do with this answer, it simply did not show the answer. If you want to see the result, you should **Print it** instead. **Print it** actually compiles the expression, executes it, sends the message `printString` to the result, and displays the resulting string.

Select 3 + 4 and **Print it** (Cmd-P). This time we see the result we expect.

```
3 + 4
>>> 7
```

We use the notation >>> as a convention in this book to indicate that a particular Pharo expression yields a given result when you **Print it**.

3.6 Inspect

Select or place the cursor on the line of 3 + 4, and this time **Inspect it** (Cmd-I).

Now you should see a new window titled "Inspector on 7" as shown in Figure 3-5. The inspector is an extremely useful tool that allows you to browse and interact with any object in the system. The subtitle of the window, "a SmallInteger (7)", tells us that 7 is an instance of the class `SmallInteger`. The top

3.7 Other operations

Figure 3-6 Inspecting a Morph using `Inspect`.

panel allows us to browse the instance variables of an object and their values. The bottom panel can be used to write expressions to send messages to the inspected object. Try typing `self squared` in the bottom panel of the inspector and then **Print it**.

The inspector presents specific tabs that show different information and views on an object depending on the kind of object you are inspecting. Inspect `Morph new openInWorld` you should get something similar to Figure 3-6.

3.7 Other operations

Other right-click options that may be used are the following:

- **Do it and go** additionally opens a *navigable* inspector on the side of the playground. It allows us to navigate the object structure. Try it with the previous expression `Morph new openInWorld` and then navigate the structure.
- **Basic Inspect it** opens the classic inspector that offers a more minimal interface and live updates of changes to the object.
- **Debug it** opens the debugger on the code.
- **Profile it** profiles the code with the Pharo profile tool, showing you how much time is spent for each message that is sent.

A quick tour of Pharo

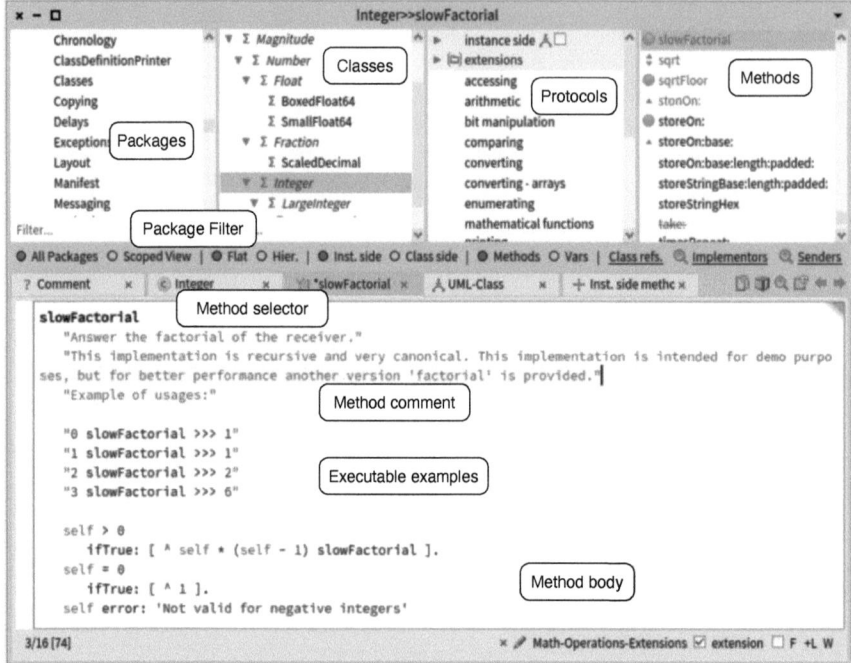

Figure 3-7 The System Browser shows the `slowFactorial` method of the class `Integer`.

- **Code search** offers several options provided by System Browser, such as browsing the source code of an expression, searching for senders and implementors, and so on.

3.8 Calypso: the System Browser

The **System Browser**, also known as the "Class Browser", is one of the key tools used for programming in Pharo. As we shall see, there are actually several interesting browsers available in Pharo, but this is the basic one you will find in any image. The current implementation of the System Browser is called **Calypso**. The previous version of the System Browser was called **Nautilus**.

Opening the System Browser on a given method

This is not the usual way that we open a browser on a method: we can use much more advanced tools! But for the sake of this exercise, please execute

3.8 Calypso: the System Browser

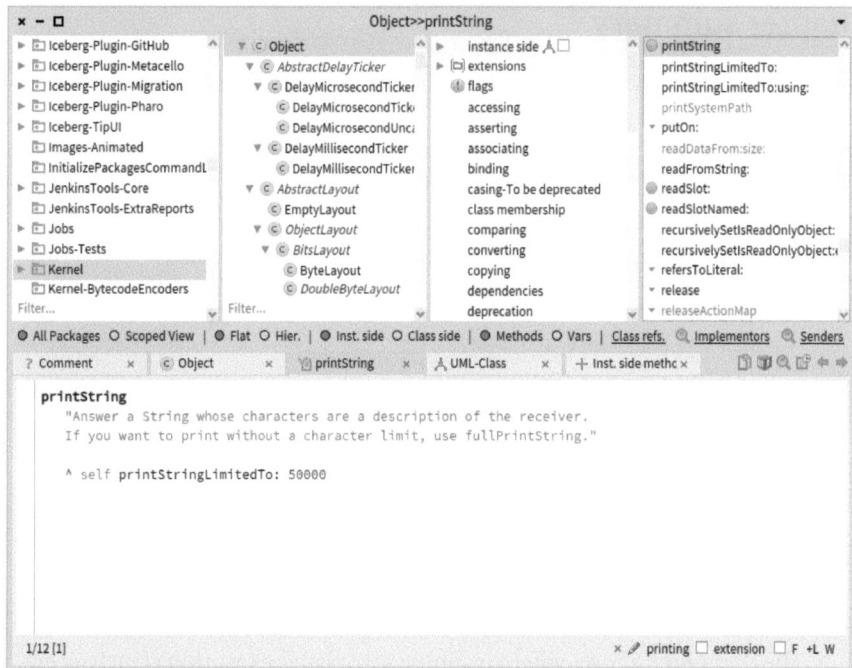

Figure 3-8 The System Browser showing the `printString` method of class Object.

the following code snippet:

```
[ClyFullBrowserMorph openOnMethod: Integer>>#slowFactorial
```

It will open a System Browser on the method `slowFactorial`, showing something like in Figure 3-7. The title bar of 'Integer»#slowFactorial' indicates that we are browsing the class `Integer` and its method `slowFactorial`. Figure 3-7 shows the different entities displayed by the browser: packages, classes, protocols, methods, and the method definition.

In Pharo, the default System Browser is Calypso. However, as we have mentioned, it is possible to have other System Browsers installed in the Pharo environment. Each System Browser may have its own GUI that may be very different from the Calypso GUI. From now on, we will use the terms 'Browser', 'System Browser' and 'Calypso' interchangeably.

3.9 Chapter summary

This chapter has been a whirlwind tour to introduce you to the Pharo environment and some of the major tools you will use to program in it. You have also seen a little of Pharo's syntax, even though you may not understand it all yet. Here's a little summary of what we've learned:

- You can click on the Pharo background to bring up the **World Menu** and launch various tools.
- A **Playground** is a tool for writing and evaluating snippets of code. You can also use it to store arbitrary text.
- You can use keyboard shortcuts on text in the Playground, or any other tool, to evaluate code. The most important of these are **Do it** (Cmd-D), **Print it** (Cmd-P), **Inspect it** (Cmd-I), and **Browse it** (Cmd-B).
- The **System Browser** is the main tool for browsing Pharo code and for developing new code.
- The **Test Runner** is a tool for running unit tests, and aids in Test-Driven Development.
- The **Debugger** allows you to examine errors and exceptions (such as errors or failures encountered when running tests). You can even create new methods right in the debugger.

CHAPTER 4

Finding information in Pharo

In this short chapter we will show you some ways to find information in Pharo.

4.1 Navigating using the System Browser

There are ways to get to the class or method you're looking for in Pharo fast - very fast indeed. Later on we'll introduce you to **Spotter**, one of the quickest ways to find an object in Pharo. But for now, while we're still learning, let's try taking the slow road by only using the System Browser to find the printString method defined in the class Object. At the end of the navigation, we will get the situation depicted in 3-8:

- **Open the Browser**: Either by using the World Menu or the shortcut Cmd-O Cmd-B. When a new System Browser window first opens, all panes but the leftmost are empty. This first pane lists all known **packages**, which contain groups of related classes.

- **Filter packages**: Type part of the name of the package in the left most filter. It filters the list of packages to be shown in the list above it. Type 'Kern' for example.

- **Expand the Kernel package and select the Objects element**: When we select a package, it causes the second pane to show a list of all of the **classes** in the selected package. You should see the class hierarchy of ProtoObject.

- **Select the Object class**: When a class is selected, the remaining two panes will be populated. The third pane displays the **protocols** of the currently selected class. These are convenient groupings of related methods which we'll discuss further later in the book. If no protocol is selected you should see all methods in the fourth pane.

- **Select the `printing` protocol**: You may have to scroll down to find it - Object is a pretty important class and has lots of protocols. You can also click on the third pane and type pr, to typeahead-find the printing protocol. Now select it, and in the fourth pane you will see only the methods related to printing.

- **Select the `printString` method**: Now we see in the bottom pane the source code of the `printString` method, shared by all objects in the system (except those that override it).

There are much better way to find a method, for example, just type it in a Playground and select the word and use **Implementors of it** in the **Code search** context menu item, which you can bring up with an action-click, or just use the keyboard shortcut Cmd-M.

4.2 Finding classes

There are several ways to find a class in Pharo. The first, as we have just seen above, is to know (or guess) what package it is in, and to navigate to it using the Browser.

A second way is to send the `browse` message to an instance or the class itself, asking it to open a Browser on itself. Suppose we want to browse the class Point:

- **Using the Message browse**: Type `Point browse` into a Playground and then **Do it**. A Browser will open on the Point class. You can do the same with 10@20 (which is an instance of the class Point).

- **Using Cmd-B:** There is also a keyboard shortcut Cmd-B that you can use in any text pane; select the word and press Cmd-B. Use this keyboard shortcut to browse the class Point.

Notice that, when the Point class is selected but no protocol or method is selected, instead of the source code of a method we see a class definition. This is nothing more than an ordinary message that is sent to the parent class, asking it to create a subclass. If you click on the **Comments** button at the bottom of the class pane, you can see the class comment in a dedicated pane.

In addition the system supports the following mouse shortcuts:

- Cmd-Click on a word (Alt-Right click on Windows and Linux): open the definition of a class when the word is a class name. You get also the

4.2 Finding classes

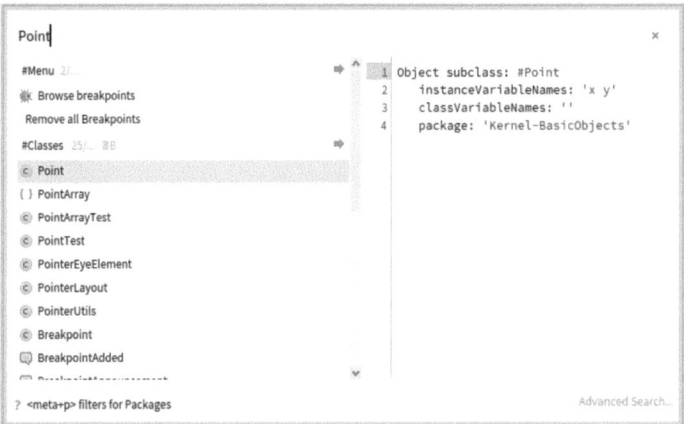

Figure 4-1 Using Spotter `Shift-Enter` to browse the class `Point`.

implementors of the message when you click on a selector that is in the body of a method.

- `Shift-Cmd-Click` on a word (`Shift-Alt-Right` click on Windows and Linux): open a list browser with all the refs of the class when the word is a class name. You get also the senders of the message when you click on a selector that is in the body of a method.

Using Spotter

The fastest (and probably the coolest) way to find a class is to use **Spotter**. Pressing `Shift-Enter` opens **Spotter**, a very powerful tool for finding classes, methods, and many other related actions. Figure 4-1 shows Spotter being used to look for `Point`.

Spotter offers several possibilities as shown in Figure 4-1. You can specify to Spotter the kind of *category* you are interested in. For example, using `#Classes` followed by the word you match against for, indicates that you are interested in classes.

Figure 4-2 shows how we can ask **Spotter** to show all the implementors of a given messages. We do not have to type the full category name. Other categories are

- `#Menu`, matching entries from the World Menu
- `#Packages`, matching packages in the system
- `#Implementors`, the implementors of a matching method

Figure 4-2 Looking for implementors matching `printString`.

- `#Senders`, the senders of matching messages
- `#Help`, matching documents in Pharo's help system

You can also just type the beginning of the category to identify it, i.e. `#sen printOn:` will give all the senders of the message `printOn:`.

By default, Spotter shows matches from multiple categories, all grouped together under their category heading. You can navigate through each category to see more results.

Using 'Find class' in the System Browser

In the System Browser you can also search for a class by its name. For example, suppose that you are looking for some unknown class that represents dates and times.

In the System Browser, click anywhere in the package pane or the class pane, and launch the Class Search window by typing `Cmd-F`, or selecting **Find class** from the right-click context menu. Type `time` in the dialog box. A list of classes is displayed, whose names contain the substring `time`. Choose one (say, `Time`), and click **OK** (or press `Enter`), and the Browser will show it.

4.3 Finding methods

Sometimes you can guess the name of a method, or at least part of the name of a method, more easily than the name of a class. For example, if you are interested in the current time, you might expect that there would be a method

4.3 Finding methods

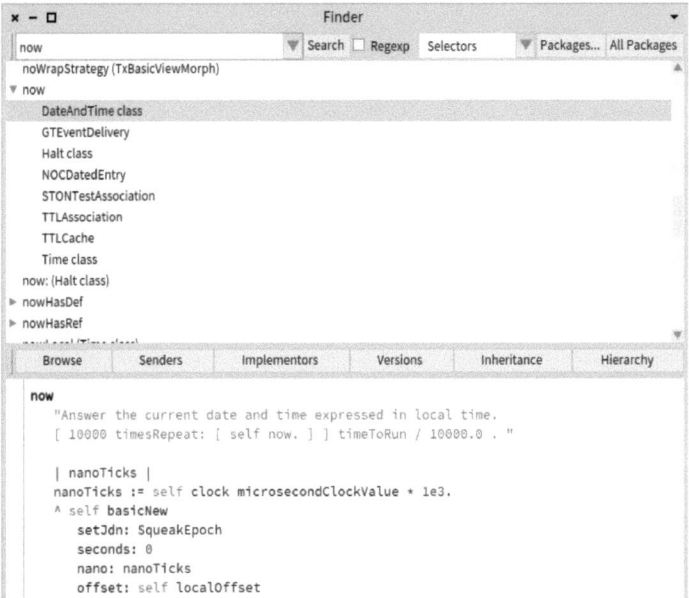

Figure 4-3 The Finder tool

called now, or at least one containing "now" as a substring. But where might it be? **Spotter** and **Finder** can help you!

With Spotter

As we've already said, Spotter can also find methods. You can use the #Implementors category to search for methods - just type #Implementors aMethodName. It will display all the methods that are implemented and have a similar or the same name. For instance, you will see all the methods starting with "now" if you type #imp now.

With Finder

Open the **Finder**, either through the **Browse** menu on the menu bar, or through the World Menu. Type now in the top left search box, cick **Search** (or just press the Enter key). You should see a list of results similar to the one in Figure 4-3.

The Finder will display a list of all the method names that contain the substring "now". To scroll to now itself, move the cursor to the list and type "n"; this type-ahead trick works in all scrolling windows. Expanding the "now" item shows you the classes that implement a method with this name. Select-

31

Finding information in Pharo

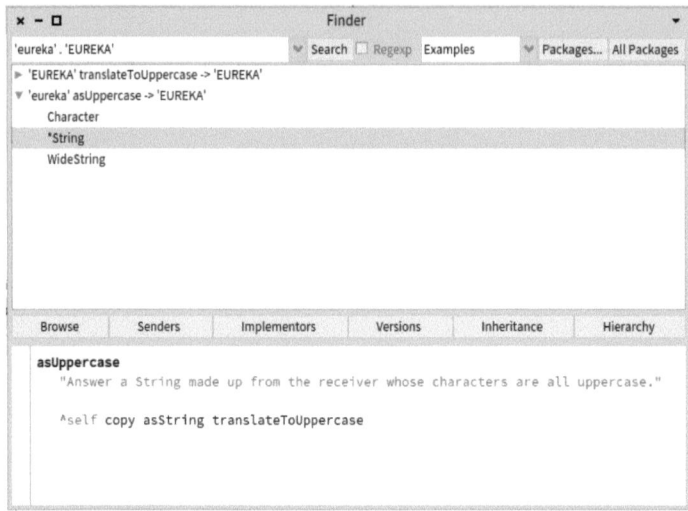

Figure 4-4 Looking for a method that given the string `'eureka'` returns the string `'EUREKA'`.

ing any one of them will display the source code for the implementation in the code pane on the bottom. It is also possible to search for the exact match, by typing "now" in the top left search bar; by using quotes you will only get the exact match.

4.4 Finding Methods using Examples

Using the Finder you can look for classes or methods based on their names as mentioned above. You can also look for a string inside the whole method bodies, comments included.

But the Finder also offers a unique and powerful facility. At times you may have an inkling that a method exists, but have no idea what it might be called; you know how it should behave, but you don't know what it's called. But the Finder can still help! Suppose that you want to find a method that up-cases a string (for example, transforming `'eureka'` into `'EUREKA'`). We can give Finder the inputs and expected outputs of a method and it will (try to) find it for you.

In the Finder, select the **Examples** mode using the second drop-down box (the one that shows **Selectors** by default).

Type `'eureka'` . `'EUREKA'` into the search box and press the Enter key or click the **Search** button (don't forget the single quotes!).

The Finder will then suggest a method that does what you were looking for, as well as display a list of classes that implement methods with the same name. In this case, it determined that the `asUppercase` method is the one that performed the operation that fit your example as shown in Figure 4-4.

Click on the `'eureka' asUppercase -> 'EUREKA'` line, to show the list of classes that implement the method `asUppercase`.

An asterisk at the beginning of a line in the list of classes indicates that this method is the one that was actually used to obtain the desired result. So the asterisk in front of `String` lets us know that the method `asUppercase` defined in the class `String` was executed and returned the result we wanted. The classes that do not have an asterisk are just the other implementors of `asUppercase`, which share the method name but did *not* return the result you wanted. So the method `asUppercase` defined in `Character` was not executed in our example, because `'eureka'` is not a `Character` instance (it's a `String`).

You can also use the Finder to search for methods with one or more arguments. For example, if you are looking for a method that will find the greatest common factor of two integers, you might try 25 . 35 . 5. You can also give Finder multiple examples to narrow the search space; the help text in the bottom pane explains how.

4.5 Conclusion

- The **Spotter** is a powerful tool to navigate the system and find information.
- The **Finder** allows you to look for classes, methods and more. In addition it lets you find methods based on the object receiving the message, the message arguments, and the returned object.

CHAPTER 5

A first tutorial: Developing a simple counter

To start off in Pharo, let's write a simple counter by following the steps given below. In this exercise you will learn how to create packages, classes, methods, instances, unit tests and more. This tutorial covers most of the important actions you will perform when developing in Pharo. You can also watch the companion videos available in the Pharo MOOC at http://mooc.pharo.org, which help illustrate this tutorial.

Note that the development flow promoted by this little tutorial is *traditional* in the sense that you will define a package, a class, *then* define its instance variables, *then* define its methods, and *then* finally execute it. Now in Pharo, developers usually follow a different workflow called Test-Driven Development (much as we saw in the last chapter): they execute an expression that raises an error. These errors are caught by the Debugger and the developer codes directly in the debugger, allowing the system to define instance variables and methods on the fly for them.

We will also show you how to save your code with git hosting services such as GitHub using Iceberg.

Once you finish this tutorial, and you feel more confident in Pharo, we strongly suggest you do the exercise again using TDD. Again, there is another video showing this powerful method of coding.

5.1 Our use case

Here is our use case: We want to be able to create a counter, increment it twice, decrement it and check that its value is as expected. The following example shows this in action, and will make a perfect unit test - you will define one later.

```
| counter |
counter := Counter new.
counter increment; increment.
counter decrement.
counter count = 1
```

We will write all of the necessary classes and methods to support this example.

5.2 Create a package and class

In this part, you will create your first class. In Pharo, a class is defined in a package, so we'll need to create a package first to put the class in. The steps are the same every time we create a class, so pay attention.

Create a package

Use the Browser to create a package (right-click in the package pane, select **New Package**). The system will ask you for a name, write MyCounter. This new package is then created, added to the package list, and selected by default. Figure 5-1 shows the expected result.

Create a class

The lower pane of the Browser should now be open with a tab showing the template for a class definition. To create a new class, you just need to edit this template and compile the class. There are **five** parts you might want to change:

- **Superclass Specification.** This describes the superclass of the class you're creating. It defaults to Object, the least specialized of all classes in Pharo, which is what we want for our new Counter class. This won't always be the case: often you'll want to base a class on a more specific class.
- **Class Name.** Next, you should fill in the name of your class by replacing #MyClass with #Counter. Take care that the name of the class starts with a capital letter and that you do not remove the # sign in front of #Counter. This is because we name our classes using a **Symbol**, a unique string in Pharo which we write starting with a #.

5.2 Create a package and class

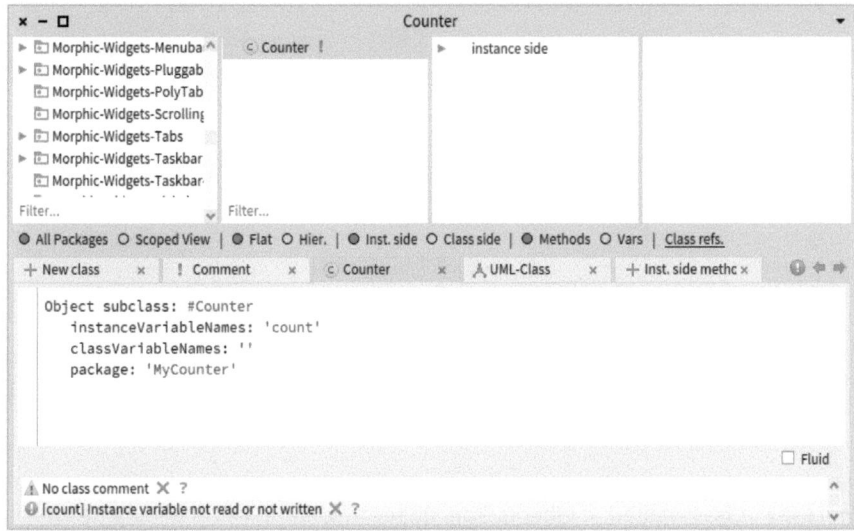

Figure 5-1 Package created and class creation template.

- **Instance Variable Specification.** Then, you should fill in the names of the instance variables of this class next to `instanceVariableNames`. We need only one instance variable called `'count'`. Take care that you leave in the quotes!
- **Class Variable Specification.** These are declared next to `classVariableNames:`; make sure it's an empty string as we will not need any class variables.

You should get the following class definition:

```
Object subclass: #Counter
    instanceVariableNames: 'count'
    classVariableNames: ''
    package: 'MyCounter'
```

We now have a class definition for the class Counter. To define it in our system we still have to *compile* it - either through the context menu in the lower panel, or the shortcut Cmd-S. The class Counter is now compiled and immediately added to the system.

Figure 5-2 illustrates the resulting situation that the browser should show.

The Pharo code critic tool will run automatically and shows some errors; don't worry about them for now, they're mainly about our class not being used yet.

A first tutorial: Developing a simple counter

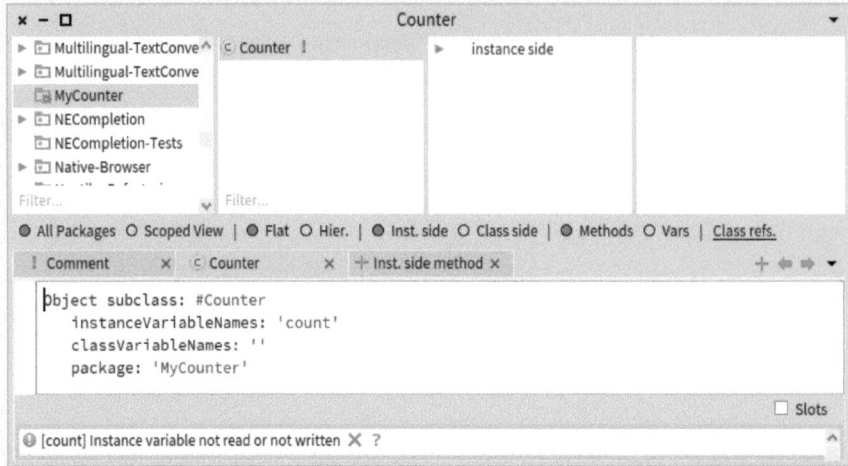

Figure 5-2 Class created: It inherits from Object class and has one instance variable named count.

As we are disciplined developers, we will add a comment to our Counter class by clicking the **Comment** pane and the **Toggle Edit / View comment** toggle. You can write the following comment:

```
`Counter` is a simple concrete class which supports incrementing and
    decrementing.
Its API is
- `decrement` and `increment`
- `count`
Its creation message is `startAt:`
```

Comments are written in Microdown, a dialect of Markdown that should be quite intuitive. They render nicely in the Browser. Again, accept these changes either through the menu or by hitting Cmd-S.

Figure 5-3 shows the class with its comment.

5.3 Defining protocols and methods

In this part you will use the Browser to learn how to add protocols and methods.

The class we have defined has one instance variable named count, and we're going to use that variable to keep count. We'll increment it, decrement it, and show its current value. But in Pharo we need to remember three things:

5.4 Create a method

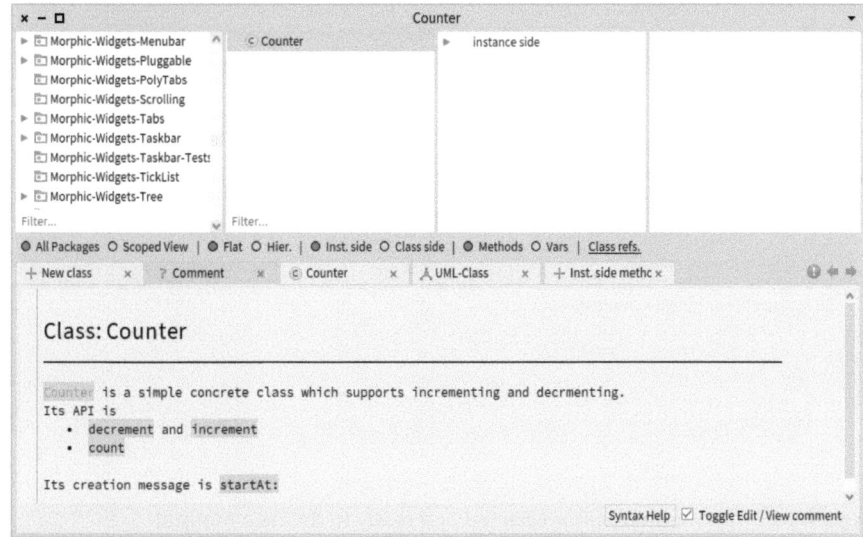

Figure 5-3 Counter class has now a comment! Well done.

1. *Everything* is an object
2. Instance variables are *completely private* to the object
3. The *only* way to interact with an object is by *sending messages* to it

And so there is no other mechanism to access our instance variable from outside of our counter than by sending a message to the object. What must do is define a method that returns the value of the instance variable. Such methods are called *getter* methods. So, let's define an accessor method for our instance variable count.

A method is usually placed into a *protocol*. These protocols are just a group of methods - they have no meaning in Pharo, but they do convey important information to the readers of your class. Although protocols can have any name, Pharo programmers follow certain conventions when naming protocols. If you define a method and are not sure what protocol it should be in, first take a look through existing code and see if you can find an appropriate protocol that already exists.

5.4 Create a method

Now let us create the getter method for the instance variable count. Start by selecting the class Counter in a Browser, and make sure you are editing the

A first tutorial: Developing a simple counter

Figure 5-4 The method editor selected and ready to define a method.

instance side of the class (i.e., we define methods on *instances* of our class) by selecting the instance side tab. Then define your method.

Figure 5-4 shows the method editor ready to define a method.

As a general hint, double click at the end of or beginning of the text and start typing your method: this automatically replaces the template.

Write the following method definition:

```
count
    ^ count
```

This defines a method called `count`, which takes no arguments and returns the value of the instance variable `count`. Then choose *accept* in the menu to compile the method. The method is automatically categorized in the protocol *accessing*.

Figure 5-5 shows the state of the system once the method is defined.

You can now test your new method by typing and evaluating the next expression in a Playground:

```
Counter new count
>>> nil
```

This expression first creates a new instance of `Counter`, and then sends the message `count` to it. It retrieves the current value of the counter. This should return `nil` (the default value for non-initialized instance variables). Afterwards we will create instances with a reasonable default initialization value.

5.5 Adding a setter method

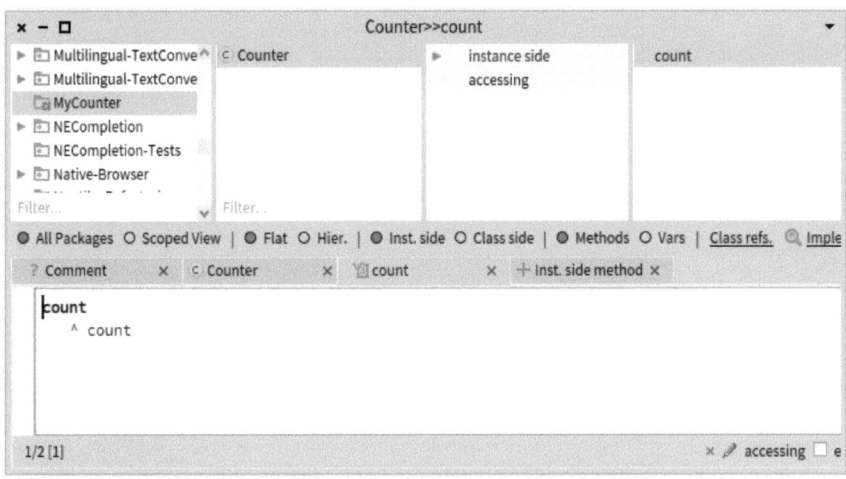

Figure 5-5 The method count defined in the protocol *accessing*.

5.5 Adding a setter method

Complementing the getter method we find the *setter* method. These are used to change the value of an instance variable from outside the object. For example, the expression Counter new count: 7 first creates a new Counter instance and then sets its value to 7 by sending it the message count: 7. Getters and setters are collectively referred to as *accessor* methods.

This example shows a setter method in action:

```
| c |
c := Counter new count: 7.
c count
>>> 7
```

The setter method does not currently exist, so as an exercise create the method count: such that, when invoked on an instance of Counter, the instance variable is set to the argument of the message. Test your method by evaluating the example above in a Playground.

5.6 Define a Test Class

Writing tests - whether you do it before or after you write your code - isn't really optional these days. A collection of well-written tests will support the evolution of your application, and give you confidence that your program does the things you expect it to do. Writing tests for your code is a good invest-

A first tutorial: Developing a simple counter

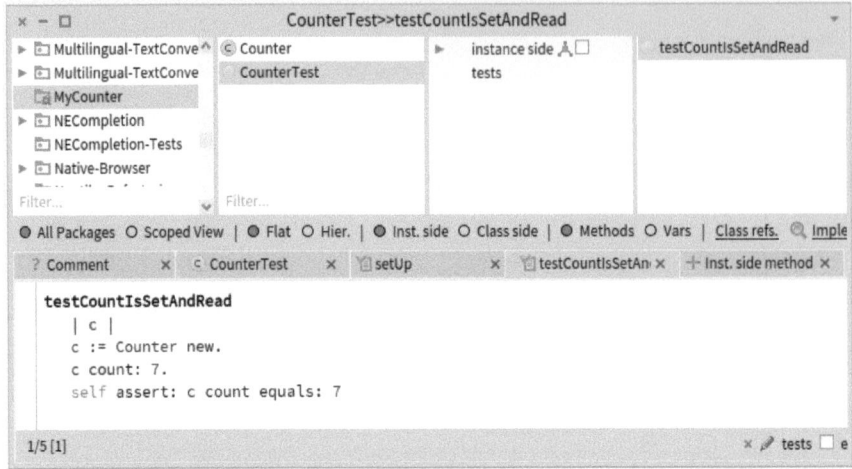

Figure 5-6 A first test is defined and it passes.

ment; test code is written once and executed a million times. For example, if we turned the example above into a test we could have checked automatically that our new setter method is working as expected.

Our test cases, written as methods, need to live inside a test class that inherits from TestCase. So we define a class named CounterTest as follows:

```
TestCase subclass: #CounterTest
    instanceVariableNames: ''
    classVariableNames: ''
    package: 'MyCounter'
```

Now we can write our first test by defining a method. Test methods should start with *test* to be automatically executed by the Test Runner or to get the little clickable circle next to the method name that lets you run the test.

Figure 5-6 shows the definition of the method testCountIsSetAndRead in the class CounterTest.

Define the following method for our test case. It first creates an instance of a Counter, sets its value and then verifies that the value has been set. The message assert:equals: is a message implemented in our test class. It verifies a fact (in this case that two objects are equal), and will fail the test if the fact isn't true.

```
CounterTest >> testCountIsSetAndRead
    | c |
    c := Counter new.
    c count: 7.
    self assert: c count equals: 7
```

A typographic convention

Pharoers frequently use the notation `ClassName >> methodName` to identify the class to which a method belongs. For example, the `count` method we wrote above in our class `Counter` would be referred to as `Counter >> count`. Just keep in mind that this is not *exactly* Pharo syntax, but more like a convenient notation we use to indicate "the instance method `count` which belongs to the class `Counter`".

From now on, when we show a method in this book, we will write the name of the method in this form. Of course, when you actually type the code into the browser, you don't have to type the class name or the >>; instead, you just make sure that the appropriate class is selected in the class pane.

Verify that the test passes by executing either pressing the circle icon in front of the method (as shown by Figure 5-6) or using the Test Runner available in the **Tools** menu.

As you now have your first green test, it's a good time to save your work.

5.7 Saving your code as a git repository with Iceberg

Saving your work in the Pharo image is good, but it's not ideal for sharing your work or collaborating with others. Much of modern software development is mediated through git, an open-source version control system. Services such as GitHub are built on top of git, providing places where developers can work together building open source projects - like Pharo!

Pharo works with git through the tool **Iceberg**. This section will show you how to create a local git repository for your code, commit your changes to it, and also push those changes to a remote repository such as GitHub.

Open Iceberg

Open Iceberg through the **Sources** menu, or by hitting `Cmd-O,I`.

You should now see something similar to Figure 5-7 which shows the top-level Iceberg pane. It shows the Pharo project, and a few other projects that also come with your image, and indicates that it could not find a local repository for them by showing 'Local repository missing'. You do not have to worry

A first tutorial: Developing a simple counter

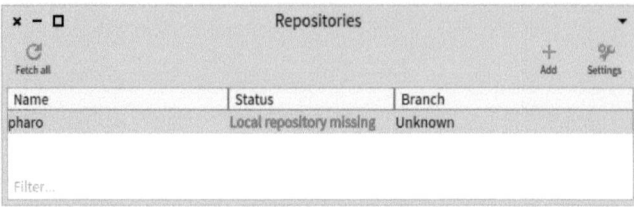

Figure 5-7 Iceberg *Repositories* browser on a fresh image indicates that if you want to version modifications to Pharo itself you will have to tell Iceberg where the Pharo clone is located. But you do not care.

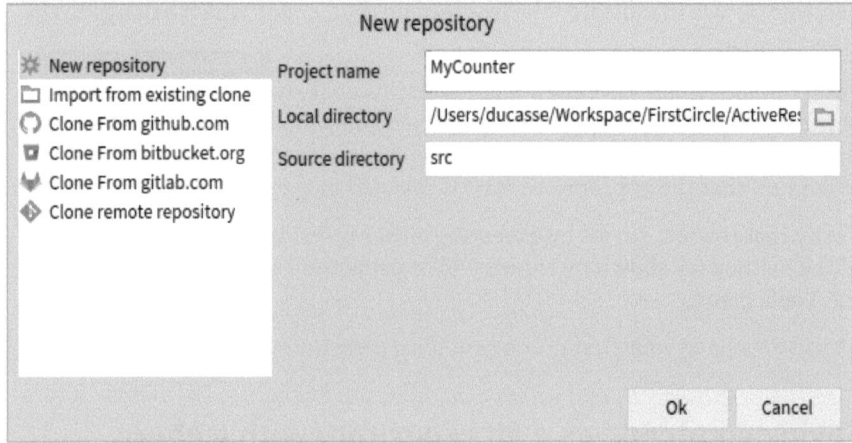

Figure 5-8 Add and create a project named MyCounter and with the `src` subdirectory.

about the Pharo project or having a local repository if you do not want to contribute to Pharo.

We're going to create a new project of our own.

Add and configure a project

Press the button Add to create a new project. Select 'New Repository' from the left and you should see a configuration pane similar to the one in Figure 5-8. Here we name our project, declare a directory on our local disk where the project's source should be saved, and also a subdirectory in the project itself which will be used to keep the Pharo code in - conventionally this is the `src` directory.

5.7 Saving your code as a git repository with Iceberg

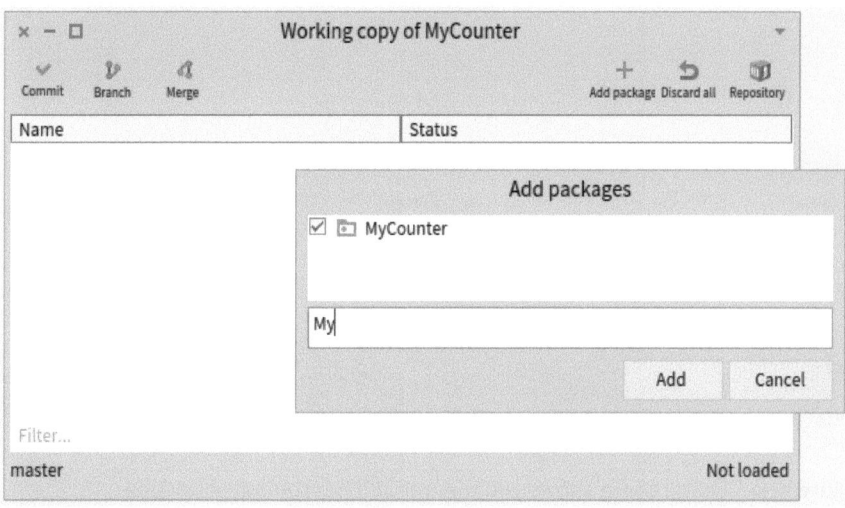

Figure 5-9 Selecting the Add package iconic button, add your package MyCounter to your project.

Add your package to the project

Once added, the Iceberg *Working copy* browser should show you an empty pane because we still haven't added any packages to our project. Click on the **Add package** button and select the package MyCounter as shown by Figure 5-9.

Commit your changes

Once you package is added, Iceberg shows you that there is uncommitted code in the packages managed by your project, as shown in Figure 5-10. Press the **Commit** button. Iceberg will show you all the changes that are about to be saved (Figure 5-11). Enter a commit message and commit your changes.

Code saved

Once you have committed, Iceberg indicates that your system and local repository are in sync.

Nicely done! We'll take a look at how to push these changes to a remote repository in a bit. But for now let's get back to our Counter.

45

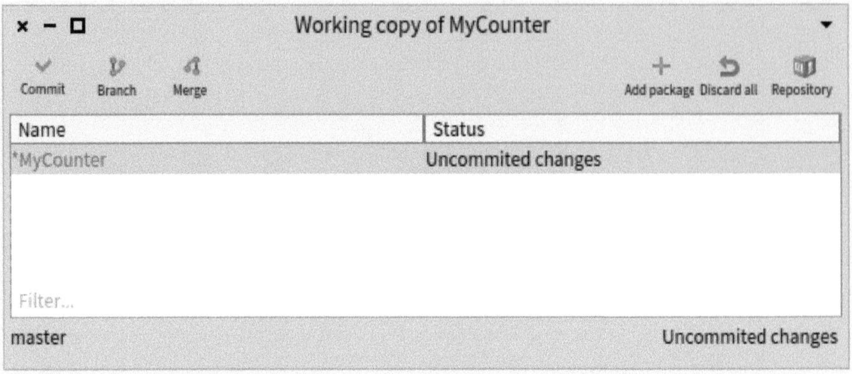

Figure 5-10 Now Iceberg shows you that you did not commit your code.

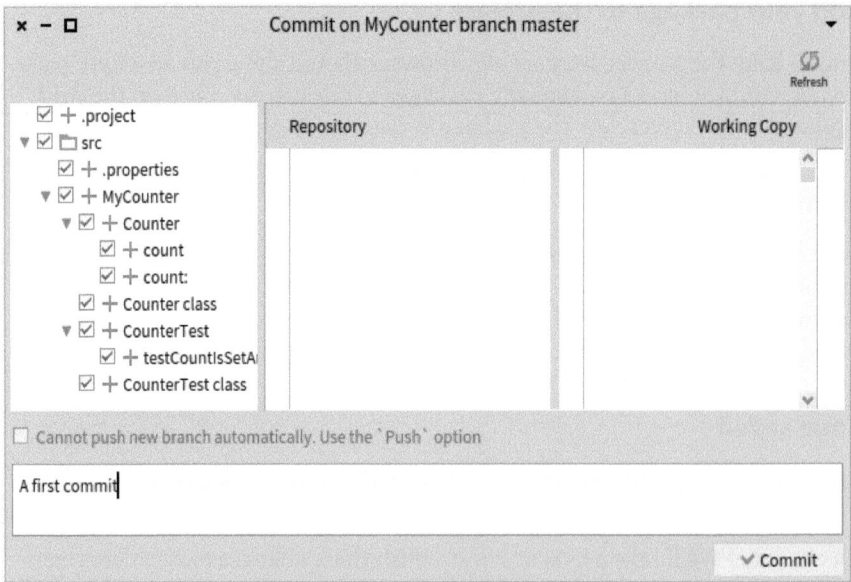

Figure 5-11 Iceberg shows you the changes about to be committed.

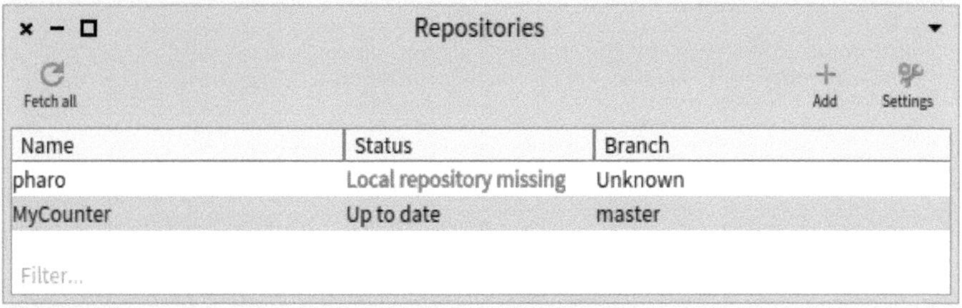

Figure 5-12 Once you save your change, Iceberg shows you that .

5.8 Adding more messages

We're going to test-drive the following messages for our Counter class. First, here's a test for the increment message:

```
CounterTest >> testIncrement
    | c |
    c := Counter new.
    c count: 0 ; increment; increment.
    self assert: c count equals: 2
```

Now you try it! Write a definition for the method increment that makes the test pass.

And when you've done that, try and write a test for the message decrement, then make *it* pass by implementing the method on the Counter class.

Solution

```
Counter >> increment
    count := count + 1
```

```
Counter >> decrement
    count := count - 1
```

Your tests should all pass (as shown in Figure 5-13). Again, this is a good moment to save your work. Saving at point where tests are green is always good practice. To save your changes, you just have to commit them using Iceberg.

5.9 Instance initialization method

Right now the initial value of our counter is not set as the following expression shows:

A first tutorial: Developing a simple counter

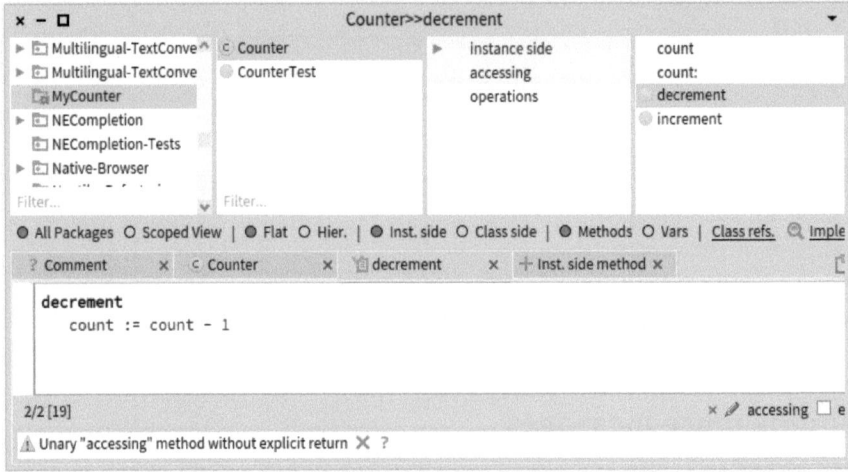

Figure 5-13 Class with more green tests.

```
Counter new count
>>> nil
```

Let's write a test that asserts that a newly created Counter instance has 0 as the count:

```
CounterTest >> testInitialize
    self assert: Counter new count equals: 0
```

This time the test will turn *yellow*, indicating a test failure - the test ran fine, but the assertion did not pass. This is different to the *red* tests we've seen so far, where the tests have failed because an error occurred (when a method has not been implemented, for instance).

5.10 Define an initialize method

Now we have to write an initialization method that sets a default value of the count instance variable. However, as we mentioned, the initialize message is sent to the newly created instance. This means that the initialize method should be defined on the *instance side*, just like any method that is sent to an instance of Counter (increment and decrement). The initialize method is responsible for setting up the default values of instance variables.

And so, on the instance side of Counter, and in the initialization protocol, write the following method (the body of this method is left blank. Fill it in!).

48

```
Counter >> initialize
    "set the initial value of the value to 0"

    "Your code here""
```

If you do this right, our `testInitialize` test will now pass.

As always, save your work before moving on to the next step.

5.11 Define a new instance creation method

We just discussed how the `initialize` method is defined on the *instance side* of our class, as it is responsible for altering an instance of `Counter`. Now let's take a look at defining a method on the *class side* of a class. Class methods will be executed as a result of sending messages to the class itself, rather than to instances of the class. To define the method on the class, we need to toggle the Code Browser over to the class side by selecting **Class side**.

Define a new instance creation method called `startingAt:`. This method receives an integer as an argument and returns a new instance of `Counter` with the count set to the specified value.

What do we do first? Why, we define a test of course:

```
TestCounter >> testCounterStartingAt5
    self assert: (Counter startingAt: 5) count equals: 5
```

Here the message `startingAt:` is sent to the class `Counter` itself.

Your implementation should look something like:

```
Counter class >> startingAt: anInteger
    ^ self new count: anInteger.
```

Here we see the notation for identifying a *class side* method in our text: `ClassName class >> methodName` just means "the class side method `startingAt:` on the class `Counter`".

What does `self` refer to here? As always, `self` refers to the object that the method is defined in, and so here it refers to the `Counter` class itself.

Let's write another test just to make sure that everything is working:

```
CounterTest >> testAlternateCreationMethod
    self assert: ((Counter startingAt: 19) increment ; count) equals: 20
```

A first tutorial: Developing a simple counter

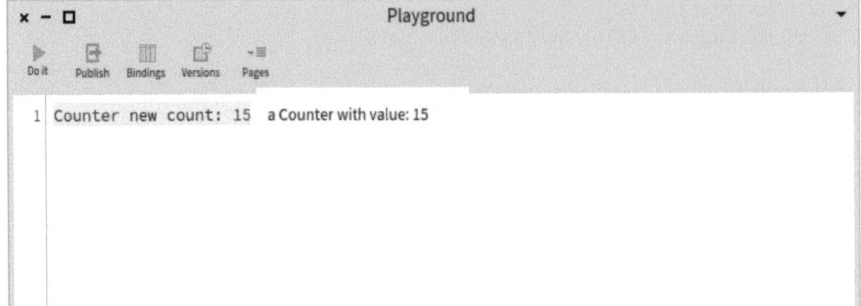

Figure 5-14 Counter instance better description.

5.12 Better object description

When you inspect a Counter instance, either through the Debugger or through opening an Inspector with Cmd-I on a Counter new expression, or even when you just run a **Print it** on a Counter new, you will see a very simplistic representation of your counter; it will just say 'a Counter':

```
Counter new
>>> a Counter
```

We would like a much richer representation, one that, for example, shows the counter's value. Implement the following method under the protocol printing:

```
Counter >> printOn: aStream
    super printOn: aStream.
    aStream nextPutAll: ' with value: ', count printString.
```

Note the message printOn: is sent to any object when it is printed using **Print it** (See Figure 5-14) or inspected in an Inspector. By implementing the method printOn: on instances of Counter we can control how they are displayed, and we *override* the default implementation defined in the Object class, which has been doing all the work up until now. We'll look at these ideas in more detail, as well as learn more about streams and super, later in the book.

In this case we'll let you define a test case for this method. A tip: send the message printString to Counter new to get its string representation, as generated by printOn:.

```
Counter new printString
>>> a Counter with value: 0
```

Now let's save our code again, but this time on a remote git server.

5.13 Saving your code on a remote server

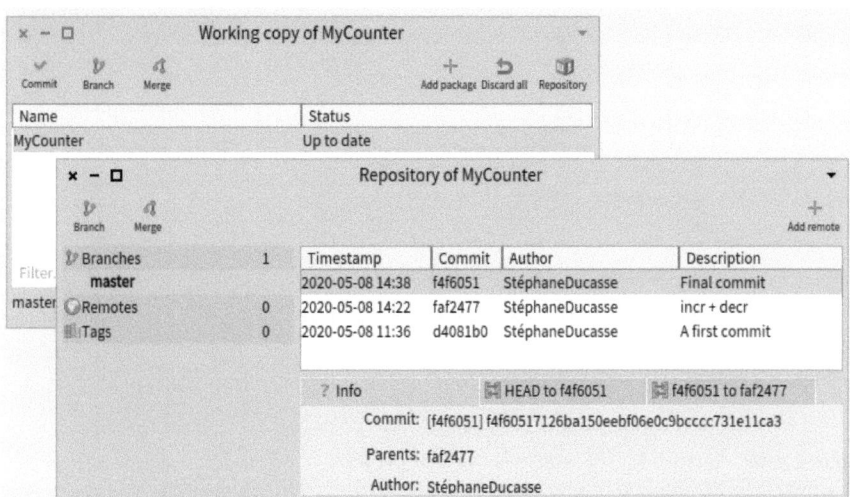

Figure 5-15 A *Repository* browser opened on your project.

5.13 Saving your code on a remote server

Up until now you saved your code on your local disc. We will now show how you can save your code on a remote git repository such as the one you can create on GitHub http://github.com or GitLab.

Create a project on the remote server

First you should create a project on your remote git server. Don't put anything in it! Things could get confusing. Name it something simple and obvious like "Counter" or "Pharo-Counter". This is the place we're going to send our Iceberg project to.

Add a remote repository in HTTPS access

In Iceberg, go to the Working Copy browser of your Counter repository by double-clicking on the repository. Then click on the icon that looks like a box, labeled **Repository**. This opens the Repository browser for the Counter project, as shown in Figure 5-15.

Then you just have to add a remote repository for the project, which is as simple as clicking the big plus icon marked **Add remote.** You will be asked to give a name for the remote, which is just the label that git uses locally to identify it, and a URL for the remote. You can use HTTPS access (a URL that starts

A first tutorial: Developing a simple counter

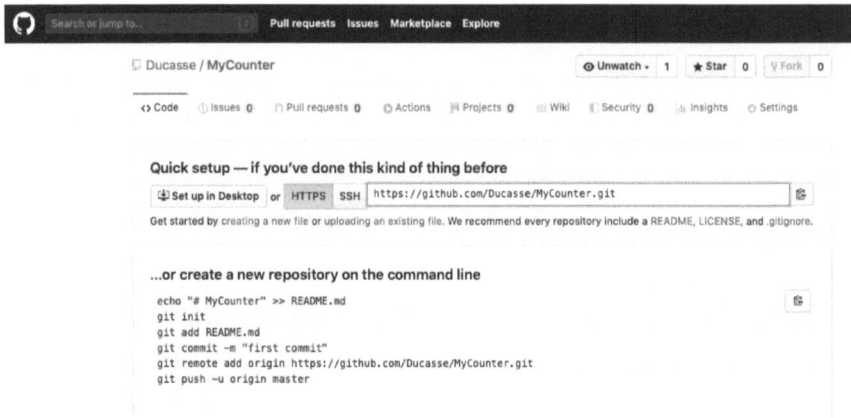

Figure 5-16 GitHub HTTPS address our our project.

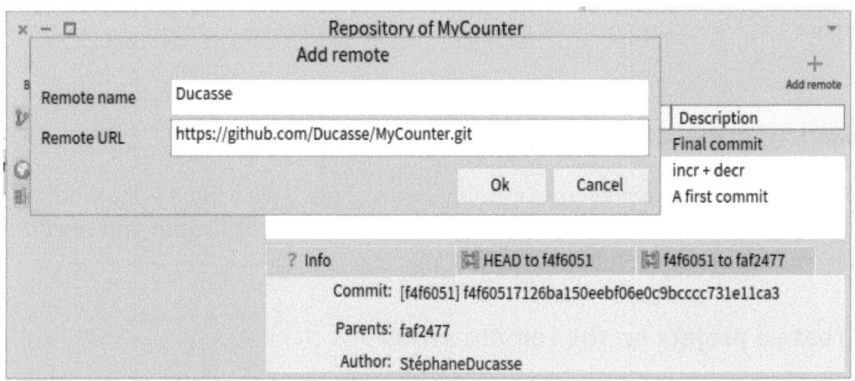

Figure 5-17 Using the GitHub HTTPS address.

with https://github.com for GitHub), or SSH access (a URL that starts with git@github.com). SSH will require you to set up your SSH agent on your machine with the correct credentials (please consult your git remote provider for the details of how to achieve this), HTTPS will require you to enter your user name and password; Pharo can store these for you if you would like. See in Figures 5-16 and 5-17 for using HTTPS.

Push

As soon as you add a valid server address, Iceberg will show a small red indicator on the **Push** button. This shows that you have changes in your local repos-

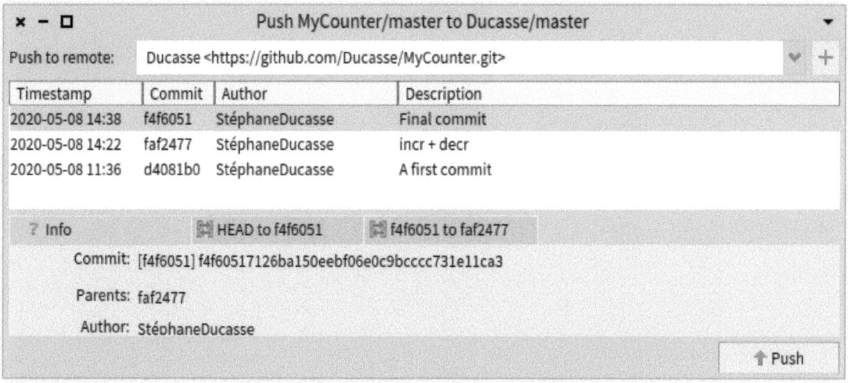

Figure 5-18 Commits sent to the remote repository.

itory that have not yet been pushed to your remote repository. Al you have to do is press the **Push** button; Iceberg will show you the commits that will be pushed to the server as shown in Figure 5-18.

Now you *really* saved your code will be able to reload from another machine or location. This skill will enable you to work remotely, and to share and collaborate with others.

5.14 Conclusion

In this tutorial, you learned how to define packages, classes, methods, and tests. The workflow of programming that we chose for this first tutorial is similar to most programming languages. However, in Pharo, smart and agile developers use a different workflow: Test-Driven Development (TDD). We suggest you redo this whole exercise by defining a test first, executing it, defining a method in the debugger, and then repeating. Watch the second "Counter" video of the Pharo MOOC available at http://mooc.pharo.org to get a better understanding of the workflow.

CHAPTER 6

Building a little game

In this chapter we will develop a simple game: Lights Out (http://en.wikipedia.org/wiki/Lights_Out_(game)). In doing so, we will increase our familiarity with the Browser, the Inspector, the Debugger, and versioning code with Iceberg. It's important to become proficient with these core tools. Once again, we will encourage you to take a test-first approach to developing this game by using Test-Driven Development.

A word of warning: this chapter contains a few deliberate mistakes in order for us to demonstrate how to handle errors and find bugs. Sorry if you find this a bit frustrating, but do try and follow along, as these are also important techniques that we need to see in action.

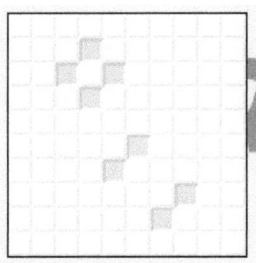

Figure 6-1 The Lights Out game board.

Building a little game

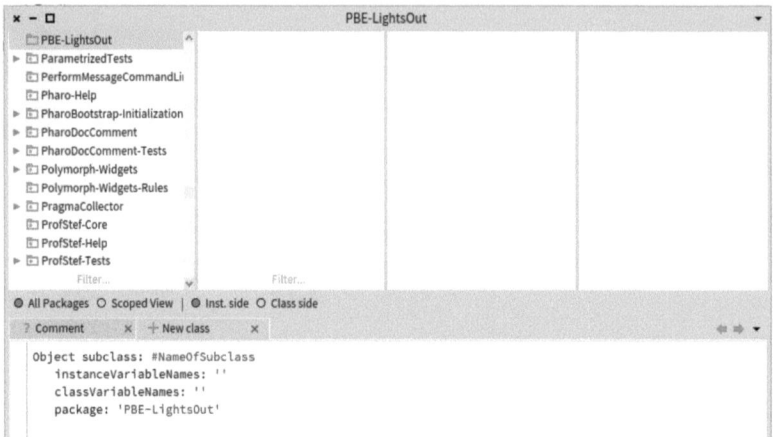

Figure 6-2 Create a Package and class template.

6.1 The Lights Out game

The game board consists of a rectangular array of light yellow cells. When you click on one of the cells, the four surrounding cells turn blue. Click again, and they toggle back to light yellow. The object of the game is to turn as many cells blue as possible.

"Lights Out" is made up of two kinds of objects: the game board itself, and 100 individual cell objects. The Pharo code to implement the game will contain two classes: one for the game and one for the cells.

6.2 Creating a new package

We'll need to define a package, which we'll do once again in the Browser. If you need a reminder of how to do this, consult Chapter : A Quick Tour of Pharo and Chapter : Developing a simple counter.

We'll call this package `PBE-LightsOut`. It might be a good idea to filter the package list once you've created the new package: just type `PBE` into the filter and you should only see our package.

6.3 Defining the class LOCell

At this point there are, of course, no classes in the new package. However, the main editing pane displays a template to make it easy to create a new class (see Figure 6-3). Let's fill it in with what we need.

6.4 Creating a new class

Figure 6-3 Filtering our package to work more efficiently.

Listing 6-4 LOCell class definition

```
SimpleSwitchMorph subclass: #LOCell
    instanceVariableNames: 'mouseAction'
    classVariableNames: ''
    package: 'PBE-LightsOut'
```

6.4 Creating a new class

The code in 6-4 contains the new class definition we're going to use:

Let's think for a minute about what you're looking at with this template. Is this a special form we fill in to create a class? Is it a new syntax? No, it's just another message being sent to another object! The message is subclass:instanceVariableNames:classVariableNames:package, which is a bit of a mouthful, and we're sending it to the class SimpleSwitchMorph. The arguments are all strings, apart from the name of the subclass we're creating, which is the symbol #LOCell. The package is our new package, and the mouseAction instance variable is going to be used to define what action the cell should take when it gets clicked on.

So why are we subclassing SimpleSwitchMorph rather than Object? We'll see the benefits of subclassing already specialized classes very soon. And we'll find out what that mouseAction instance variable is all about.

To send the message, accept the code either through the menu or the Cmd-S shortcut. The message is sent, the new class compiles, and we get something like 6-5.

The new class appears in the class pane of the browser, and the editing pane

Building a little game

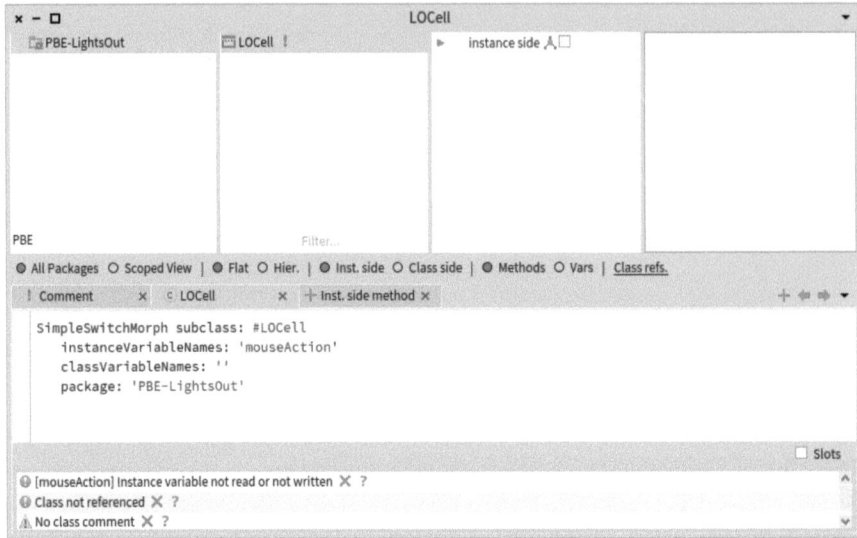

Figure 6-5 The newly-created class LOCell.

now shows the class definition. At the bottom of the window you'll get the Quality Assistant's feedback: it automatically runs some quality checks on your code and reports them. Don't worry about it too much for now.

6.5 About comments

Pharoers put a very high value on the readability of their code to help explain what's going on, but also on good comments.

Method comments

There's been a tendency in the recent past to believe that well-written, expressive methods don't need comments; the intent and meaning should be obvious just by reading it. This is just plain wrong and encourages sloppiness. Of course, crufty and hard-to-understand code should be worked on, renamed, and refactored.

A good comment does not excuse hard to read code. And obviously, writing comments for trivial methods makes no sense; a comment should not just be the code written again in English. Your comments should aim to be an explanation of what the method is doing, its context, and possibly the rationale behind its implementation. A reader should be comforted by your comment, it

Listing 6-6 Initializing instance of LOCell
```
LOCell >> initialize
  super initialize.
  self label: ''.
  self borderWidth: 2.
  bounds := 0 @ 0 corner: 16 @ 16.
  offColor := Color paleYellow.
  onColor := Color paleBlue darker.
  self useSquareCorners.
  self turnOff
```

should show that what they assumed about the code was correct and should dispel any confusion they might have.

Class comments

For the class comment, Pharo offers you a template with some suggestions on what makes a good class comment. So, read it! The format is based on Class (or Candidate) Responsibility Collaborator cards (CRC cards), developed by Kent Beck and Ward Cunningham from many influences while they were working in Smalltalk in the 1980s (see their paper "A Laboratory For Teaching Object-Oriented Thinking"[1] for more details). In a nutshell, the idea is to state the *responsibility* of the class in a couple of sentences, and how it *collaborates* with other classes to achieve this. In addition, we can state the class' API (the main messages an object understands), give an example of the class being used (usually in Pharo we define examples as class methods), and some details about the internal representation or the rationale behind the implementation.

6.6 Adding methods to a class

Now let's add some methods to our class. First, let's add the Listing 6-6 as instance side method:

Recall from previous chapters that we use the syntax `ClassName >> methodName` to explicitly show which class the method is defined in.

Note that the characters on line 3 are two separate single quotes with nothing between them, not a double quote! `''` is the empty string. Another way to create an empty string is `String new`. Do not forget to compile the method!

There's a lot going on in this method, let's go through it all.

---

[1] https://c2.com/doc/oopsla89/paper.html

Building a little game

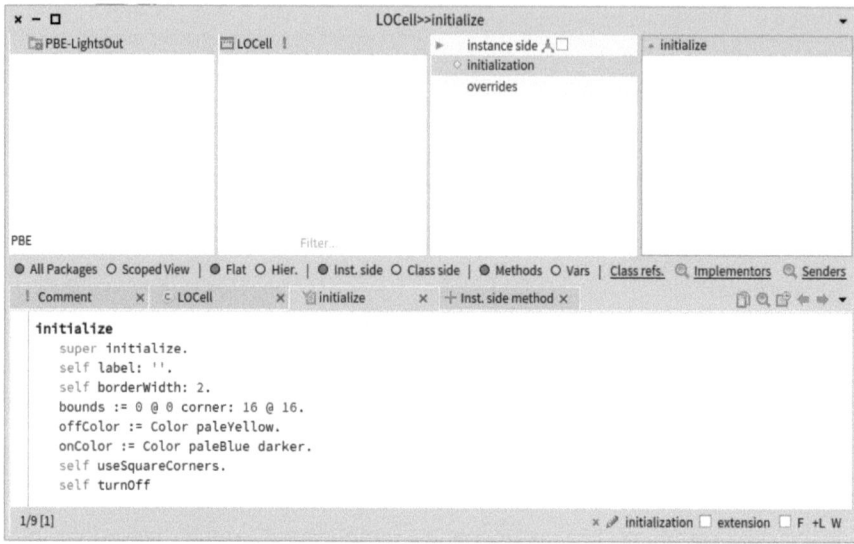

Figure 6-7 The newly-created method `initialize`.

Initialize methods

First off, it's another `initialize` method as we saw with our counter in the last chapter. As a reminder, these methods are special as, by convention, they're executed straight after an instance is created. So, when we execute `LOCell new`, the message `initialize` is sent automatically to the newly created object. `initialize` methods are used to set up the state of objects, typically to set their instance variables, and this is exactly what we are doing here.

Invoking superclass initialization

But the first thing this method does is to execute the `initialize` method of its superclass, `SimpleSwitchMorph`. The idea here is that any inherited state from the superclass will be properly initialized by the `initialize` method of the superclass. It is *always* a good idea to initialize inherited state by sending a `super initialize` before doing anything else. We don't know exactly what `SimpleSwitchMorph`'s `initialize` method will do when we call it, *and we don't care*, but it's a fair bet that it will set up some instance variables to hold reasonable default values that a `SimpleSwitchMorph` is going to need. So we had better call it, or we risk our new object starting off in an invalid state.

The rest of the method sets up the state of this object. Sending `self label: ''`, for example, sets the label of this object to the empty string.

About point and rectangle creation

The expression 0@0 corner: 16@16 needs some explanation. 0@0 constructs a Point object with its x and y coordinates both set to 0. In fact, 0@0 sends the message @ to the number 0 with argument 0. The effect will be that the number 0 will ask the Point class to create a new instance with the coordinates (0,0). Now we send this newly created point the message corner: 16@16, which causes it to create a Rectangle with corners 0@0 and 16@16. This newly created rectangle will be assigned to the bounds variable, inherited from the superclass. And this bounds variable determines how big our Morph is going to be - in effect we're just saying "be a 16 by 16 pixel square".

Note that the origin of the Pharo screen is at the top left, and the y coordinate increases as we go down the screen.

About the rest

The rest of the method should be self-explanatory. Part of the art of writing good Pharo code is picking good method names so that the code can be read like (very basic) English. You should be able to imagine the object talking to itself and saying "Self, use square corners!", "Self, turn off!".

Notice that there is a little green arrow next to your method (see Figure 6-7). This means the method exists in the superclass and is overridden in your class.

6.7 Inspecting an object

You can immediately test the effect of the code you have written by creating a new LOCell object and inspecting it: Open a Playground, type the expression LOCell new, and inspect it.

In the **Raw** tab of the Inspector The left-hand column shows a list of instance variables, and the value of the instance variable is shown in the right column (see Figure 6-8). Other tabs show other aspects of the LOCell, take a look at them and experiment.

If you click on an instance variable, the Inspector will open a new pane with the details of the instance variable (see Figure 6-9).

Executing expressions

The bottom pane of the Inspector acts as a mini-playground. It's useful because in this playground the pseudo-variable self is bound to the object selected.

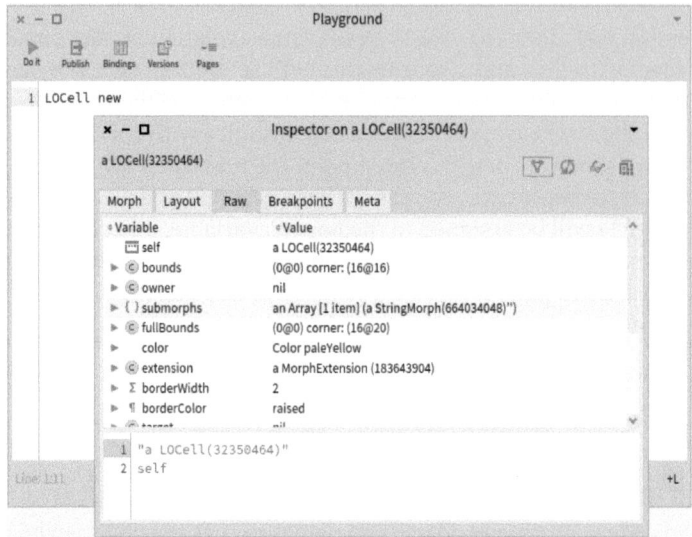

Figure 6-8 The inspector used to examine a LOCell object.

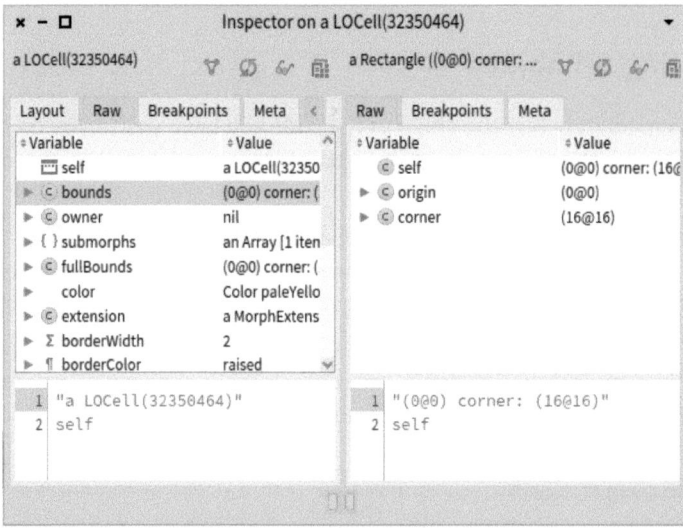

Figure 6-9 When we click on an instance variable, we inspect its value (another object).

6.7 Inspecting an object

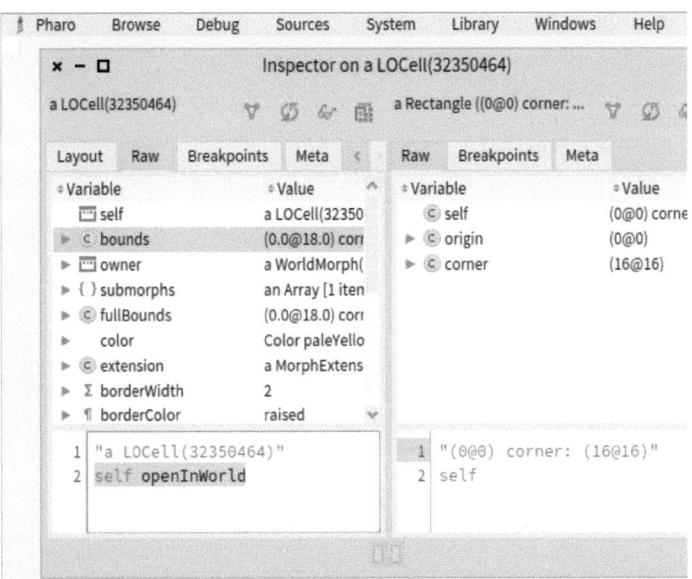

Figure 6-10 A LOCell opened in the **World**.

Go to that Playground at the bottom of the pane and type the text `self bounds: (200 @ 200 corner: 250 @ 250)` and then "Do it". To refresh the values, click on the `update` button (the blue little circle) at the top right of the pane. The `bounds` variable should change in the inspector. Now type the text `self openInWorld` in the mini-playground and **Do it**.

The Morphic Halo

The cell should appear near the top left-hand corner of the screen (as shown in Figure 6-10) and exactly where its bounds say that it should appear - i.e. 200 pixels down from the top and 200 pixels in from the left.

Meta-click (`Option-Shift-Click`) on the cell to bring up the **Morphic Halo**. The Morphic halo represents a visual way to interact with a Morph, using the 'handles' that now surround the Morph. Rotate the cell with the blue handle (next to the bottom-left) and resize it with the yellow handle (bottom-right). Notice how the bounds reported by the inspector also change (you may have to click refresh to see the new bounds value). Delete the cell by clicking on the x in the pink handle.

Listing 6-11 Defining the LOGame class

```
BorderedMorph subclass: #LOGame
    instanceVariableNames: ''
    classVariableNames: ''
    package: 'PBE-LightsOut'
```

Listing 6-12 Initialize the game

```
LOGame >> initialize
    | sampleCell width height n |
    super initialize.
    n := self cellsPerSide.
    sampleCell := LOCell new.
    width := sampleCell width.
    height := sampleCell height.
    self bounds: (5 @ 5 extent: (width * n) @ (height * n) + (2 * self
        borderWidth)).
    cells := Array2D
            new: n
            tabulate: [ :i :j | self newCellAt: i at: j ]
```

6.8 Defining the class LOGame

Now let's create the other class that we need for the game, LOGame.

Make the class definition template visible in the Browser main window. Do this by clicking on the package name, or right-clicking on the Class pane. Edit the code so that it reads as in Listing 6-11, and accept it.

Here, we subclass BorderedMorph. Morph is the superclass of all of the graphical shapes in Pharo. We've already seen a SimpleSwitchMorph, which is a Morph that can be toggled on and off, and (unsurprisingly) a BorderedMorph is a Morph with a border. We could also insert the names of the instance variables between the quotes on the second line, but for now, let's just leave that list empty.

6.9 Initializing our game

Let's define an initialize method for LOGame. Type the contents of 6-12 into the Browser as a method for LOGame and **Accept** it.

That's a lot, but don't worry about it for now. We're going to fill in the details as we go on.

Pharo will complain that it doesn't know the meaning of cells (see Figure 6-13). It will offer you a number of ways to fix this. Choose **Declare new instance variable**, because we want cells to be an instance variable.

6.10 Taking advantage of the Debugger

Figure 6-13 Declaring cells as a new instance variable.

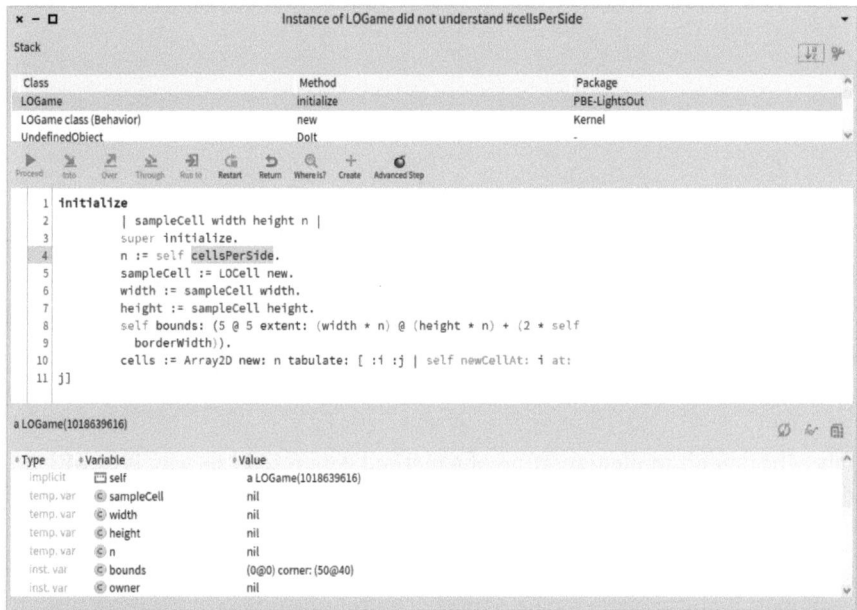

Figure 6-14 Pharo detecting an unknown selector.

6.10 Taking advantage of the Debugger

At this stage if you open a Playground, type LOGame new, and **Do it**, Pharo will complain that it doesn't know the meaning of some of the terms in the method(see Figure 6-14). It will tell you that LOGame doesn't understand the message cellsPerSide, it will open a Debugger. But cellsPerSide is not a mistake; it is just a method that we haven't yet defined. We will do so.

Do not close the Debugger. Click on the button Create in the Debugger and, when prompted, select LOGame, the class which will contain the method. Click on **Ok**, then when prompted for a method protocol enter accessing. The Debugger will create the method cellsPerSide on the fly and invoke it immedi-

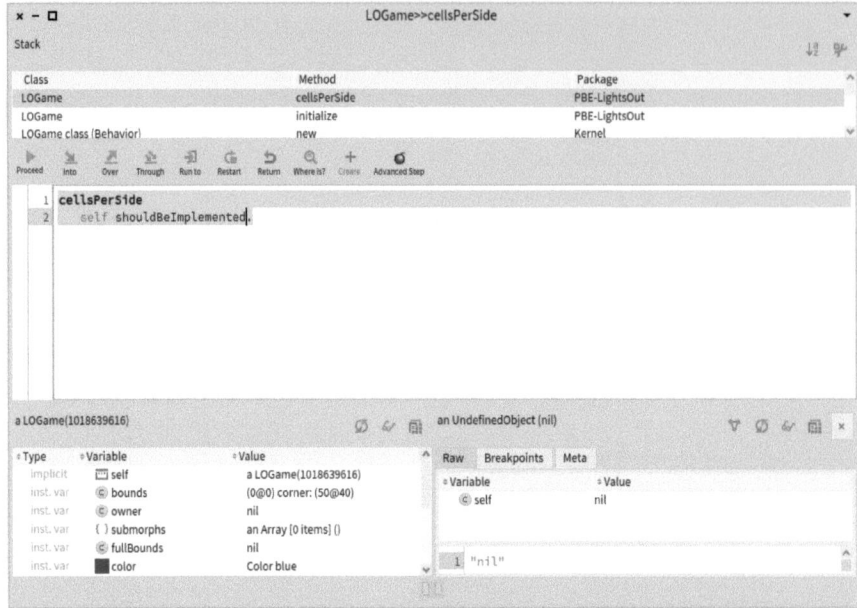

Figure 6-15 The system created a new method with a body to be defined.

ately. The default implementation of a method generated this way is to with a body of self shouldBeImplemented. This is then evaluated, which raises an exception and opens... the Debugger again on the method definition.

Here you can write your new method's definition. This method could hardly be simpler: it always returns the number 10. One advantage of representing constants as methods is that, if the program evolves so that the constant then depends on some other features, the method can be changed to calculate this value.

```
LOGame >> cellsPerSide
  "The number of cells along each side of the game"
  ^ 10
```

Do not forget to compile the method definition by using **Accept** when you've written it. You should end up with something looking like Figure 6-16. If you press the button **Proceed** the program will continue its execution, and it will stop again as we haven't defined the method newCellAt:.

We could use the same process but for now we'll stop to explain what we've done so far. Close the Debugger, and look at the class definition once again (which you can do by clicking on **LOGame** on the second pane of the **System Browser**). You will see that the browser has modified it to include the instance

6.11 Studying the initialize method

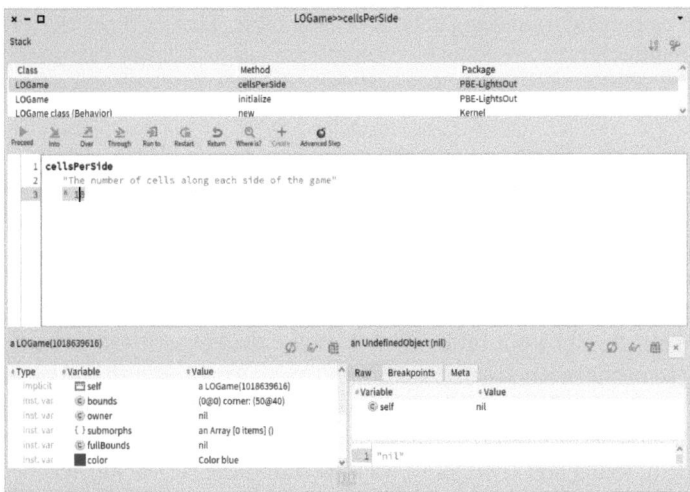

Figure 6-16 Defining `cellsPerSide` in the debugger.

Listing 6-17 Initialize the game

```
LOGame >> initialize
  | sampleCell width height n |
  super initialize.
  n := self cellsPerSide.
  sampleCell := LOCell new.
  width := sampleCell width.
  height := sampleCell height.
  self bounds: (50 @ 50 extent: (width * n) @ (height * n) + (2 * self
    borderWidth)).
  cells := Array2D
    new: n
    tabulate: [ :i :j | self newCellAt: i at: j ]
```

variable `cells`.

6.11 Studying the initialize method

Let's take a closer look at the `initialize` method on a `LOGame`.

Line 2

At line 2, the expression `| sampleCell width height n |` declares four temporary variables. They are called temporary variables because their scope and lifetime are entirely limited to the method. Well named temporary variables can be helpful in making code more readable. Lines 4-7 set the value of these variables.

Line 4

How big should our game board be? Big enough to hold some number of cells, and big enough to draw a border around them. And how many cells is the right number? 5? 10? 100? We just don't know yet, and if even if we thought we did know, we'd probably want change our minds later on. So we delegate the responsibility for knowing that number to a method, `cellsPerSide`, which we'll write in a bit. Don't be put off by this: it's very good practice to write code by referring to other methods that we haven't yet defined. Why? Well, it wasn't until we started writing the `initialize` method that we realized that we needed it. So when we realize that we're going to need it we can just give it a meaningful name and then move on to defining the rest of our method without interrupting our flow of thoughts. Deferring these decisions and implementations is a superpower.

And so line 4, `n := self cellsPerSide.`, sends the message `cellsPerSide` to `self`. The response, which will be the number of cells per side of the game board, is assigned to the temporary variable `n`.

The next three lines create a new `LOCell` object, and then we assign its width and height our `width` and `height` temporary variables. Why? We're using this instance of `LOCell` to find out what the dimensions of a cell are, because the most appropriate place to hold that information is in a `LOCell` itself.

Line 8

Line 8 sets the bounds of our new `LOGame`. Without worrying too much about the details just yet, believe us that the expression in parentheses creates a square with its origin (i.e., its top-left corner) at the point (50,50) and its bottom-right corner far enough away to allow space for the right number of cells.

Last line

The last line sets the `LOGame` object's instance variable `cells` to a newly created `Array2D` with the right number of rows and columns. We do this by sending the message `new:tabulate:` to the `Array2D` class. We know that `new:tabulate:` takes two arguments because it has two colons (:) in its name. The arguments go after each of the colons. If you are used to languages that put all of the arguments together inside parentheses, this may seem weird at first. Don't panic, it's only syntax! It turns out to be a very good syntax because the name of the method can be used to explain the roles of the arguments. For example, it is pretty clear that `Array2D rows: 5 columns: 2` has 5 rows and 2 columns, and not 2 rows and 5 columns.

`Array2D new: n tabulate: [ :i :j | self newCellAt: i at: j ]` creates a new n by n two-dimensional array (a matrix), and initializes its elements. The initial value of each element will depend on its coordinates. The $(i,j)^{th}$ element will be initialized to the result of evaluating `self newCellAt: i at: j`.

6.12 Organizing methods into protocols

Before we define any more methods, let's take a quick look at the third pane at the top of the browser. In the same way that the first pane of the browser lets us categorize classes into packages, the protocol pane lets us categorize methods so that we are not overwhelmed by a very long list of method names in the method pane. These groups of methods are called "protocols".

By default, you will have the `instance side` virtual protocol, which contains all of the methods in the class.

If you have followed along with this example, the protocol pane may well contain the `initialization` and `overrides` protocols. These protocols are added automatically when you override `initialize`. The Pharo Browser organizes the methods automatically, and adds them to the appropriate protocol whenever possible.

How does the Browser know that this is the right protocol? Well, in general Pharo can't know exactly. But if, for example, there is also an `initialize` method in the superclass, it will assume that our `initialize` method should be in the same protocol as the method it overrides.

The protocol pane may also contain the protocol **as yet unclassified**. Methods that aren't organized into protocols can be found here. You can right-click in the protocol pane and select **categorize all uncategorized** to fix this, or you can just organize things yourself manually.

6.13 Finishing the game

Now let's define the other methods that are used by `LOGame >> initialize`. You could either do this through the Browser or through the Debugger, but either way let's start with `LOGame >> newCellAt:at:`, in the `initialization` protocol:

Listing 6-18 The callback method

```
LOGame >> toggleNeighboursOfCellAt: i at: j

  i > 1
    ifTrue: [ (cells at: i - 1 at: j) toggleState ].
  i < self cellsPerSide
    ifTrue: [ (cells at: i + 1 at: j) toggleState ].
  j > 1
    ifTrue: [ (cells at: i at: j - 1) toggleState ].
  j < self cellsPerSide
    ifTrue: [ (cells at: i at: j + 1) toggleState ]
```

```
LOGame >> newCellAt: i at: j

  "Create a cell for position (i,j) and add it to my on-screen
    representation at the appropriate screen position. Answer the new
    cell"

  | c origin |
  c := LOCell new.
  origin := self innerBounds origin.
  self addMorph: c.
  c position: ((i - 1) * c width) @ ((j - 1) * c height) + origin.
  c mouseAction: [ self toggleNeighboursOfCellAt: i at: j ].
```

Note: the previous code is not correct. It will produce an error - this is on purpose.

Formatting

As you can see there is some indentation and empty lines in our method definition. Pharo can take care of this formatting for you: you can right-click on the method edit area and click on Format (or use Cmd-Shift-F shortcut). This will format your method nicely.

Toggle neighbors

The method defined above created a new LOCell, initialized to position (i, j) in the Array2D of cells. The last line defines the new cell's mouseAction to be the block [self toggleNeighboursOfCellAt: i at: j]. In effect, this defines the callback behavior to perform when the mouse is clicked. And so the corresponding method also needs to be defined:

The method toggleNeighboursOfCellAt:at: toggles the state of the four cells to the north, south, west and east of cell (i, j). The only complication is

6.14 Final LOCell methods

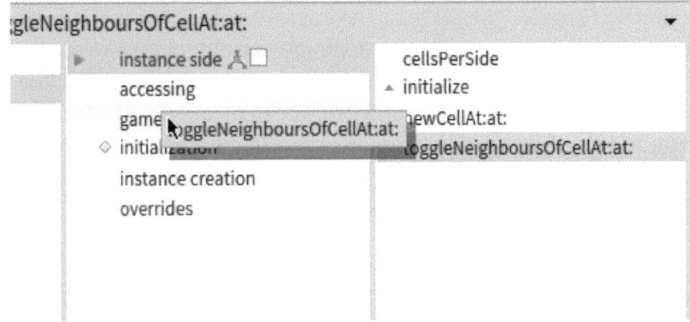

Figure 6-19 Drag a method to a protocol.

Listing 6-20 A typical setter method
```
LOCell >> mouseAction: aBlock
    mouseAction := aBlock
```

Listing 6-21 An event handler
```
LOCell >> mouseUp: anEvent

    self toggleState.
    mouseAction value
```

that the board is finite, so we have to make sure that a neighboring cell exists before we toggle its state.

Place this method in a new protocol called game logic. (Right-click in the protocol pane to add a new protocol). To move (re-classify) a method, you can simply click on its name and drag it to the newly-created protocol (see Figure 6-19).

6.14 Final LOCell methods

To complete the Lights Out game, we need to define two more methods in class LOCell this time to handle mouse events.

First, mouseAction: in Listing 6-20 is a simple accessor method:

We should put it in the accessing protocol.

Finally, we need to override the mouseUp: method. This will be called automatically by the GUI framework if the mouse button is released while the cursor is over this cell on the screen:

First, this method toggles the state of the current cell. Then it sends the message `value` to the object stored in the instance variable `mouseAction`. In `LOGame >> newCellAt: i at: j` we created the block `[self toggleNeighboursOfCellAt: i at: j ]` which will all the neighbors of a cell when it is evaluated, and we assigned this block to the `mouseAction` instance variable of the cell. Therefore sending the `value` message causes this block to be evaluated, and consequently the state of the neighboring cells will toggle.

6.15 Using the Debugger

That's it: the Lights Out game is complete! If you have followed all of the steps, you should be able to play the game, consisting of just two classes and seven methods. In a Playground, type `LOGame new openInHand` and **Do it** .

The game will open, and you should be able to click on the cells and see how it works. Well, so much for theory... When you click on a cell, a Debugger will appear. In the upper part of the debugger window you can see the execution stack, showing all the active methods. Selecting any one of them will show, in the middle pane, the code being executed in that method, with the part that triggered the error highlighted.

Click on the line labeled `LOGame >> toggleNeighboursOfCellAt: at:` (near the top). The Debugger will show you the execution context within this method where the error occurred (see Figure 6-22).

At the bottom of the Debugger is an area for all the variables in scope. You can inspect the object that is the receiver of the message that caused the selected method to execute, so you see here the values of the instance variables. You can also see the values of the method arguments, as well as intermediate values that have been calculated during execution.

Using the Debugger, you can evaluate the code step by step, inspect objects in parameters and local variables, evaluate code just as you can in a playground, and, most surprisingly to those used to other debuggers, actually change the code while it is being debugged. Some Pharoers program in the Debugger rather than the Browser almost all the time. The advantage of this is that you see the method that you are writing as it will be executed, with real parameters in the actual execution context.

In this case we can see in the first line of the top panel that the `toggleState` message has been sent to an instance of `LOGame`, while it should clearly have been an instance of `LOCell`. The problem is most likely with the initialization of the cells matrix. Browsing the code of `LOGame >> initialize` shows that `cells` is filled with the return values of `newCellAt:at:`, but when we look at that method, we see that there is no return statement there! By default, a

6.15 Using the Debugger

Figure 6-22 The Debugger, with the method `toggleNeighboursOfCell:at:` selected.

Listing 6-23 Fixing the bug.

```
LOGame >> newCellAt: i at: j
  "Create a cell for position (i,j) and add it to my on-screen
    representation at the appropriate screen position. Answer the new
    cell"

  | c origin |
  c := LOCell new.
  origin := self innerBounds origin.
  self addMorph: c.
  c position: ((i - 1) * c width) @ ((j - 1) * c height) + origin.
  c mouseAction: [ self toggleNeighboursOfCellAt: i at: j ].
  ^ c
```

method returns self, which in the case of `newCellAt:at:` is indeed an instance of LOGame. The syntax to return a value from a method in Pharo is `^`.

Close the Debugger window and add the expression `^ c` to the end of the method `LOGame >> newCellAt:at:` so that it returns c:

Often, you can fix the code directly in the Debugger window and click Proceed to continue running the application. In our case, because the bug was in the initialization of an object, rather than in the method that failed, the easiest thing to do is to close the Debugger window, destroy the running instance of the game (by opening the halo with Alt-Shift-Click and selecting the pink

Listing 6-24 Overriding mouse move actions

```
[ LOCell >> mouseMove: anEvent
```

x), and then create a new one.

Execute `LOGame new openInHand` again because if you use the old game instance it will still contain the blocks with the old logic.

Now the game should work properly... or nearly so. If we happen to move the mouse between clicking and releasing, then the cell the mouse is over will also be toggled. This turns out to be behavior that we inherit from `SimpleSwitchMorph`. We can fix this simply by overriding `mouseMove:` to do nothing as in Listing 6-24

And now finally we are done!

About the Debugger

By default, when an error occurs in Pharo, the system displays a Debugger. However, we can fully control this behavior and make it do something else. For example, we can write the error to a file, or we can even serialize the execution stack to a file, zip it and then reopen it in another Pharo image. When we are developing our software, the Debugger is available to let us go as fast as possible. But in a production system, developers will often want to control the Debugger to prevent their mistakes interfering too much with their users' work.

6.16 And if all else fails...

First, do not stress! It's perfectly normal to make a mess of things when you program. If anything, it's the rule and not the exception. Probably the most annoying thing that can happen when you're starting to experiment with graphical elements in Pharo is that the screen becomes cluttered with seemingly indestructible widgets. Don't panic. Try and get an Inspector up on one of them by using a meta-click (`Option-Shift-Click` or equivalent) to open the Morphic halo, select the menu handle, "debug > inspect". Once you get an Inspector open you're home free:

- if you are inspecting the game itself: `self delete`.
- if you are inspect a game cell: `self owner delete`.

6.17 Saving and sharing Pharo code

Now that you have **Lights Out** working, you probably want to save it somewhere so that you can archive it and share it with your friends. Of course, you can save your whole Pharo image and show off your first program by running it, but your friends probably have their own code in their images, and don't want to give that up to use your image. What you need is a way of getting the source code out of your Pharo image so that other programmers can bring it into theirs.

We showed you the basics of using Iceberg and Git to save, share, and version your projects, and you should feel free to do that again with Lights Out. If you would like to learn more about Iceberg, and you're feeling impatient, then you should feel free to skip ahead to Chapter 7.

If you're still reading this, we're now going to take a look at exporting your Pharo code as files.

6.18 Saving code in a file

You can also save the code of your package by writing it to a file, an action commonly called "filing out" by all Pharoers, Squeakers and related communities. The right-click menu in the Package pane will give you the option to select **Extra > File Out** the whole of the `PBE-LightsOut` package. The resulting file is more or less human readable, but is really intended for computers, not humans. You can email this file to your friends, and they can "file it in" with their own image.

File out the `PBE-LightsOut` package (see Figure 6-25). You should now find a file named `PBE-LightsOut.st` in the same folder on disk where your image is saved. Have a look at this file with a text editor to get a feel for what the code looks like when it's in a file. If you don't want to leave Pharo to look at the file, try inspecting `'PBE-LightsOut.st' asFileReference` in a Playground.

Open a fresh Pharo image and use the **File Browser** tool (**System > File Browser**) to file in the `PBE-LightsOut.st` fileout (see Figure 6-26). Right-click on the file and select **Install into the image**. Verify that the game now works in the new image.

6.19 Accessor conventions

If you are used to getters and setters in other programming languages, you might expect these methods to be called `setMouseAction` and `getMouseAction`. The Pharo convention is different. A getter always has the same name as the variable it gets, and a setter is named similarly, but with a trailing ":" to

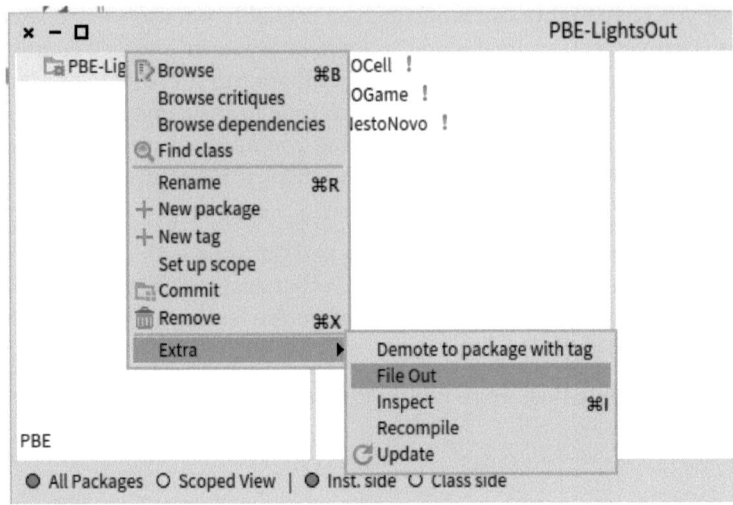

Figure 6-25 File out the `PBE-LightsOut` package.

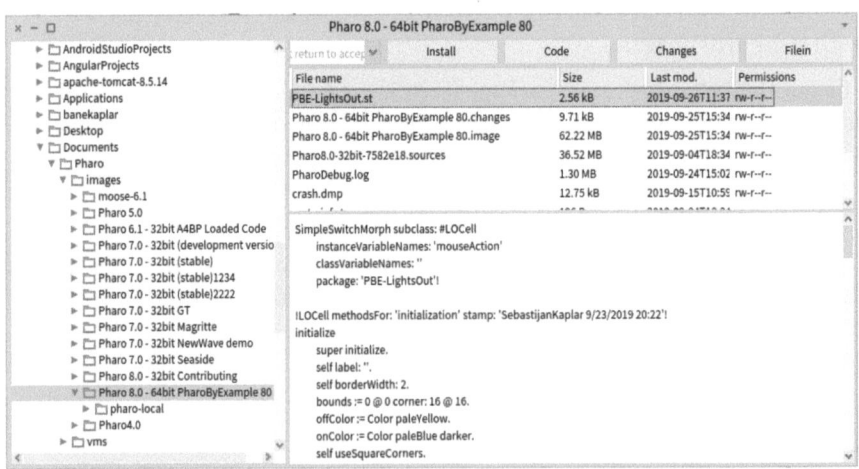

Figure 6-26 Import your code with the file browser.

allow it to take an argument, hence `mouseAction` and `mouseAction:`. Collectively, setters and getters are called *accessor methods*, and by convention they should be placed in the `accessing` protocol. In Pharo, *all* instance variables are private to the object that owns them, so the only way for another object to read or write those variables is through accessor methods. Instance variables can of course be accessed in subclasses too, but you can never access another object's instance variables - not even ones in another instance of your class, or the class object itself.

6.20 Chapter summary

In this chapter, we've had a chance to reinforce what we've learned about Pharo so far, and to apply it to writing a simple game using the Morphic framework. We've learned how to open the Morphic halo around graphical elements on the screen, how to manipulate them, and (importantly) how to get rid of them. We've also learned how to "file out" and "file in" Pharo packages for quick sharing.

CHAPTER 7

Publishing and packaging your first Pharo project

In this chapter we will explain in more detail how you can publish your project on GitHub using Iceberg. Iceberg is a tool and library that supports the handling of Git repositories; it does more than just save and publish your files. Then we will briefly show how to make sure that you or other developers can load your code without having to understand its internal dependencies.

We will not explain basic concepts like commit, push/pull, merging, or cloning, please refer to a Git tutorial for this. A strong prerequisite for reading this chapter is that you must be able to publish from the command line to your Git hosting service. If you cannot, do not expect Iceberg to fix it for you. If you have some problems with your SSH configuration (which is the default way to push using GitHub) you can either use HTTPS instead, or read the *Manage your code with Iceberg* booklet that you can find on http://books.pharo.org. Let us get started.

7.1 For the impatient

If you do not want to read through everything below, and you feel pretty confident, here is an executive summary of how to get your code published:

- Create a project on GitHub or any Git-based platform.
- [Optional] Configure Iceberg to use custom SSH keys.
- Add a project to Iceberg.

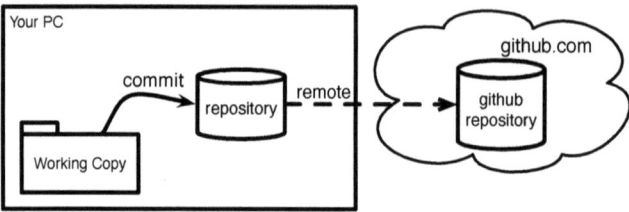

Figure 7-1 Git: A distributed versioning system.

- [Optional (but strongly recommended)] In the cloned repository, create a directory named `src` on your file system. This is a good convention.
- In Iceberg, open your project and add your packages.
- Commit your project.
- [Optional] Add a baseline to your project.
- Push your changes to the remote repository.

And you're done. But now let's explain these steps more calmly.

7.2 Basic architecture

As Git is a distributed versioning system, you need a *local* clone of the repository and a *working copy*. Your working copy and local repository are usually on your machine. Your changes to the working copy will be committed to the local repository before being pushed to your remote repository or repositories (Figure 7-1). Pharo complicates this situation a little, which is why we use Iceberg. In a nutshell, Pharo classes and methods are objects that get modified on the fly. When you modify a class source code, the Git working copy is not automatically modified. It is as though you have two working copies: the object one in your image, and the Git-file based one. Iceberg is here to help you synchronize and manage them both.

Create a new project on GitHub

While you can save locally first and then later create a remote repository, we're going to create a new project on GitHub first – we'll explain the other option later.

Figure 7-2 shows the creation of a project on GitHub. The order does not really matter, but you will use different options when you add a repository to Iceberg as we will show later.

7.2 Basic architecture

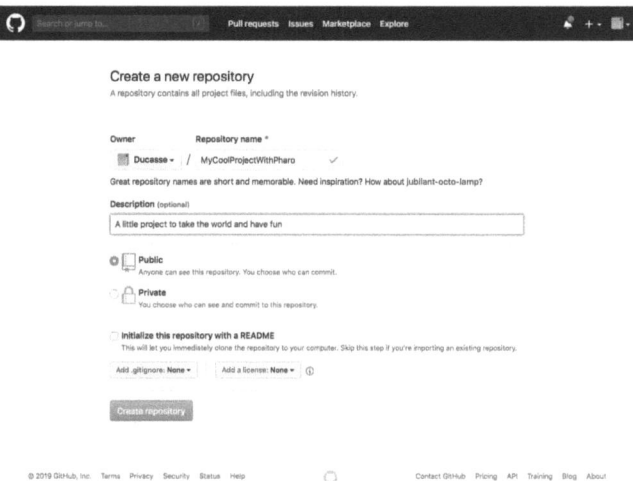

Figure 7-2 Create a new project on GitHub.

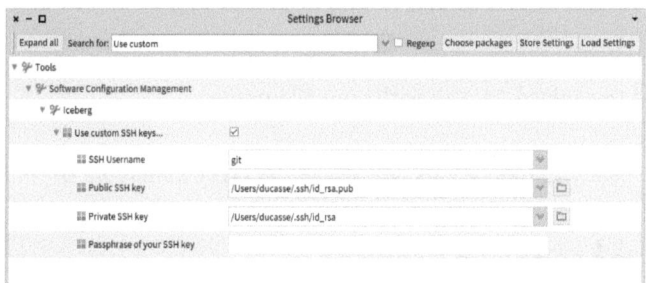

Figure 7-3 Use Custom SSH keys settings.

[Optional] SSH setup: tell Iceberg to use your keys

To be able to commit to your Git project, you should either use HTTPS or you will need to set up valid SSH credentials in your system. If you do use SSH (the default way), you will need to make sure those keys are available to your GitHub account, and that the shell adds them for smoother communication with the server.

Go to settings browser, search for "Use custom SSH keys" and enter your data there as shown in Figure 7-3).

Alternatively, you can execute the following expressions in your image Playground or add them to your Pharo system preference file:

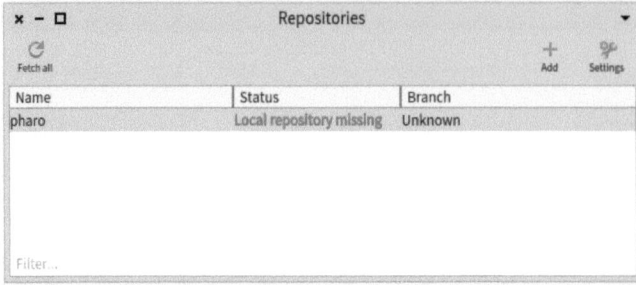

Figure 7-4 Iceberg *Repositories* browser on a fresh image indicates that if you want to version modifications to Pharo itself you will have to tell Iceberg where the Pharo clone is located. But you do not care.

```
IceCredentialsProvider useCustomSsh: true.
IceCredentialsProvider sshCredentials
  publicKey: 'path\to\ssh\id_rsa.pub';
  privateKey: 'path\to\ssh\id_rsa'
```

> **Note** This method can also be used if you have a non-default key file. You just need to replace `id_rsa` with your file name.

Now we are ready to have a look at Iceberg the layer managing Git in Pharo.

7.3 Iceberg repositories browser

Figure 7-4 shows the top level pane for Iceberg. It shows that, for now, you do not have any projects defined or loaded. It shows the Pharo project (among others), but indicates that it could not find a local repository for it by displaying 'Local repository missing'.

First, don't worry about the missing repository for Pharo: you'll only need it if you want to contribute to the Pharo language project, which you're more than welcome to do but maybe let's finish this chapter first. Here's what's going on: the Pharo system does not know where the corresponding Git repository for its classes is. But Pharo works just fine without a local repository; you can still browse system classes and methods, and make changes, because Pharo has its own internal source management in the image. This warning just indicates that if you want to version Pharo system code using Git, then you should tell to the system where the local clone and working copy of Pharo are located on your local machine. But if you don't plan to modify and share the Pharo system code, you don't have to worry.

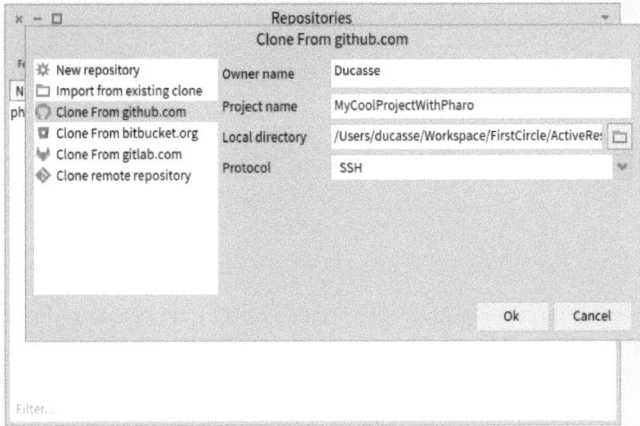

Figure 7-5 Cloning a project hosted on GitHub via SSH.

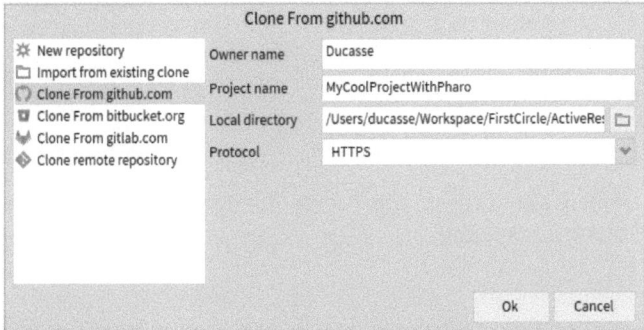

Figure 7-6 Cloning a project hosted on GitHub via HTTPS.

7.4 Add a new project to Iceberg

The first step is to add a project to Iceberg:

- Press the + button to the right of the Iceberg main window.
- Select the source of your project. In our example, since you did not clone your project yet, choose the GitHub option.

Notice that you can either use SSH (Figure 7-5) or HTTPS (Figure 7-6).

This instructs Iceberg to clone the repository we just created on GitHub. We specify the owner, project, and physical location where the Git local clone and working copy will be on your disk.

Publishing and packaging your first Pharo project

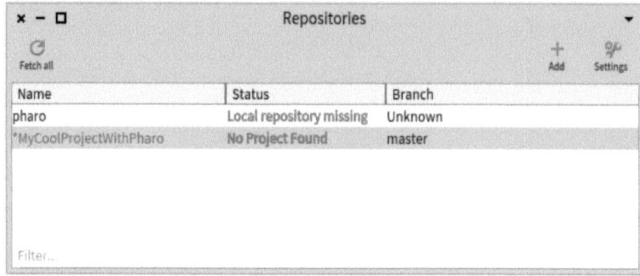

Figure 7-7 Just after cloning an empty project, Iceberg reports that the project is missing information.

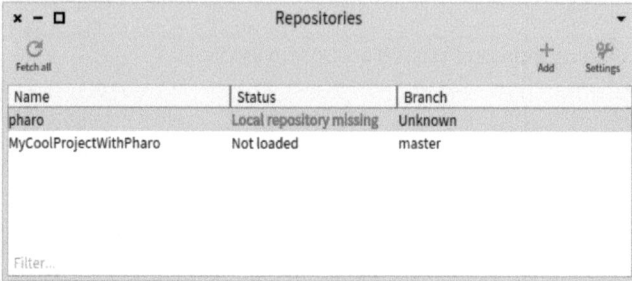

Figure 7-8 Adding a project with some contents shows that the project is not loaded - not that it is not found.

Iceberg has now added your project to its list of managed projects and cloned an empty repository to your disk. You will see the status of your project, as in Figure 7-7. Here is a breakdown of what you are seeing:

- `MyCoolProjectWithPharo` has a star and is green. This usually means that you have changes which haven't been committed yet, but may also happen in unrelated edge cases like this one. Don't worry about this for now.

- The Status of the project is **'No Project Found'** and this is more important. This is normal since the project is empty. Iceberg cannot find its metadata. We will fix this soon.

Later on, when you have committed changes to your project and you want to load it in another image by cloning it again, you will see that Iceberg will just report that the project is not loaded as shown in Figure 7-8.

7.4 Add a new project to Iceberg

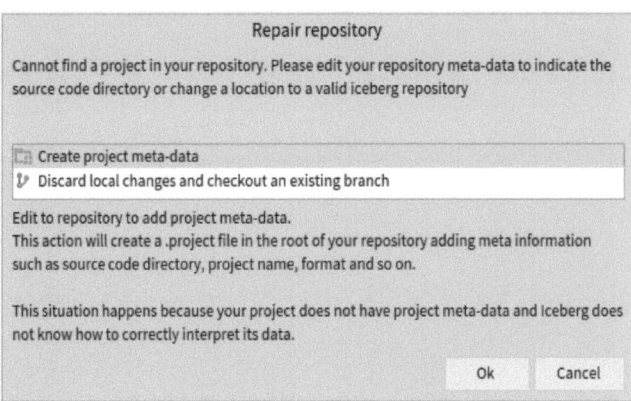

Figure 7-9 Create project metadata action and explanation.

Repair to the rescue

Iceberg is a smart tool that helps you fix the problems you may encounter while working with Git. As a general principle, each time you get a status with red text (such as **'No Project Found'** or **'Detached Working Copy'**), you should ask Iceberg to fix it using the **Repair** command.

Iceberg cannot solve all situations automatically, but it will propose and explain possible repair actions. The actions are ranked from most to least likely to be right one. Each action offers an explanation and the consequences of using it. It is *always* a good idea to read them. Setting up your repository the right way makes it extremely hard to lose any piece of code with Iceberg and Pharo, since Pharo contains its own copy of the code. Extremely hard... but not impossible. So pay attention!

Create project metadata

Iceberg reported that it could not find the project because some metadata was missing, such as the file encoding for your code, and the example location inside the repository. When we activate the repair command, we get Figure 7-9. It shows the **Create project metadata** action and its explanation.

When you choose to create the project metadata, Iceberg shows you the filesystem of your project as well as the repository format as shown in Figure 7-10. Tonel is the preferred format for Pharo projects: it has been designed to work across multiple filesystems, so only change it if you know what you are doing!

Before accepting the changes it is a good idea to add a source folder to your repository, by convention `src`. Do that by pressing the + icon. You will be

Publishing and packaging your first Pharo project

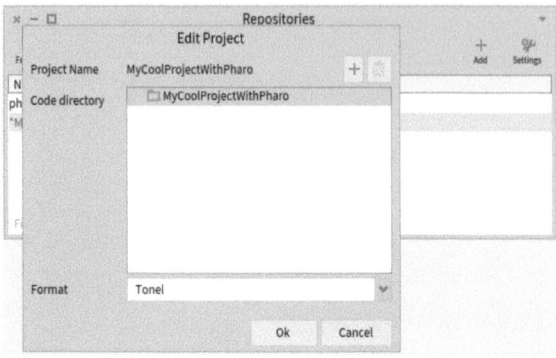

Figure 7-10 Showing where the metadata will be saved and the file encoding.

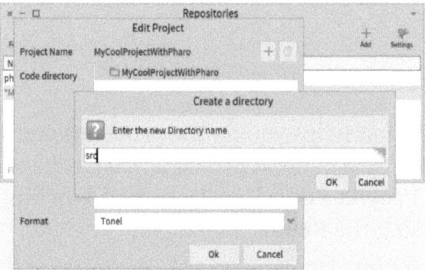

Figure 7-11 Adding a src repository for code storage.

prompted to specify the folder for code as shown in Figure 7-11. Do not forget to select the src folder once you created it. Iceberg will show you the exact structure of your project as shown in Figure 7-12.

After accepting the project details, Iceberg shows you the files that you will be committing as shown in Figure 7-13.

Once you have committed the metadata, Iceberg shows you that your project has been repaired but has not bee loaded, as shown in Figure 7-8. This is normal since we haven't added any packages to our project yet. You can still push your changes to your remote repository at this point if you want to.

Your local repository is ready, let's move on to the next part.

7.5 Add and commit your package using the 'Working copy' browser

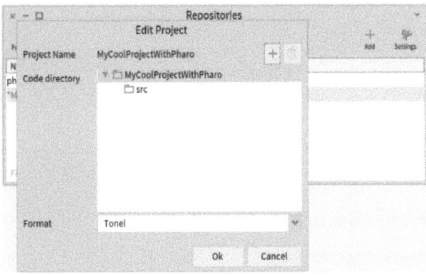

Figure 7-12 Resulting situation with a src folder: Pay attention to select it.

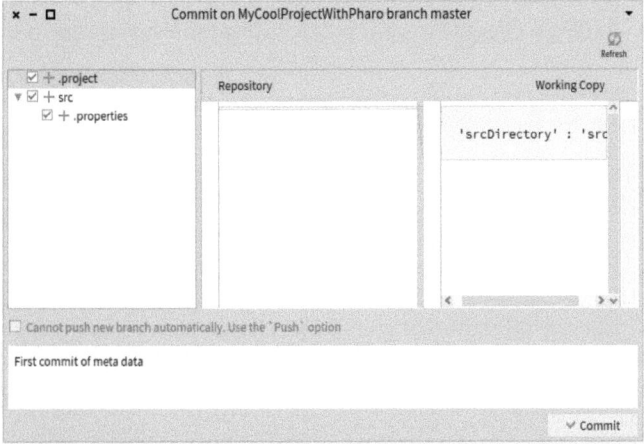

Figure 7-13 Details of metadata commit.

7.5 Add and commit your package using the 'Working copy' browser

Once your project contains Iceberg metadata, Iceberg will be able to manage it easily. Double click on your project to bring up a **Working copy** browser for your project. It lists all the packages that compose your project. Right now you have none. Add a package by pressing the + button as shown by Figure 7-14.

Again, Iceberg shows that your package contains changes that are not committed by using the green color and the star in front of the package name as showing in Figure 7-15.

Publishing and packaging your first Pharo project

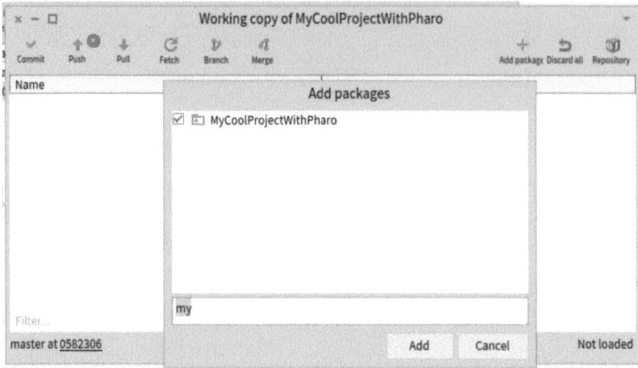

Figure 7-14 Adding a package to your project using the *Working copy* browser.

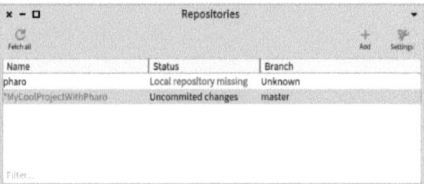

Figure 7-15 Iceberg indicates that your project has unsaved changes – indeed you just added your package.

Commit the changes

Commit the changes to your local repository using the Commit button as shown in Figure 7-16. Iceberg lets you chose the changed entities you want to commit. It might not be necessary but it's an important feature. Iceberg will show the result of the commit action by removing the star and changing the color. It now shows that the code in the image is in sync with your local repository as shown by Figure 7-17. You can commit several times if needed.

Publish your changes to your remote

Publish your changes from your local directory to your remote repository using the **Push button**. You may be prompted for credentials if you used HTTPS.

When you push your changes, Iceberg will show you all the commits awaiting publication and will push them to your remote repository as shown in Figure 7-18.

Now you're basically done. You know the essential aspects of managing your

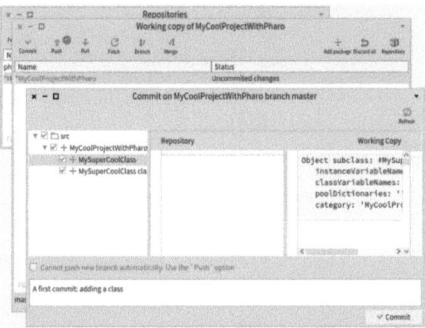

Figure 7-16 When you commit changes, Iceberg shows you the code about to be committed and you can chose the code entities that will effectively be saved.

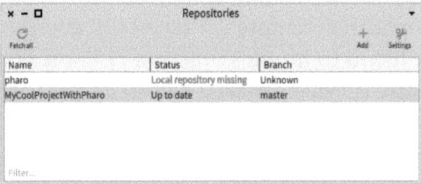

Figure 7-17 Once changes committed, Iceberg reflects that your project is in sync with the code in your local repository.

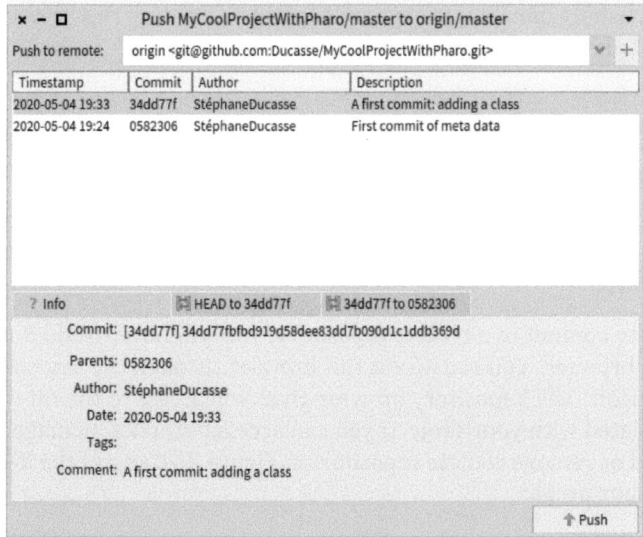

Figure 7-18 Publishing your committed changes.

Publishing and packaging your first Pharo project

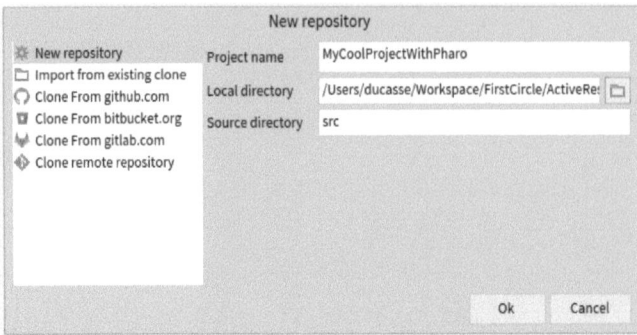

Figure 7-19 Creating a local repository without pre-existing remote repository.

code with GitHub or any other remote Git service. Iceberg has been designed to guide you so please listen to it unless you really know what you are doing. You are now ready to use services offered by GitHub and others to improve your code control and quality!

7.6 What if I did not create a remote repository?

We started by creating a remote repository on GitHub. Then we asked Iceberg to add a project by cloning it from GitHub. So how do we do this the other way around, publishing our local project without a pre-existing repository. This is actually quite simple, so let's give it a whirl.

Create a new repository

When you add a new repository use the **New repository** option as shown in 7-19.

Add a remote

If you want to commit to a remote repository, you will have to add it using the **Repository** browser. You can access this browser through the associated menu item or the icon. The Repository browser gives you access to the Git repositories associated with your project: you can access branches, manage them, and also add or remove remote repositories. Figure 7-20 shows the Repository browser on our project.

Pressing the **Add remote** button adds a remote; you just need to fill in the information that you can find in your remote Git project. Figure 7-21 shows it for the sample project using SSH and Figure 7-22 for HTTPS.

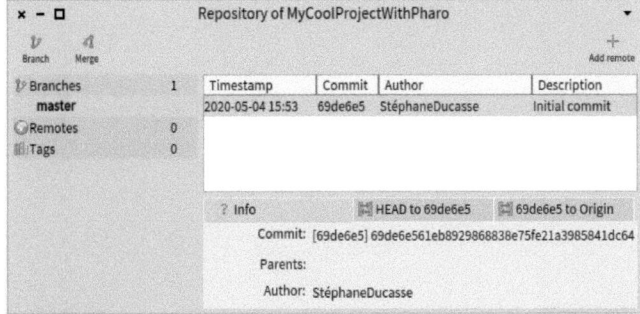

Figure 7-20 Opening the repository browser let you add and browse branches as well as remote repositories.

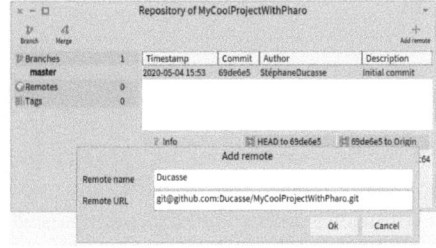

Figure 7-21 Adding a remote using the *Repository* browser of your project (SSH version).

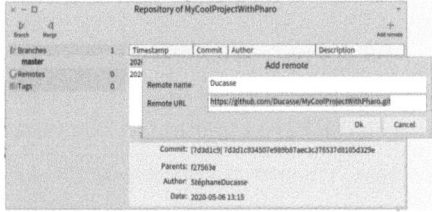

Figure 7-22 Adding a remote using the *Repository* browser of your project (HTTP version).

Publishing and packaging your first Pharo project

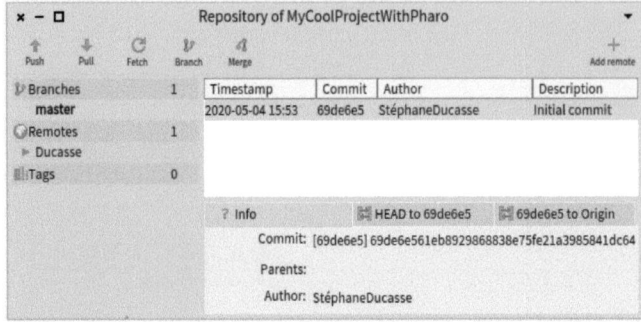

Figure 7-23 Once you pushed you changes to the remote repository.

Push to the remote

Now you can push your changes and versions to the remote repository using the **Push** button. Once you have pushed you can see that you have one remote as shown in Figure 7-23.

7.7 Configuring your project

Versioning code is just the first part of making sure that you and other developers can reload your code. We will now describe how to define a *Baseline*: a project map that you will use to define the dependencies within your project and its dependencies on other projects.

Defining a `BaselineOf`

A Baseline is a description of a project architecture. You express the dependencies between your packages and other projects so that all the dependent projects are loaded without the user having to understand them or the links between them.

A baseline is expressed as a subclass of BaselineOf and packaged in a package named 'BaselineOfXXX' (where 'XXX' is the name of your project). So if you have no dependencies, you can have something as simple as this:

```
BaselineOf subclass: #BaselineOfMyCoolProjectWithPharo
    ...
    package: 'BaselineOfMyCoolProjectWithPharo'
```

7.8 Loading from an existing repository

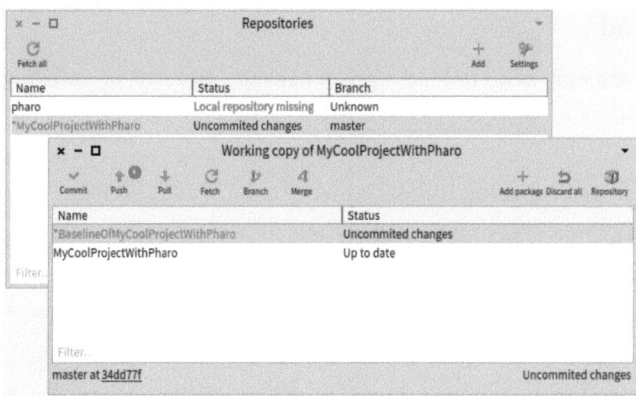

Figure 7-24 Added the baseline package to your project using the *Working copy* browser.

```
BaselineOfMyCoolProjectWithPharo >> baseline: spec
  <baseline>
  spec
    for: #common
    do: [ spec package: 'MyCoolProjectWithPharo' ]
```

Once you have defined your baseline, you should add its package to your project using the Working Copy browser as explained above. You should end up with something like Figure 7-24.

Now, commit it and push your changes to your remote repository.

More information about what you can achieve with Baseline is available on the Pharo wiki at: https://github.com/pharo-open-documentation/pharo-wiki/.

7.8 Loading from an existing repository

There are several ways to load your versioned code into a new Pharo image:

Loading Baseline using Iceberg

To load a project interactively, you can use the **Metacello** menu item in Iceberg, seen when action-clicking the name of your repository. It lets you load a Baseline and execute it to load the project's packages. This way you are sure that all the required sub-projects are loaded.

Manual load

Sometimes you may need to load a given package directly, or your project may not have defined a Baseline. You can use Iceberg to load a specific package as follows:

- Add the project using Iceberg as we previously explained.
- Open the "Working copy" browser by double clicking on the project in the Repositories browser.
- Select a package and manually load it.

Scripting the load

The second way is to use a Metacello script:

```
Metacello new
    baseline: 'MyCoolProjectWithPharo';
    repository: 'github://Ducasse/MyCoolProjectWithPharo/src';
    load
```

For projects with metadata, like the one we just created, that's all you have to do. Notice that we not only give the GitHub path but also the code folder (src in this case).

7.9 Stepping back...

When working in Pharo on a package that's being managed with Iceberg, you need to understand that you are not editing your local working copy directly: you are actually modifying objects that represent classes and methods within the running Pharo environment. And so it's like you have two working copies: the running Pharo image and the Git working copy on disk.

When you use Git to manage your project outside of Pharo and Iceberg, with the git command line tool for instance, you need to remember that there is the code in the Pharo image *and* the code in the working copy (and the code in your local clone). To update your image, you *first* have to update your Git working copy and *then* load code from the working copy to the image. To save your code you *first* have to save the code in your image as files, *then* add them to your Git working copy, and *then* finally commit them to your clone.

The beauty of Iceberg is that it manages all of this for you transparently. All the tedious synchronization between the two working copies is done behind the scenes.

The architecture of the Iceberg system is as follows:

- You have your code in the Pharo image.
- Pharo is acting as a working copy (it contains the contents of the local Git repository).
- Iceberg manages the publication of your code to the Git working copy and the Git local repository.
- Iceberg manages the publication of your code to remote repositories.
- Iceberg manages the re-synchronization of your image with the Git local repository, Git remote repositories and the Git working copy.

7.10 Conclusion

This chapter presented the most important aspects of how to publish and package your code correctly. This will help you to reload it in other images, as well as collaborate with other Pharo developers.

CHAPTER 8

Syntax in a nutshell

Pharo adopts a syntax very close to that of its ancestor, Smalltalk.

The syntax is designed so that program text can be read aloud as though it were a kind of pidgin English. The following method of the class Week shows an example of the syntax. It checks whether DayNames already contains the argument, i.e., if this argument represents a correct day name. If this is the case, it will assign it to the class variable StartDay.

```
startDay: aSymbol

    (DayNames includes: aSymbol)
        ifTrue: [ StartDay := aSymbol ]
        ifFalse: [ self error: aSymbol, ' is not a recognised day name' ]
```

Pharo's syntax is minimal. Essentially there is syntax only for sending messages (i.e., expressions). Expressions are built up from a very small number of primitive elements (message sends, assignments, closures, returns...). There are only 6 reserved keywords, i.e., pseudo-variables, and there are no dedicated syntax constructs for control structures or declaring new classes. Instead, nearly everything is achieved by sending messages to objects.

For instance, instead of an if-then-else control structure, conditionals are expressed as messages (such as ifTrue:) sent to Boolean objects. New subclasses are created by sending a message to their superclass.

8.1 Syntactic elements

Expressions are composed of the following building blocks:

1. The six *pseudo-variables*: `self`, `super`, `nil`, `true`, `false`, and `thisContext`
2. Constant expressions for *literal* objects including numbers, characters, strings, symbols and arrays
3. Variable declarations
4. Assignments
5. Block closures
6. Messages
7. Method returns

We can see examples of the various syntactic elements in the table below.

Syntax expression	What it represents
`startPoint`	a variable name
`Transcript`	a global variable name
`self`	pseudo-variable
`1`	decimal integer
`2r101`	binary integer
`1.5`	floating point number
`2.4e7`	number in exponential notation
`$a`	the character `'a'`
`'Hello'`	the string `'Hello'`
`#Hello`	the symbol `#Hello`
`#(1 2 3)`	a literal array
`{ 1 . 2 . 1 + 2 }`	a dynamic array
`"a comment"`	a comment
`| x y |`	declaration of variables x and y
`x := 1`	assign 1 to x
`[:x	x + 2]`	a block that evaluates to x + 2
`<primitive: 1>`	a method annotation (here primitive)
`3 factorial`	unary message `factorial`
`3 + 4`	binary message `+`
`2 raisedTo: 6 modulo: 10`	keyword message `raisedTo:modulo:`
`^ true`	return the value `true`

8.1 Syntactic elements

`x := 2 . x := x + x`	two expressions separated by separator (.)
`Transcript show: 'hello'; cr`	two cascade messages separated by (;)

Local variables. `startPoint` is a variable name, or identifier. By convention, identifiers are composed of words in "camelCase" (i.e., each word except the first starting with an upper case letter). The first letter of an instance variable, method or block parameters, or temporary variable must be lower case. This indicates to the reader that the variable has a private scope.

Shared variables. Identifiers that start with upper case letters are global variables, class variables, pool dictionaries or class names. `Transcript` is a global variable, an instance of the class `ThreadSafeTranscript`.

The message receiver. `self` is a pseudo-variable that refers to the object that receives the message (that led to the execution of the method using `self`). It gives us a way send messages to it. We call `self` "the receiver" because this object will receive the message that causes the method to be executed. Finally, `self` is called a "pseudo-variable" since we cannot directly change its values or assign to it.

Integers. In addition to ordinary decimal integers like 42, Pharo also provides a radix notation. `2r101` is 101 in radix 2 (i.e., binary), which is equal to decimal 5.

Floating point numbers. Such numbers can be specified with their base-ten exponent: `2.4e7` is 2.4×10^7.

Characters. A dollar sign introduces a literal character: `$a` is the literal for the character `'a'`. Instances of special, non-printing characters can be obtained by sending appropriately named messages to the `Character` class, such as `Character space` and `Character tab`.

Strings. Single quotes `' '` are used to define a literal string. If you want a string with a single quote inside, just double the quote, as in `'G''day'`.

Symbols. Symbols are like Strings, in that they contain a sequence of characters. However, unlike a string, a literal symbol is guaranteed to be globally unique. There is only one `Symbol` object `#Hello` but there may be multiple `String` objects with the value `'Hello'`.

Compile-time literal arrays. They are defined by `#( )`, surrounding space-separated literals. Everything within the parentheses must be a compile-time constant. For example, `#(27 (true) abc 1+2)` is a literal array of 6 elements: the integer 27, the compile-time array containing the object `true` (non-changeable Boolean), the symbol `#abc`, the integer 1, the symbol `+` and the integer 2. Note that this is the same as `#(27 #(true) #abc 1 #+ 2)`.

Run-time dynamic arrays. Curly braces `{ }` define a dynamic array whose elements are expressions, separated by periods, and evaluated at run-time.

So `{ 1. 2. 1 + 2 }` defines an array with elements 1, 2, and 3 the result of evaluating 1+2.

Comments. They are enclosed in double quotes " ". "hello" is a comment, not a string, and is ignored by the Pharo compiler. Comments may span multiple lines but they cannot be nested.

Local variable definitions. Vertical bars `|  |` enclose the declaration of one or more local variables before the beginning of a method or a block body.

Assignment. The two characters `:=` specify that a variable refers to an object.

Blocks. Square brackets `[ ]` define a block, also known as a block closure or a lexical closure, which is a first-class object representing a function. As we shall see, blocks may take arguments (`[:i | ...]`) and can have local variables (`[| x | ...]`). Blocks also close over their definition environment, i.e., they can refer to variables that where reachable at the time of their definition.

Pragmas and primitives. `< primitive: ... >` is a method annotation. This specific one denotes the invocation of a virtual machine (VM) primitive. In the case of a primitive the code following it, it either to explain what the primitive is doing (for essential primitives) or is executed only if the primitive fails (for optional primitive). The same syntax of a message within `< >` is also used for other kinds of method annotations also called pragmas.

Unary messages. These consist of a single word (like `factorial`) sent to a receiver (like 3). In `3 factorial`, 3 is the receiver, and `factorial` is the message selector.

Binary messages. These are messages sent to a receiver with a single argument, and whose selector looks like mathematical operator (for example: +). In `3 + 4`, the receiver is 3, the message selector is +, and the argument is 4.

Keyword messages. Their selectors consist of one or more keywords (like `raisedTo: modulo:`), each ending with a colon and taking a single argument. In the expression `2 raisedTo: 6 modulo: 10`, the message selector `raisedTo:modulo:` takes the two arguments 6 and 10, one following each colon. We send the message to the receiver 2.

Sequences of statements. A period or full-stop (.) is the statement separator. Putting a period between two expressions turns them into independent statements like in `x := 2. x := x + x`. Here we first assign value 2 to the variable x, and then duplicate its value by assigning a value of `x + x` to it.

Cascades. Semicolons (;) are used to send a cascade of messages to a single receiver. In `stream nextPutAll: 'Hello World'; close` we first send the keyword message `nextPutAll: 'Hello World'` to the receiver `stream`, and then we send the unary message `close` to the same receiver.

Method return. ^ is used to *return* a value from a method.

The basic classes Number, Character, String and Boolean are described in Chapter : Basic Classes.

8.2 Pseudo-variables

In Pharo, there are 6 pseudo-variables: nil, true, false, self, super, and thisContext. They are called pseudo-variables because they are predefined and cannot be assigned to. true, false, and nil are constants, while the values of self, super, and thisContext vary dynamically as code is executed.

- true and false are the unique instances of classes True and False which are the subclasses of class Boolean. See Chapter : Basic Classes for more details.
- self always refers to the receiver of the message and denotes the object in which the corresponding method will be executed. Therefore, the value of self dynamically changes during the program execution, but can not be assigned in the code.
- super also refers to the receiver of the message too, but when you send a message to super, the method-lookup changes so that it starts from the superclass of the class containing the method that sends message to super. For further details see Chapter : The Pharo Object Model.
- nil is the undefined object. It is the unique instance of the class UndefinedObject. Instance variables, class variables and local variables are, by default, initialized to nil.
- thisContext is a pseudo-variable that represents the top frame of the execution stack and gives access to the current execution point. thisContext is normally not of interest to most programmers, but it is essential for implementing development tools such as the debugger, and it is also used to implement exception handling and continuations.

8.3 Messages and message sends

As we described, there are three kinds of messages in Pharo with predefined precedence. This distinction has been made to reduce the number of mandatory parentheses.

Here we give a brief overview on message kinds and ways for sending and executing them, while more detailed description is provided in Chapter : Understanding messages.

1. *Unary* messages take no argument. 1 factorial sends the message factorial to the object 1. Unary message selectors consist of alphanumeric characters, and start with a lower case letter.

2. *Binary* messages take exactly one argument. 1 + 2 sends the message + with argument 2 to the object 1. Binary message selectors consist of one or more characters from the following set: + - / * ~ < > = @ % | & ? ,

3. *Keyword* messages take an arbitrary number of arguments. 2 raisedTo: 6 modulo: 10 sends the message consisting of the message selector raisedTo:modulo: and the arguments 6 and 10 to the object 2. Keyword message selectors consist of a series of alphanumeric keywords, where each keyword starts with a lower-case letter and ends with a colon.

Message precedence

Unary messages have the highest precedence, then binary messages, and finally keyword messages, while brackets can be used to change the evaluation order.

Thus, in the following example we first send factorial to 3 which will give us result 6. Afterwards we send + 6 to 1 which gives the result 7, and finally we send raisedTo: 7 to 2.

```
2 raisedTo: 1 + 3 factorial
>>> 128
```

Precedence aside, for the messages of the same kind, execution is strictly from left to right. Hence, as we have two binary messages, the following example return 9 and not 7.

```
1 + 2 * 3
>>> 9
```

Parentheses must be used to alter the order of evaluation as follows:

```
1 + (2 * 3)
>>> 7
```

8.4 Sequences and cascades

All expressions may be composed in sequences separated by period, while message sends may be also composed in cascades by semi-colons. A period separated sequence of expressions causes each expression in the series to be evaluated as a separate *statement*, one after the other.

```
Transcript cr.
Transcript show: 'hello world'.
Transcript cr
```

This will send cr to the Transcript object, then send to Transcript the message show: 'hello world', and finally send it another cr, again.

When a series of messages is being sent to the *same* receiver, then this can be expressed more succinctly as a *cascade*. The receiver is specified just once, and the sequence of messages is separated by semi-colons as follows:

```
Transcript
  cr;
  show: 'hello world';
  cr
```

This cascade has precisely the same effect as the sequence in the previous example.

8.5 Method syntax

Whereas expressions may be evaluated anywhere in Pharo (for example, in a playground, in a debugger, or in a browser), methods are normally defined in a browser window, or in the debugger. Methods can also be filed in from an external medium, but this is not the usual way to program in Pharo.

Programs are developed one method at a time, in the context of a given class. A class is defined by sending a message to an existing class, asking it to create a subclass, so there is no special syntax required for defining classes.

Here is the method lineCount defined in the class String. The usual *convention* is to refer to methods as ClassName>>methodName. Here the method is then String>>lineCount. Note that ClassName>>methodName is not part of the Pharo syntax just a convention used in books to clearly define a method within a class in which it is defined.

```
String >> lineCount
  "Answer the number of lines represented by the receiver, where every
    cr adds one line."

  | cr count |
  cr := Character cr.
  count := 1 min: self size.
  self do: [:c | c == cr ifTrue: [count := count + 1]].
  ^ count
```

Syntactically, a method consists of:

1. the method pattern, containing the name (i.e., `lineCount`) and any parameters (none in this example),
2. comments which may occur anywhere, but the convention is to put one at the top that explains what the method does,
3. declarations of local variables (i.e., `cr` and `count`), and
4. any number of expressions separated by dots (here there are four).

The execution of any expression preceded by a ^ (a caret or upper arrow, which is Shift-6 for most keyboards) will cause the method to exit at that point, returning the value of the expression that follows the ^. A method that terminates without explicitly returning value of some expression will implicitly return `self` object.

Parameters and local variables should always start with lower case letters. Names starting with upper-case letters are assumed to be global variables. Class names, like `Character`, for example, are simply global variables referring to the object representing that class.

8.6 Block syntax

Blocks (lexical closures) provide a mechanism to defer the execution of expressions. A block is essentially an anonymous function with a definition context. A block is executed by sending it the message `value`. The block answers the value of the last expression in its body, unless there is an explicit return (with ^) in which case it returns the value of the returned expression.

```
[ 1 + 2 ] value
>>> 3
```

```
[ 3 = 3 ifTrue: [ ^ 33 ]. 44 ] value
>>> 33
```

Blocks may have parameters each of which is declared with a leading colon. A vertical bar separates the parameters declaration from the body of the block. To evaluate a block with one parameter, you must send it the message `value:` with one argument. A two-parameter block must be evaluated by sending `value:value:` with two arguments, and so on, up to 4 arguments.

```
[ :x | 1 + x ] value: 2
>>> 3
```

```
[ :x :y | x + y ] value: 1 value: 2
>>> 3
```

If you have a block with more than four parameters, you must use `value-WithArguments:` and pass the arguments in an array. However, a block with a large number of parameters is often a sign of a design problem.

In blocks there may be also declared local variables, surrounded by vertical bars, just like local variable declarations in a method. Local variables are declared after arguments and vertical bar separator, and before the block body. In the following example, x y are parameters, and z is local variable.

```
[ :x :y |
  | z |
  z := x + y.
  z ] value: 1 value: 2
>>> 3
```

Blocks are actually lexical closures, since they can refer to variables of the surrounding environment. The following block refers to the variable x of its enclosing environment:

```
| x |
x := 1.
[ :y | x + y ] value: 2
>>> 3
```

Blocks are instances of the class `BlockClosure`. This means that they are objects, so they can be assigned to variables and passed as arguments just like any other object.

8.7 Conditionals and loops

Pharo offers no special syntax for control constructs. Instead, these are typically expressed by sending messages to booleans, numbers and collections, with blocks as arguments.

Some conditionals

Conditionals are expressed by sending one of the messages `ifTrue:`, `ifFalse:` or `ifTrue:ifFalse:` to the result of a boolean expression. See Chapter : Basic Classes, for more about booleans.

```
(17 * 13 > 220)
  ifTrue: [ 'bigger' ]
  ifFalse: [ 'smaller' ]
>>>'bigger'
```

Some loops

Loops are typically expressed by sending messages to blocks, integers or collections. Since the exit condition for a loop may be repeatedly evaluated, it should be a block rather than a boolean value. Here is an example of a very procedural loop:

```
n := 1.
[ n < 1000 ] whileTrue: [ n := n*2 ].
n
>>> 1024
```

`whileFalse:` reverses the exit condition.

```
n := 1.
[ n > 1000 ] whileFalse: [ n := n*2 ].
n
>>> 1024
```

`timesRepeat:` offers a simple way to implement a fixed number of iterations through the loop body:

```
n := 1.
10 timesRepeat: [ n := n*2 ].
n
>>> 1024
```

We can also send the message `to:do:` to a number which then acts as the initial value of a loop counter. The two arguments are the upper bound, and a block that takes the current value of the loop counter as its argument:

```
result := String new.
1 to: 10 do: [:n | result := result, n printString, ' '].
result
>>> '1 2 3 4 5 6 7 8 9 10 '
```

High-order iterators

Collections comprise a large number of different classes, many of which support the same protocol. The most important messages for iterating over collections include `do:`, `collect:`, `select:`, `reject:`, `detect:` and `inject:into:`. These messages represent high-level iterators that allow one to write very compact code.

An **Interval** is a collection that lets one iterate over a sequence of numbers from the starting point to the end. `1 to: 10` represents the interval from 1 to 10. Since it is a collection, we can send the message `do:` to it. The argument is a block that is evaluated for each element of the collection.

```
result := String new.
(1 to: 10) do: [:n | result := result, n printString, ' '].
result
>>> '1 2 3 4 5 6 7 8 9 10 '
```

`collect:` builds a new collection of the same size, transforming each element. You can think of `collect:` as the Map in the MapReduce programming.

```
(1 to:10) collect: [ :each | each * each ]
>>> #(1 4 9 16 25 36 49 64 81 100)
```

`select:` and `reject:` build new collections, each containing a subset of the elements of the iterated collection that satisfies, or not, respectively, the boolean block condition.

`detect:` returns the first element in the collection that satisfies the condition.

Don't forget that strings are also collections (of characters), so you can iterate over all the characters.

```
'hello there' select: [ :char | char isVowel ]
>>> 'eoee'
```

```
'hello there' reject: [ :char | char isVowel ]
>>> 'hll thr'
```

```
'hello there' detect: [ :char | char isVowel ]
>>> $e
```

Finally, you should be aware that collections also support a functional-style fold operator in the `inject:into:` method. You can also think of it as the Reduce in the MapReduce programming model. This lets you generate a cumulative result using an expression that starts with a seed value and injects each element of the collection. Sums and products are typical examples.

```
(1 to: 10) inject: 0 into: [ :sum :each | sum + each]
>>> 55
```

This is equivalent to 0+1+2+3+4+5+6+7+8+9+10.

More about collections can be found in Chapter : Collections.

8.8 Method annotations: Primitives and pragmas

In Pharo methods can be annotated too. Method annotation are delimited by < and >. There are used for two main scenarios: execution specific metadata for the primitives of the language and metadata.

Primitives

In Pharo everything is an object, and everything happens by sending messages. Nevertheless, at certain points we hit rock bottom. Certain objects can only get work done by invoking virtual machine primitives. Such primitives are essential primitives since they cannot be expressed in Pharo.

For example, the following are all implemented as primitives: memory allocation (new, new:), bit manipulation (bitAnd:, bitOr:, bitShift:), pointer and integer arithmetic (+, -, <, >, *, /, =, ==...), and array access (at:, at:put:).

When a method with a primitive is executed, the primitive code is executed in place of the method. A method using such a primitive may include additional Pharo code, which will be executed only if the primitive fails (for the case the primitive is an optional one).

In the following example, we see the code for SmallInteger>>+. If the primitive fails, the expression super + aNumber will be evaluated and its value returned.

```
+ aNumber
    "Primitive. Add the receiver to the argument and answer with the
        result
    if it is a SmallInteger. Fail if the argument or the result is not a
    SmallInteger Essential No Lookup. See Object documentation
        whatIsAPrimitive."

    <primitive: 1>
    ^ super + aNumber
```

Pragmas

In Pharo, the angle bracket syntax is also used for method annotations called pragmas. Once a method has been annotated with a pragma, the annotations can be collected using a collection (see the class PragmaCollector).

8.9 Chapter summary

- Pharo has only six reserved identifiers known as pseudo-variables: true, false, nil, self, super, and thisContext.
- There are five kinds of literal objects: numbers (5, 2.5, 1.9e15, 2r111), characters ($a), strings ('hello'), symbols (#hello), and arrays (#('hello' #hi) or { 1 . 2 . 1 + 2 })
- Strings are delimited by single quotes, comments by double quotes. To get a quote inside a string, double it.

8.9 Chapter summary

- Unlike strings, symbols are guaranteed to be globally unique.
- Use #(...) to define a literal array at compile time. Use { ... } to define a dynamic array at runtime. Note that #(1+2) size >>> 3, but {12+3} size >>> 1. To observe why, compare #(12+3) inspect and {1+2} inspect.
- There are three kinds of messages: unary (e.g., 1 asString, Array new), binary (e.g., 3 + 4, 'hi', ' there'), and keyword (e.g., 'hi' at: 2 put: $o)
- A cascaded message send is a sequence of messages sent to the same target, separated by semi-colons: OrderedCollection new add: #calvin; add: #hobbes; size >>> 2
- Local variables declarations are delimited by vertical bars. Use := for assignment. |x| x := 1
- Expressions consist of message sends, cascades and assignments, evaluated left to right (and optionally grouped with parentheses). Statements are expressions separated by periods.
- Block closures are expressions enclosed in square brackets. Blocks may take arguments and can contain temporary variables. The expressions in the block are not evaluated until you send the block a value message with the correct number of arguments. [:x | x + 2] value: 4
- There is no dedicated syntax for control constructs, just messages whose sends conditionally evaluate blocks.

CHAPTER 9

Understanding message syntax

Although Pharo's message syntax is extremely simple, it is unconventional and can take some time getting used to. This chapter offers some guidance to help you get acclimatized to the syntax for sending messages. If you already feel comfortable with the syntax, you may choose to skip this chapter, or come back to it later. The Pharo's syntax is closed to the one of Smalltalk, so Smalltalk programmers can be familiar with Pharo's syntax.

9.1 Identifying messages

In Pharo, except for the syntactic elements listed in Chapter 8 (:= ^ . ; # () {} [: |]), everything is a message send. You can define operators like + for your own classes, but all operators, existing and defined ones, have the same precedence. In fact, in Pharo there is no operators! Just messages of a given kind: *unary*, *binary* or *keywords*. Moreover, you cannot change the arity of a message selector. The selector "-" is always the selector of a binary message; there is no way to have a unary - for unary messages.

In Pharo, the order in which messages are sent is determined by the *kind* of message. There are just three kinds of messages: *unary*, *binary*, and *keyword messages*. Unary messages are always sent first, then binary messages and finally keyword ones. As in most languages, parentheses are used to change the execution order. These rules make Pharo code as easy to read as possible. And most of the time you do not have to think about the rules.

As most computation in Pharo is done by message passing, correctly identifying messages is crucial. The following terminology will help us:

Understanding message syntax

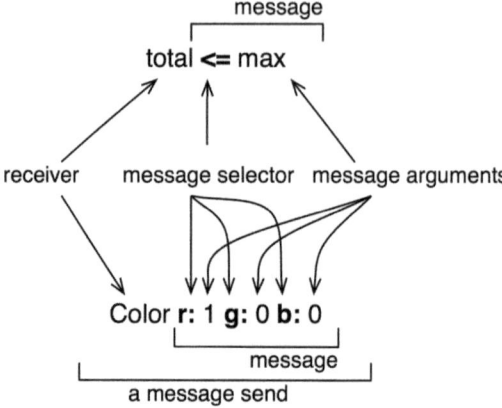

Figure 9-1 Two message sends composed of a receiver, a method selector, and a set of arguments.

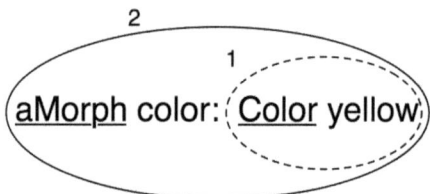

Figure 9-2 Two messages: `Color yellow` and `aMorph color: Color yellow`.

- A message is composed of a message *selector* and optional message arguments.
- A message is sent to a *receiver*.
- The combination of a message and its receiver is called a *message send* as shown in Figure 9-1.

A message is always sent to a receiver, which can be a single literal, a block or a variable or the result of evaluating another message. To help you identify the receiver of a message, we will underline it for you. We will also surround each message send with an ellipse and number message sends starting from the first one that will be sent to help you see the order in which messages are sent.

Figure 9-2 represents two message sends, `Color yellow` and `aMorph color: Color yellow`, hence there are two ellipses. The message send `Color yellow` is executed first so its ellipse is numbered 1. There are two receivers: aMorph which receives the message `color:` ... and `Color` which receives the message `yellow`. Both receivers are underlined.

A receiver can be the first element of a message, such as `100` in the message send `100 + 200` or `Color` in the message send `Color yellow`. However, a receiver can also be the result of other messages. For example in the message `Pen new go: 100`, the receiver of the message `go: 100` is the object returned by the message send `Pen new`. In all the cases, a message is sent to an object called the *receiver* which may be the result of another message send.

Message send	Message type	Result
`Color yellow`	unary	Creates color yellow.
`aPen go: 100`	keyword	The pen moves forward 100 pixels.
`100 + 20`	binary	100 is increased by 20
`Browser open`	unary	Opens a new browser.
`Pen new go: 100`	unary and keyword	Creates and moves a pen 100 pixels forward.
`aPen go: 100 + 20`	keyword and binary	The pen moves forward 120 pixels.

The table shows several examples of message sends. You should note that:

- Not all message sends have arguments. Unary messages like `open` do not have arguments.

- Single keyword and binary messages like `go: 100` and `+ 20` each have one argument.

- There are also simple messages and composed ones. `Color yellow` and `100 + 20` are simple: a message is sent to an object, while the message send `aPen go: 100 + 20` is composed of two messages: `+ 20` is sent to `100` and `go:` is sent to `aPen` with the argument being the result of the first message.

- A receiver can be an expression (such as an assignment, a message send or a literal) which returns an object. In `Pen new go: 100`, the message `go: 100` is sent to the object that results from the execution of the message send `Pen new`.

9.2 Three kinds of messages

Pharo defines a few simple rules to determine the order in which the messages are sent. These rules are based on the distinction between 3 different kinds of messages:

- *Unary messages* are messages that are sent to an object without any other information. For example in 3 factorial, factorial is a unary message. A sent unary message may execute a basic unary operation or an arbitrary functionality, but it is always sent without arguments.
- *Binary messages* are messages consisting of operators (often arithmetic) and executing basic binary operations. They are binary because they always involve only two objects: the receiver and the argument object. For example in 10 + 20, + is a binary message sent to the receiver 10 with argument 20.
- *Keyword messages* are messages consisting of one or more keywords, each ending with a colon (:) and taking an argument. For example in anArray at: 1 put: 10, the message selector is at:put:. The keyword at: takes the argument 1 and the keyword put: takes the argument 10.

It is important to note that:

- There are no keyword messages that are sent without arguments. All messages that are sent without arguments are unary ones.
- There is a difference between keyword messages that are sent with exactly one argument and binary ones - Basically a keyword message contains a colon to identify each of its arguments.

Unary messages

Unary messages are messages that do not require any argument. They follow the syntactic template: receiver messageName. The selector is simply made up of a succession of characters not containing a colon ():) *e.g.,* factorial, open, class.

```
89 sin
>>> 0.860069405812453
```

```
3 sqrt
>>> 1.732050807568877
```

```
Float pi
>>> 3.141592653589793
```

```
'blop' size
>>> 4
```

```
true not
>>> false
```

```
Object class
>>> Object class    "The class of Object is Object class (BANG)"
```

> **Important** Unary messages follow the syntactic template: receiver **selector**

Binary messages

Binary messages are messages that require exactly one argument *and* whose selector consists of a sequence of one or more characters from the set: +, -, *, /, &, =, >, |, <, ~, and @. Note that -- is not allowed for parsing reasons.

```
100@100
>>> 100@100  "creates a Point object"
```

```
3 + 4
>>> 7
```

```
10 - 1
>>> 9
```

```
4 <= 3
>>> false
```

```
(4/3) * 3 == 4
>>> true  "equality is just a binary message, and Fractions are exact"
```

```
(3/4) == (3/4)
>>> false  "two equal Fractions are not the same object"
```

> **Important** Binary messages follow the syntactic template: receiver **selector** argument

Keyword messages

Keyword messages are messages that require one or more arguments and whose selector consists of one or more keywords each ending in a colon (:).

In the following example, message between:and: is composed of two keywords: between: and and:. The full message selector is between:and: and it is sent to numbers.

```
2 between: 0 and: 10
>>> true
```

Each keyword takes an argument. Hence r:g:b: is a message with three arguments, playFileNamed: and at: are messages with one argument, and at:put: is a message with two arguments. To create an instance of the class Color one can use the message r:g:b: as in Color r: 1 g: 0 b: 0, which creates the color red. Note that the colons are part of the selector.

```
Color r: 1 g: 0 b: 0
>>> Color red  "creates a new color"
```

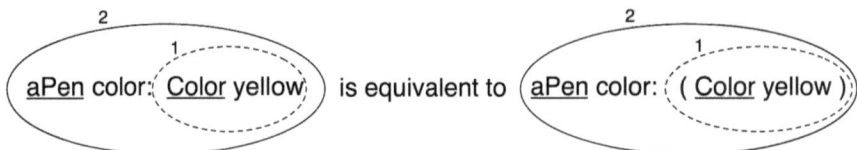

Figure 9-3 Unary messages are sent first so Color yellow is sent. This returns a color object which is passed as argument of the message aPen color:.

In a Java like syntax, the Pharo message send `Color r: 1 g: 0 b: 0` would correspond to a method invocation written as `Color.rgb(1,0,0)`.

```
1 to: 10
>>> (1 to: 10)   "creates an interval"
```

```
| nums |
nums := Array newFrom: (1 to: 5).
nums at: 1 put: 6.
nums
>>> #(6 2 3 4 5)
```

> **Important** Keyword messages follow the syntactic template: receiver **selectorWordOne:** argumentOne **wordTwo:** argumentTwo ... **wordN:** argumentN

9.3 Message composition

The three kinds of messages each have different precedence, which allows them to be composed in an elegant way.

- Unary messages are always sent first, then binary messages and finally keyword messages.
- Messages in parentheses are sent prior to any kind of messages.
- Messages of the same kind are evaluated from left to right.

These rules lead to a very natural reading order. Now if you want to be sure that your messages are sent in the order that you want you can always put more parentheses as shown in Figure 9-3. In this figure, the message `yellow` is an unary message and the message `color:` a keyword message, therefore the message send `Color yellow` is sent first. However as message sends in parentheses are sent first, putting (unnecessary) parentheses around `Color yellow` just emphasizes that it will be sent first. The rest of the section illustrates each of these points.

Unary > Binary > Keywords

Unary messages are sent first, then binary messages, and finally keyword messages. We also say that unary messages have a higher priority over the other kinds of messages.

> **Important** Unary > Binary > Keyword

As these examples show, Pharo's syntax rules generally ensure that message sends can be read in a natural way:

```
1000 factorial / 999 factorial
>>> 1000
```

```
2 raisedTo: 1 + 3 factorial
>>> 128
```

Unfortunately the rules are a bit too simplistic for arithmetic message sends, so you need to introduce parentheses whenever you want to impose a priority over binary operators:

```
1 + 2 * 3
>>> 9
```

```
1 + (2 * 3)
>>> 7
```

We will dedicate a section to arithmetic inconsistencies.

The following example, which is a bit more complex (!), offers a nice illustration that even complicated expressions can be read in a natural way:

```
[:aClass | aClass methodDict keys select: [:aMethod |
    (aClass>>aMethod) isAbstract ]] value: Boolean
>>> an IdentitySet(#or: #| #and: #& #ifTrue: #ifTrue:ifFalse:
    #ifFalse: #not #ifFalse:ifTrue:)
```

Here we want to know which methods of the Boolean class are abstract. We ask some argument class, aClass, for the keys of its method dictionary, and select those methods of that class that are abstract. Then we bind the argument aClass to the concrete value Boolean. We need parentheses only to send the binary message >>, which selects a method from a class, before sending the unary message isAbstract to that method. The result shows us which methods must be implemented by Boolean's concrete subclasses True and False.

In fact, we could also have written the equivalent but simpler expression:
Boolean methodDict select: [:each | each isAbstract] thenCollect: [:each | each selector].

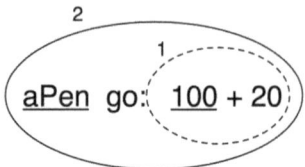

Figure 9-4 Binary messages are sent before keyword messages.

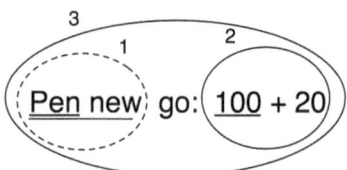

Figure 9-5 Decomposing Pen new go: 100 + 20.

Example. In the message aPen color: Color yellow, there is one *unary* message yellow sent to the class Color and a *keyword* message color: sent to aPen. Unary messages are sent first so the message send Color yellow is sent (1). This returns a color object which is passed as argument of the message aPen color: aColor (2). Figure 9-3 shows graphically how messages are sent.

```
Decomposing the execution of aPen color: Color yellow
         aPen color: Color yellow
(1)      Color yellow           "unary message is sent first"
              >>> aColor
(2)      aPen color: aColor     "keyword message is sent next"
```

Example. In the message aPen go: 100 + 20, there is a *binary* message + 20 and a *keyword* message go:. Binary messages are sent prior to keyword messages so 100 + 20 is sent first (1): the message + 20 is sent to the object 100 and returns the number 120. Then the message aPen go: 120 is sent with 120 as argument (2). The following example shows how the message send is executed.

```
         aPen go: 100 + 20
(1)      100 + 20           "binary message first"
              >>>   120
(2)      aPen go: 120       "then keyword message"
```

Example. As an exercise we let you decompose the execution of the message send Pen new go: 100 + 20 which is composed of one unary, one keyword

9.3 Message composition

and one binary message (see Figure 9-5).

Parentheses first

Messages within parentheses are sent prior to other messages.

> **Important** (Msg) > Unary > Binary > Keyword

Here are some examples.

The first example shows that parentheses are not needed when the order is the one we want, *i.e.* that result is the same if we write this with or without parentheses. Here we compute tangent of 1.5, then we round it and convert it as a string.

```
1.5 tan rounded asString = (((1.5 tan) rounded) asString)
>>> true
```

The second example shows that `factorial` is executed prior to the sum and if we want to first perform the sum of 3 and 4 we should use parentheses as shown below.

```
3 + 4 factorial
>>> 27    "(not 5040)"
```

```
(3 + 4) factorial
>>> 5040
```

Similarly in the following example, we need the parentheses to force sending `lowMajorScaleOn:` before `play`.

```
(FMSound lowMajorScaleOn: FMSound clarinet) play
"(1) send the message clarinet to the FMSound class to create a
    clarinet sound.
 (2) send this sound to FMSound as argument to the lowMajorScaleOn:
    keyword message.
 (3) play the resulting sound."
```

Example.   The message send `(65@325 extent: 134@100) center` returns the center of a rectangle whose top left point is (65, 325) and whose size is 134*100. The following example shows how the message is decomposed and sent. First the message between parentheses is sent: it contains two binary messages `65@325` and `134@100` that are sent first and return points, and a keyword message `extent:` which is then sent and returns a rectangle. Finally the unary message `center` is sent to the rectangle and a point is returned. Evaluating the message without parentheses would lead to an error because the object `100` does not understand the message `center`.

119

Understanding message syntax

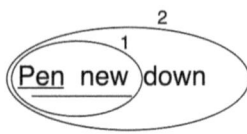

Figure 9-6 Decomposing Pen new down.

```
Example of Parentheses.
      (65@325 extent: 134@100) center
(1)   65@325
      "binary"
      >>> aPoint
(2)                              134@100                        "binary"
                                 >>> anotherPoint
(3)   aPoint extent: anotherPoint                               "keyword"
      >>> aRectangle
(4)   aRectangle center                                         "unary"
      >>> 132@375
```

From left to right

Now we know how messages of different kinds or priorities are handled. The final question to be addressed is how messages with the same priority are sent. They are sent from the left to the right. Note that you already saw this behaviour in the example `1.5 tan rounded asString` where all unary messages are sent from left to right which is equivalent to `(((1.5 tan) rounded) asString)`.

> **Important** When the messages are of the same kind, the order of execution is from left to right.

Example. In the message sends `Pen new down` all messages are unary messages, so the leftmost one, `Pen new`, is sent first. This returns a newly created pen to which the second message `down` is sent, as shown in Figure 9-6.

Arithmetic inconsistencies

The message composition rules are simple. There is no notion of mathematical precedence because arithmetic messages are just messages as any other ones. So their result may look in inconsistent when executed them. Here we see the common situations where extra parentheses are needed.

```
3 + 4 * 5
>>> 35     "(not 23)  Binary messages sent from left to right"
```

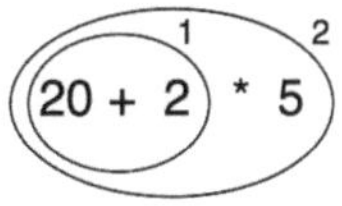

9.3 Message composition

Figure 9-7 Default execution order.

```
3 + (4 * 5)
>>> 23
```
```
1 + 1/3
>>> (2/3)     "and not 4/3"
```
```
1 + (1/3)
>>> (4/3)
```
```
1/3 + 2/3
>>> (7/9)     "and not 1"
```
```
(1/3) + (2/3)
>>> 1
```

Example. In the message sends 20 + 2 * 5, there are only binary messages + and *. However in Pharo there is no specific priority for the operations + and *. They are just binary messages, hence * does not have priority over +. Here the leftmost message + is sent first (1) and then the * is sent to the result as shown in below.

```
    "As there is no priority among binary messages, the leftmost message +
        is evaluated first even if by the rules of arithmetic the * should
        be sent first."

        20 + 2 * 5
(1)     20 + 2 >>> 22
(2)     22      * 5 >>> 110
```

As shown in the previous example the result of this message send is not 30 but 110. This result is perhaps unexpected but follows directly from the rules used to send messages. This is the price to pay for the simplicity of the model. To get the correct result, we should use parentheses. When messages are enclosed in parentheses, they are evaluated first. Hence the message send 20 + (2 * 5) returns the result as shown.

```
Decomposing 20 + (2 * 5)
"The messages surrounded by parentheses are evaluated first therefore
    * is sent prior
to + which produces the correct behaviour."

    20 + (2 * 5)
```

Understanding message syntax

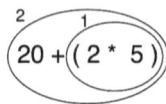

Figure 9-8 Changing default execution order using parentheses.

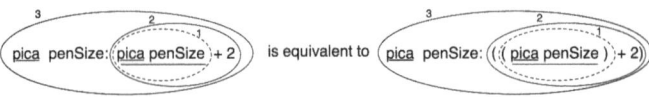

Figure 9-9 Equivalent messages using parentheses.

Figure 9-10 Equivalent messages using parentheses.

```
(1)        (2 * 5)  >>> 10
(2) 20 + 10          >>> 30
```

> **Important** In Pharo, arithmetic operators such as + and * do not have different priority. + and * are just binary messages, therefore * does not have priority over +. Use parentheses to obtain the desired result.

Implicit precedence	Explicitly parenthesized equivalent
aPen color: Color yellow	aPen color: (Color yellow)
aPen go: 100 + 20=	Pen go: (100 + 20)
aPen penSize: aPen penSize + 2	aPen penSize: ((aPen penSize) + 2)
2 factorial + 4	(2 factorial) + 4

Note that the first rule stating that unary messages are sent prior to binary and keyword messages avoid the need to put explicit parentheses around them. Table above shows message sends written following the rules and equivalent message sends if the rules would not exist. Both message sends result in the same effect or return the same value.

9.4 Hints for identifying keyword messages

Often beginners have problems understanding when they need to add parentheses. Let's see how keywords messages are recognized by the compiler.

Parentheses or not?

The characters [,], (and) delimit distinct areas. Within such an area, a keyword message is the longest sequence of words terminated by : that is not cut by the characters ., or ;. When the characters [and], (and) surround some words with colons, these words participate in the keyword message *local* to the area defined.

In this example, there are two distinct keyword messages: rotatedBy:magnify:smoothing: and at:put:.

```
aDict
    at: (rotatingForm
            rotateBy: angle
            magnify: 2
            smoothing: 1)
    put: 3
```

Hints.   If you have problems with these precedence rules, you may start simply by putting parentheses whenever you want to distinguish two messages having the same precedence.

The following piece of code does not require parentheses because the message isNil is unary hence it is sent prior to the keyword message ifTrue:.

```
(x isNil)
    ifTrue:[...]
```

The following piece of code requires parentheses because the messages includes: and ifTrue: are both keyword messages.

```
ord := OrderedCollection new.
(ord includes: $a)
    ifTrue:[...]
```

Without parentheses the unknown message includes:ifTrue: would be sent to the collection ord!

When to use [ ] or ( )

You may also have problems understanding when to use square brackets rather than parentheses. The basic principle is that you should use [ ] when you do not know how many times, potentially zero, an expression should be evaluated. [expression] will create block closure (*i.e.*, an object) from expression, which may be evaluated any number of times (possibly zero), depending on the context. Note that an expression can either be a message send, a variable, a literal, an assignment or a block.

Hence the conditional branches of `ifTrue:` or `ifTrue:ifFalse:` require blocks. Following the same principle both the receiver and the argument of a `whileTrue:` message require the use of square brackets since we do not know how many times either the receiver or the argument should be evaluated.

Parentheses, on the other hand, only affect the order of sending messages. So in (expression), the expression will *always* be evaluated exactly once.

```
[ x isReady ] whileTrue: [ y doSomething ]   "both the receiver and the
    argument must be blocks"
4 timesRepeat: [ Beeper beep ]               "the argument is evaluated
    more than once, so must be a block"
(x isReady) ifTrue: [ y doSomething ]        "receiver is evaluated
    once, so is not a block

                                             argument does not have to
    be evaluated not even once,
                    so it is a block"
```

9.5 Expression sequences

Expressions (*i.e.*, message sends, assignments, ...) separated by periods are evaluated in sequence. Note that there is no period between a variable declaration and the following expression. The value of a sequence is the value gained by the evaluation of the last expression in the sequence. The values returned by all the expressions except the last one are ignored at the end. Note that the period is a separator and not a terminator. Therefore, a final period is optional.

```
| box |
box := 20@30 corner: 60@90.
box containsPoint: 40@50
>>> true
```

9.6 Cascaded messages

Pharo offers a way to send multiple messages to the same receiver, without stating it multiple times, by using a semicolon separator (;). This is called the cascade in Pharo jargon.

Syntactically a cascade is represented as follows:

```
aReceiverExpression msg1 ; msg2 ; msg3
```

Examples. You can program in Pharo without using cascades. It just forces you to repeat the receiver of the message. The following code snippets are equivalent:

```
Transcript show: 'Pharo is '.
Transcript show: 'fun '.
Transcript cr.
```

```
Transcript
    show: 'Pharo is';
    show: 'fun ';
    cr
```

In fact the receiver of all the cascaded messages is the receiver of the first message involved in a cascade. Note that the object receiving the cascaded messages can itself be the result of a message send. In the following example, the first cascaded message is setX:setY since it is followed by a cascade. The receiver of the cascaded message setX:setY: is the newly created point resulting from the execution of Point new, and *not* Point. The subsequent message isZero is sent to that same receiver.

```
Point new setX: 25 setY: 35; isZero
>>> false
```

9.7 Chapter summary

- A message is always sent to an object named the *receiver* which may be the result of other message sends.

- Unary messages are messages that do not require any argument. They are of the form: selector.

- Binary messages are messages that involve two objects, the receiver and another object, *and* whose selector is composed of one or more characters from the following list: +, -, *, /, |, &, =, >, <, ~, and @. They are of the form: receiver **selector** argument

- Keyword messages are messages that involve more than one object and that contain at least one colon character (:). They are of the form: receiver **selectorKeywordOne:** argumentOne **KeywordTwo:** argumentTwo ... **KeywordN:** argumentN

- **Rule One.** Unary messages are sent first, then binary messages, and finally keyword messages.

- **Rule Two.** Messages in parentheses are sent before any others.

- **Rule Three.** When the messages are of the same kind, the order of execution is from left to right.

- In Pharo, traditional arithmetic operators such as + and * have the same priority. + and * are just binary messages, therefore * does not have priority over +. You must use parentheses to obtain a correct result.

CHAPTER **10**

The Pharo object model

The Pharo language model is inspired by the one of Smalltalk. It is simple and uniform: everything is an object, and objects communicate only by sending messages to each other. Instance variables are private to the object and methods are all public and dynamically looked up (late-bound).

In this chapter, we present the core concepts of the Pharo object model. We sorted the sections of this chapter to make sure that the most important points appear first. We revisit concepts such as `self`, `super` and precisely define their semantics. Then we discuss the consequences of representing classes as objects. This will be extended in Chapter: Classes and Metaclasses.

10.1 The rules of the core model

The object model is based on a set of simple rules that are applied *uniformly* and systematically without any exception. The rules are as follows:

Rule 1 Everything is an object.

Rule 2 Every object is an instance of a class.

Rule 3 Every class has a superclass.

Rule 4 Everything happens by sending messages.

Rule 5 Method lookup follows the inheritance chain.

Rule 6 Classes are objects too and follow exactly the same rules.

Let us look at each of these rules in detail.

Listing 10-1 Sending + 4 to 3 yields the object 7.
```
3 + 4
>>> 7
```

Listing 10-2 Sending `factorial` to 20 yields a large number.
```
20 factorial
>>> 2432902008176640000
```

Listing 10-3 Sending `today` to class `Date` yields the current date
```
Date today printString
>>> '24 July 2021'
```

10.2 Everything is an Object

The mantra *everything is an object* is highly contagious. After only a short while working with Pharo, you will become surprised how this rule simplifies everything you do. Integers, for example, are objects too, so you send messages to them, just as you do to any other object. At the end of this chapter, we added an implementation note on the object implementation for the curious reader.

Here are two examples.

The object 7 is different than the object returned by `20 factorial`. 7 is an instance of `SmallInteger` while `20 factorial` is an instance of `LargePositiveInteger`. But because they are both polymorphic objects (they know how to answer to the same set of messages), none of the code, not even the implementation of `factorial`, needs to know about this.

Coming back to *everything is an object* rule, perhaps the most fundamental consequence of this rule is that classes are objects too. Classes are not second-class objects: they are really first-class objects that you can send messages to, inspect, and change as any object.

From the point of view of sending a message, there is no difference between an instance such as 7 and a class. The following example shows that we can send the message `today` to the class `Date` to obtain the current date of the system.

The following example shows that we can ask a class for the instance variables its instances will have - note that the message `allInstVarNames` returns the inherited instance variables too.

> **Important** Classes are objects too. We interact the same way with classes and objects, simply by sending messages to them.

10.3 Every object is an instance of a class

Listing 10-4 Sending `allInstVarNames` to class `Date` returns the instance variables
```
that an instance of the class will have (including inherited ones).
Date allInstVarNames
>>> #(#start #duration)
```

10.3 Every object is an instance of a class

Every object has a class and you can find out which one by sending message `class` to it.

```
1 class
>>> SmallInteger
```

```
20 factorial class
>>> LargePositiveInteger
```

```
'hello' class
>>> ByteString
```

```
(4@5) class
>>> Point
```

```
Object new class
>>> Object
```

A class defines the *structure* of its instances via instance variables, and the *behavior* of its instances via methods. Each method has a name, called its *selector*, which is unique within the class.

Since *classes are objects*, and *every object is an instance of a class*, it follows that classes must also be instances of classes. A class whose instances are classes is called a *metaclass*. Whenever you create a class, the system automatically creates a metaclass for you. The metaclass defines the structure and behavior of the class that is its instance. You will not need to think about metaclasses 99% of the time, and may happily ignore them. We will have a closer look at metaclasses in Chapter : Classes and Metaclasses.

10.4 Instance structure and behavior

Now we will briefly present how we specify the structure and behavior of instances.

Instance variables

Instance variables are accessed by name in any of the instance methods of the class that defines them, and also in the methods defined in its subclasses. This

Listing 10-5 Distance between two points.
```
Point >> distanceTo: aPoint
    "Answer the distance between aPoint and the receiver."

    | dx dy |
    dx := aPoint x - x.
    dy := aPoint y - y.
    ^ ((dx * dx) + (dy * dy)) sqrt
```

means that Pharo instance variables are similar to *protected* variables in C++ and Java. However, we prefer to say that they are private, because it is considered bad style in Pharo to access an instance variable directly from a subclass.

Instance-based encapsulation

Instance variables in Pharo are private to the *instance* itself. This is in contrast to Java and C++, which let instance variables (also known as *fields* or *member variables*) to be accessed by any other instance that happens to be of the same class. We say that the *encapsulation boundary* of objects in Java and C++ is the class, whereas in Pharo it is the instance.

In Pharo, two instances of the same class cannot access each other's instance variables unless the class defines *accessor methods*. There is no language syntax that provides direct access to the instance variables of any other object. Actually, a mechanism called reflection provides a way to ask another object for the values of its instance variables. Reflection is at the root of metaprogramming which is used for writing tools like the object inspector.

Instance encapsulation example

The method `distanceTo:` of the class `Point` computes the distance between the receiver and another point. The instance variables x and y of the receiver are accessed directly by the method body. However, the instance variables of the other point must be accessed by sending it the messages x and y.

```
1@1 dist: 4@5
>>> 5.0
```

The key reason to prefer instance-based encapsulation to class-based encapsulation is that it enables different implementations of the same abstraction to coexist. For example, the method `distanceTo:` doesn't need to know or care whether the argument aPoint is an instance of the same class as the receiver.

The argument object might be represented in polar coordinates, or as a record in a database, or on another computer in a distributed system. As long as it can respond to the messages x and y, the code of method `distanceTo:` (shown above) will still work.

Methods

All methods are *public* and *virtual* (i.e., dynamically looked up). There is no static methods in Pharo. Methods can access all instance variables of the object. Some developers prefer to access instance variables only through accessors. This practice has some value, but it also clutters the interface of your classes, and worse, exposes its private state to the world.

To ease class browsing, methods are grouped into *protocols* that indicate their intent. Protocols have no semantics from the language view point. They are just folders in which methods are stored. Some common protocol names have been established by convention, for example, `accessing` for all accessor methods and `initialization` for establishing a consistent initial state for the object.

The protocol `private` is sometimes used to group methods that should not be relied on. Nothing, however, prevents you from sending a message that is implemented by such a "private" method. However, it means that the developer may change or remove such private method.

10.5 Every class has a superclass

Each class in Pharo inherits its behaviour and the description of its structure from a single *superclass*. This means that Pharo offers single inheritance.

Here are some examples showing how can we navigate the hierarchy.

```
SmallInteger superclass
>>> Integer
```

```
Integer superclass
>>> Number
```

```
Number superclass
>>> Magnitude
```

```
Magnitude superclass
>>> Object
```

```
Object superclass
>>> ProtoObject
```

```
ProtoObject superclass
>>> nil
```

Listing 10-6 The definition of the class `Point`.
```
Object subclass: #Point
    instanceVariableNames: 'x y'
    classVariableNames: ''
    package: 'Kernel-BasicObjects'
```

Listing 10-7 Sending message + with argument 4 to integer 3.
```
3 + 4
>>> 7
```

Traditionally the root of the inheritance hierarchy is the class `Object`, since everything is an object. Most classes inherit from `Object`, which defines many additional messages that almost all objects understand and respond to.

In Pharo, the root of the inheritance tree is actually the class `ProtoObject`, but you will normally not pay any attention to this class. The class `ProtoObject` encapsulates the minimal set of messages that all objects *must* have and `ProtoObject` is designed to raise as many as possible errors (to support proxy definition). Unless you have a very good reason to do otherwise, when creating application classes you should normally subclass `Object`, or one of its subclasses.

A new class is normally created by sending the message `subclass: instanceVariableNames: ...` to an existing class as shown in 10-6. There are a few other methods to create classes. To see what they are, have a look at `Class` and its `subclass creation` protocol.

10.6 Everything happens by sending messages

This rule captures the essence of programming in Pharo.

In procedural programming (and in some static features of some object-oriented languages such as Java), the choice of which method to execute when a procedure is called is made by the caller. The caller chooses the procedure to execute *statically*, by name. In such a case there is no lookup or dynamicity involved.

In Pharo when we send a message, the caller does not decide which method will be executed. Instead, we *tell* an object to do something by sending it a message. A message is nothing but a name and a list of arguments. The *receiver* then decides how to respond by selecting its own *method* for doing what was asked. Since different objects may have different methods for responding to the same message, the method must be chosen *dynamically*, when the message is received.

10.6 Everything happens by sending messages

Listing 10-8 Sending message + with argument 4 to point (1@2).
```
(1@2) + 4
>>> 5@6
```

As a consequence, we can send the *same message* to different objects, each of which may have *its own method* for responding to the message.

In the previous examples, we do not decide how the SmallInteger 3 or the Point (1@2) should respond to the message + 4. We let the objet decide: Each has its own method for +, and responds to + 4 accordingly.

Vocabulary point

In Pharo, we do *not* say that we "invoke methods". Instead, we *send messages*. This is just a vocabulary point but it is significant. It implies that this is not the responsibility of the client to select the method to be executed, it is the one of the receiver of the message.

About other computation

Nearly everything in Pharo happens by sending messages. At some point action must take place:

- *Variable declarations* are not message sends. In fact, variable declarations are not even executable. Declaring a variable just causes space to be allocated for an object reference.
- *Variable accesses* are just accesses to the value of a variable.
- *Assignments* are not message sends. An assignment to a variable causes that variable name to be freshly bound to the result of the expression in the scope of its definition.
- *Returns* are not message sends. A return simply causes the computed result to be returned to the sender.
- *Pragmas* are not message sends. They are method annotations.

Other than these few exceptions, pretty much everything else does truly happen by sending messages.

About object-oriented programming.

One of the consequences of Pharo's model of message sending is that it encourages a style in which objects tend to have very small methods and delegate tasks to other objects, rather than implementing huge, procedural methods that assume too much responsibility.

Joseph Pelrine expresses this principle succinctly as follows:

| **Note**   Don't do anything that you can push off onto someone else.

Many object-oriented languages provide both static and dynamic operations for objects. In Pharo there are only dynamic message sends. For example, instead of providing static class operations, we simply send messages to classes (which are simply objects).

In particular, since there are no *public fields* in Pharo, the only way to update an instance variable of another object is to send it a message asking that it update its own field. Of course, providing setter and getter methods for all the instance variables of an object is not good object-oriented style, because clients can access to the internal state of objects.

Joseph Pelrine also states this very nicely:

| **Note**   Don't let anyone else play with your data.

10.7 Sending a message: a two-step process

What exactly happens when an object receives a message?

This is a two-step process: *method lookup* and *method execution*.

- **Lookup.** First, the method having the same name as the message is looked up.
- **Method Execution.** Second, the found method is applied to the receiver with the message arguments: When the method is found, the arguments are bound to the parameters of the method, and the virtual machine executes it.

The lookup process is quite simple:

1. The class of the receiver looks up the method to use to handle the message.
2. If this class does not have that method defined, it asks its superclass, and so on, up the inheritance chain.

It is essentially as simple as that. Nevertheless there are a few questions that need some care to answer:

- *What happens when a method does not explicitly return a value?*
- *What happens when a class reimplements a superclass method?*
- *What is the difference between* `self` *and* `super` *sends?*

Listing 10-9 A locally implemented method.
```
EllipseMorph >> defaultColor
    "Answer the default color/fill style for the receiver"
    ^ Color yellow
```

Listing 10-10 An inherited method.
```
Morph >> openInWorld
    "Add this morph to the world."
    self openInWorld: self currentWorld
```

- *What happens when no method is found?*

The rules for method lookup that we present here are conceptual; virtual machine implementors use all kinds of tricks and optimizations to speed up method lookup.

First let us look at the basic lookup strategy, and then consider these further questions.

10.8 Method lookup follows the inheritance chain

Suppose we create an instance of `EllipseMorph`.

```
anEllipse := EllipseMorph new.
```

If we send the message `defaultColor` to this object now, we get the result `Color yellow`.

```
anEllipse defaultColor
>>> Color yellow
```

The class `EllipseMorph` implements `defaultColor`, so the appropriate method is found immediately.

In contrast, if we send the message `openInWorld` to `anEllipse`, the method is not immediately found, since the class `EllipseMorph` does not implement `openInWorld`. The search therefore continues in the superclass, `BorderedMorph`, and so on, until an `openInWorld` method is found in the class `Morph` (see Figure 10-11).

10.9 Method execution

We mentioned that sending a message is a two-step process:

- **Lookup.** First, the method having the same name as the message is looked up.

The Pharo object model

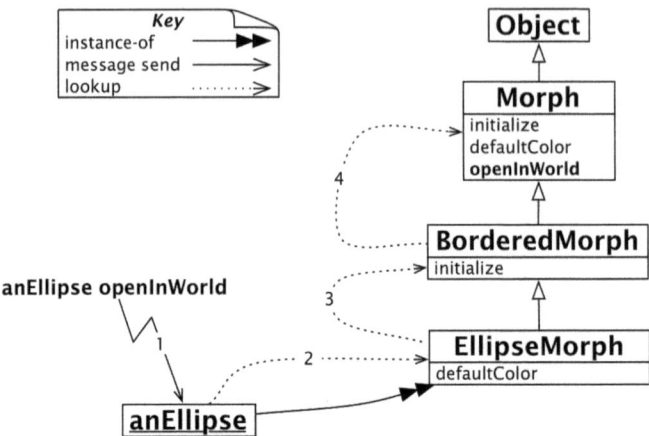

Figure 10-11 Method lookup follows the inheritance hierarchy.

Listing 10-12 Another locally implemented method.
```
EllipseMorph >> closestPointTo: aPoint
    ^ self intersectionWithLineSegmentFromCenterTo: aPoint
```

- **Method Execution.** Second, the found method is applied to the receiver with the message arguments: When the method is found, the arguments are bound to the parameters of the method, and the virtual machine executes it.

Now we explain the second point: the method execution.

When the lookup returns a method, the receiver of the message is bound to `self`, and the arguments of the message to the method parameters. Then the system executes the method body. This is true wherever the method that should be executed is found. Imagine that we send the message `EllipseMorph new closestPointTo: 100@100` and that the method is defined as in Listing 10-12.

The variable `self` will point to the new ellipse we created and `aPoint` will refer to the point `100@100`.

Now exactly the same process will happen and this even if the method found by the method lookup finds the method in a superclass. When we send the message `EllipseMorph new openInWorld`. The method `openInWorld` is found in the `Morph` class. Still the variable `self` is bound to the newly created ellipse. This is why we say that `self` always represents the receiver of the message and this independently of the class in which the method was found.

10.10 Message not understood

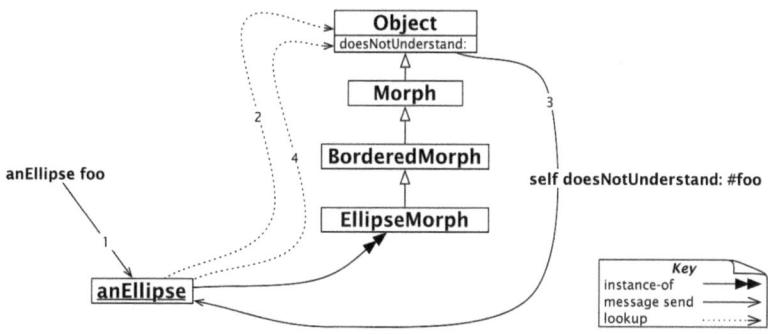

Figure 10-13 Message foo is not understood.

This is why there are two different steps during a message send: looking up the method within the class hierarchy of the message receiver and the method execution on the message receiver.

10.10 Message not understood

What happens if the method we are looking for is not found?

Suppose we send the message foo to our ellipse. First the normal method lookup will go through the inheritance chain all the way up to Object (or rather ProtoObject) looking for this method. When this method is not found, the virtual machine will cause the object to send self doesNotUnderstand: #foo (See Figure 10-13).

Now, this is a perfectly ordinary, dynamic message send, so the lookup starts again from the class EllipseMorph, but this time searching for the method doesNotUnderstand:. As it turns out, Object implements doesNotUnderstand:. This method will create a new MessageNotUnderstood object which is capable of starting a Debugger in the current execution context.

Why do we take this convoluted path to handle such an obvious error?

Well, this offers developers an easy way to intercept such errors and take alternative action. One could easily override the method Object>>doesNotUnderstand: in any subclass of Object and provide a different way of handling the error.

In fact, this can be an easy way to implement automatic delegation of messages from one object to another. A delegating object could simply delegate all messages it does not understand to another object whose responsibility it is to handle them, or raise an error itself!

Listing 10-14 Explicitly returning self.
```
Morph >> openInWorld
    "Add this morph to the world."
    self openInWorld: self currentWorld
    ^ self
```

10.11 About returning self

Notice that the method `defaultColor` of the class `EllipseMorph` explicitly returns `Color yellow`, whereas the method `openInWorld` of `Morph` does not appear to return anything.

Actually a method *always* answers a message with a value (which is, of course, an object). The answer may be defined by the ^ construct in the method, but if execution reaches the end of the method without executing a ^, the method still answers a value – it answers the object that received the message. We usually say that the method *answers self*, because in Pharo the pseudo-variable `self` represents the receiver of the message, much like the keyword `this` in Java. Other languages, such as Ruby, by default return the value of the last statement in the method. Again, this is not the case in Pharo, instead you can imagine that a method without an explicit return ends with ^ `self`.

> **Important** `self` always represents the receiver of the message.

This suggests that `openInWorld` is equivalent to `openInWorldReturnSelf`, defined in Listing 10-14.

Why is explicitly writing ^ `self` not a so good thing to do?

When you return something explicitly, you are communicating that you are returning something of interest to the sender. When you explicitly return `self`, you are saying that you expect the sender to use the returned value. This is not the case here, so it is best not to explicitly return `self`. We only return `self` on special case to stress that the receiver is returned.

This is a common idiom in Pharo, which Kent Beck refers to as *Interesting return value*: "Return a value only when you intend for the sender to use the value."

> **Important** By default (if not specified differently) a method returns the message receiver.

10.12 Overriding and extension

If we look again at the `EllipseMorph` class hierarchy in Figure 10-11, we see that the classes `Morph` and `EllipseMorph` both implement `defaultColor`. In

10.13 Self and super sends

Listing 10-15 Super initialize.
```
BorderedMorph >> initialize
    "Initialize the state of the receiver"

    super initialize.
    self borderInitialize
```

fact, if we open a new morph (`Morph new openInWorld`) we see that we get a blue morph, whereas an ellipse will be yellow by default.

We say that `EllipseMorph` *overrides* the `defaultColor` method that it inherits from `Morph`. The inherited method no longer exists from the point of view of `anEllipse`.

Sometimes we do not want to override inherited methods, but rather *extend* them with some new functionality, that is, we would like to be able to invoke the overridden method *in addition to* the new functionality we are defining in the subclass. In Pharo, as in many object-oriented languages that support single inheritance, this can be done with the help of `super` sends.

A frequent application of this mechanism is in the `initialize` method. Whenever a new instance of a class is initialized, it is critical to also initialize any inherited instance variables. However, the knowledge of how to do this is already captured in the `initialize` methods of each of the superclass in the inheritance chain. The subclass has no business even trying to initialize inherited instance variables!

It is therefore good practice whenever implementing an `initialize` method to send `super initialize` before performing any further initialization as shown in Listing 10-15.

We need `super` sends to compose inherited behaviour that would otherwise be overridden.

> **Important** It is a good practice that an `initialize` method starts by sending `super initialize`.

10.13 Self and super sends

`self` represents the receiver of the message and the lookup of the method starts in the class of the receiver. Now what is `super`? `super` is *not* the superclass! It is a common and natural mistake to think this. It is also a mistake to think that lookup starts in the superclass of the class of the receiver.

Listing 10-16 A `self` send.
```
Morph >> fullPrintOn: aStream
    aStream nextPutAll: self class name, ' new'
```

Listing 10-17 A `self` send.
```
Morph >> constructorString
    ^ String streamContents: [ :s | self fullPrintOn: s ].
```

Listing 10-18 Combining `super` and `self` sends.
```
BorderedMorph >> fullPrintOn: aStream
    aStream nextPutAll: '('.
    super fullPrintOn: aStream.
    aStream
        nextPutAll: ') setBorderWidth: ';
        print: borderWidth;
        nextPutAll: ' borderColor: ', (self colorString: borderColor)
```

> **Important** `self` represents the receiver of the message and the method lookup starts in the class of the receiver.

How do `self` sends differ from `super` sends?

Like `self`, `super` represents the receiver of the message. Yes you read it well! The only thing that changes is the method lookup. Instead of lookup starting in the class of the receiver, it starts in the *superclass of the class of the method where the* `super` *send occurs*.

> **Important** `super` represents the receiver of the message and the method lookup starts in the superclass of the class of the method where the `super` send occurs.

We shall see in the following example precisely how this works. Imagine that we define the following three methods:

First in Listing 10-16, we define the method `fullPrintOn:` on class `Morph` that just adds to the stream the name of the class followed by the string ' new' - the idea is that we could execute the resulting string and get back an instance similar to the receiver.

Second we define the method `constructorString` that sends the message `fullPrintOn:` (see Listing 10-17).

Finally, we define the method `fullPrintOn:` on the class `BorderedMorph` superclass of `EllipseMorph`. This new method extends the superclass behavior: it invokes it and adds extra behavior (see Listing 10-18).

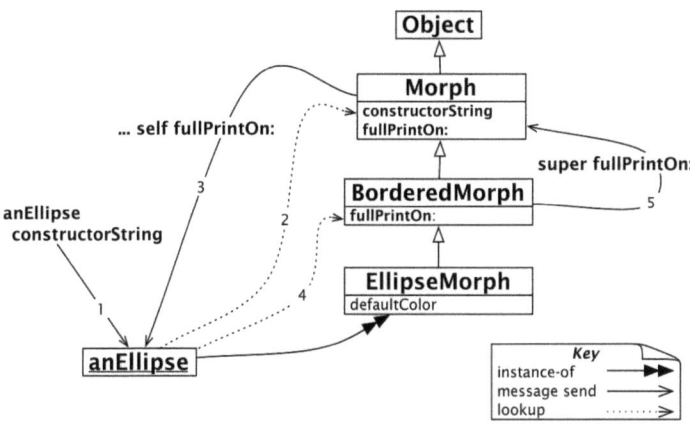

Figure 10-19 self and super sends.

Consider the message constructorString sent to an instance of EllipseMorph:

```
EllipseMorph new constructorString
>>> '(EllipseMorph new) setBorderWidth: 1 borderColor: Color black'
```

How exactly is this result obtained through a combination of self and super sends? First, anEllipse constructorString will cause the method constructorString to be found in the class Morph, as shown in Figure 10-19.

The method constructorString of Morph performs a self send of fullPrintOn:. The message fullPrintOn: is looked up starting in the class EllipseMorph, and the method fullPrintOn: BorderedMorph is found in BorderedMorph (see Figure 10-19). What is critical to notice is that the self send causes the method lookup to start again in the class of the receiver, namely the class of anEllipse.

At this point, the method fullPrintOn: of BorderedMorph does a super send to extend the fullPrintOn: behaviour it inherits from its superclass.

Because this is a super send, the lookup now starts in the superclass of the class where the super send occurs, namely in Morph. We then immediately find and execute the method fullPrintOn: of the class Morph.

10.14 Stepping back

A self send is dynamic in the sense that by looking at the method containing it, we cannot predict which method will be executed. Indeed an instance of a subclass may receive the message containing the self expression and redefine the method in that subclass. Here EllipseMorph could redefine the method fullPrintOn: and this method would be executed by method constructorString. Note that by only looking at the method constructorString, we cannot predict which fullPrintOn: method (either the one of EllipseMorph, BorderedMorph, or Morph) will be executed when executing the method constructorString, since it depends on the receiver the constructorString message.

> **Important** A self send triggers a *method lookup starting in the class of the receiver*. A self send is dynamic in the sense that by looking at the method containing it, we cannot predict which method will be executed.

Note that the super lookup did not start in the superclass of the receiver. This would have caused lookup to start from BorderedMorph, resulting in an infinite loop!

If you think carefully about super send and Figure 10-19, you will realize that super bindings are static: all that matters is the class in which the text of the super send is found. By contrast, the meaning of self is dynamic: it always represents the receiver of the currently executing message. This means that *all* messages sent to self are looked up by starting in the receiver's class.

> **Important** A super send triggers a method lookup starting in the *superclass of the class of the method performing the super send*. We say that super sends are *static* because just looking at the method we know the class where the lookup should start (the class above the class containing the method).

10.15 The instance and class sides

Since classes are objects, they have their own instance variables and their own methods. We call these *class instance variables* and *class methods*, but they are really no different from ordinary instance variables and methods: They simply operate on different objects (classes in this case).

An instance variable describes instance state and a method describes instance behavior.

Similarly, class instance variables are just instance variables defined by a metaclass (a class whose instances are classes):

- *Class instance variables* describe the state of classes. An example is the superclass instance variable that describes the superclass of a given class.
- *Class methods* are just methods defined by a metaclass and that will be executed on classes. Sending the message now to the class Date is defined

10.15 The instance and class sides

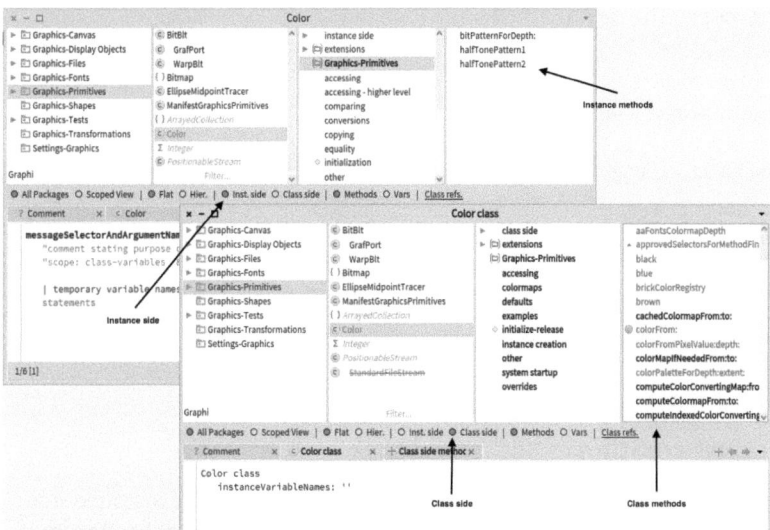

Figure 10-20 Browsing a class and its metaclass.

on the (meta)class `Date class`. This method is executed with the class `Date` as receiver.

A class and its metaclass are two separate classes, even though the former is an instance of the latter. However, this is largely irrelevant to you as a programmer: you are concerned with defining the behavior of your objects and the classes that create them.

For this reason, the browser helps you to browse both class and metaclass as if they were a single thing with two "sides": the *instance side* and the *class side*, as shown in Figure 10-20.

- By default, when you select a class in the browser, you're browsing the *instance side* i.e., the methods that are executed when messages are sent to an *instance* of `Color`.

- Clicking on the **Class side** button switches you over to the *class side*: the methods that will be executed when messages are sent to the *class* `Color` itself.

For example, `Color blue` sends the message `blue` to the class `Color`. You will therefore find the method `blue` defined on the *class side* of `Color`, not on the instance side.

143

Listing 10-21 The class method `blue` (defined on the class-side).
```
Color blue
>>> Color blue
"Color instances are self-evaluating"
```

Listing 10-22 Using the accessor method `red` (defined on the instance-side).
```
Color blue red
>>> 0.0
```

Listing 10-23 Using the accessor method `blue` (defined on the instance-side).
```
Color blue blue
>>> 1.0
```

Metaclass creation

You define a class by filling in the template proposed on the instance side. When you compile this template, the system creates not just the class that you defined, but also the corresponding metaclass (which you can then edit by clicking on the **Class side** button). The only part of the metaclass creation template that makes sense for you to edit directly is the list of the metaclass's instance variable names.

Once a class has been created, browsing its instance side lets you edit and browse the methods that will be possessed by instances of that class (and of its subclasses).

10.16 Class methods

Class methods can be quite useful, you can browse `Color class` for some good examples: You will see that there are two kinds of methods defined on a class: *instance creation methods*, like the class method `blue` in the class `Color class`, and those that perform a utility function, like `Color class>>wheel:`. This is typical, although you will occasionally find class methods used in other ways.

It is convenient to place utility methods on the class side because they can be executed without having to create any additional objects first. Indeed, many of them will contain a comment designed to make it easy to execute them.

Browse method `Color class>>wheel:`, double-click just at the beginning of the comment `"(Color wheel: 12) inspect"` and press CMD-d. You will see the effect of executing this method.

For those familiar with Java and C++, class methods may seem similar to static methods. However, the uniformity of the Pharo object model (where classes are just regular objects) means that they are somewhat different: Whereas

10.17 Class instance variables

Listing 10-24 Dog class definition.
```
Object subclass: #Dog
    instanceVariableNames: ''
    classVariableNames: ''
    package: 'Example'
```

Listing 10-25 Adding a class instance variable.
```
Dog class
    instanceVariableNames: 'count'
```

Java static methods are really just statically-resolved procedures, Pharo class methods are dynamically-dispatched methods. This means that inheritance, overriding and super-sends work for class methods in Pharo, whereas they don't work for static methods in Java.

10.17 Class instance variables

With ordinary *instance* variables, all the instances of a class have the same set of variables (though each instance has its own private set of values), and the instances of its subclasses inherit those variables.

The story is exactly the same with *class* instance variables: a class is an object instance of another class. Therefore the class instance variables are defined on such classes and each class has its own private values for the class instance variables.

Instance variables also works. Class instance variables are inherited: A subclass will inherit those class instance variables, *but a subclass will have its own private copies of those variables.* Just as objects don't share instance variables, neither do classes and their subclasses share class instance variables.

For example, you could use a class instance variable called count to keep track of how many instances you create of a given class. However, any subclass would have its own count variable, so subclass instances would be counted separately. The following section presents an example.

10.18 Example: Class instance variables and subclasses

Suppose we define the class Dog, and its subclass Hyena. Suppose that we add a count class instance variable to the class Dog (i.e., we define it on the metaclass Dog class). Hyena will naturally inherit the class instance variable count from Dog.

Now suppose we define class methods for Dog to initialize its count to 0, and to increment it when new instances are created:

The Pharo object model

Listing 10-26 Hyena class definition.
```
Dog subclass: #Hyena
    instanceVariableNames: ''
    classVariableNames: ''
    package: 'Example'
```

Listing 10-27 Initialize the count of dogs.
```
Dog class >> initialize
    count := 0.
```

Listing 10-28 Keeping count of new dogs.
```
Dog class >> new
    count := count +1.
    ^ super new
```

Now when we create a new Dog, the count value of the class Dog is incremented, and so is that of the class Hyena (but the hyenas are counted separately).

About class initialize

When you instantiate an object such as Dog new, initialize is called automatically as part of the new message send (you can see for yourself by browsing the method new in the class Behavior). But with classes, simply defining them does not automatically call initialize because it is not clear to the system if a class is fully working. So we have to call initialize explicitly here.

By default class initialize methods are automatically executed only when classes are loaded. See also the discussion about lazy initialization, below.

```
Hyena count
>>> 0
```

```
| aDog |
aDog := Dog new.
Dog count
>>> 1   "Incremented"
```

```
Hyena count
>>> 0    "Still the same"
```

Listing 10-29 Accessing to count.
```
Dog class >> count
    ^ count
```

```
Dog initialize.
Hyena initialize.
Dog count
>>> 0
```

10.19 Stepping back

Class instance variables are private to a class in exactly the same way that instance variables are private to an instance. Since classes and their instances are different objects, this has the following consequences:

1. A class does not have access to the instance variables of its own instances. So, the class `Color` does not have access to the variables of an object instantiated from it, `aColorRed`. In other words, just because a class was used to create an instance (using `new` or a helper instance creation method like `Color red`), it doesn't give *the class* any special direct access to that instance's variables. The class instead has to go through the accessor methods (a public interface) just like any other object.

2. The reverse is also true: an *instance* of a class does not have access to the class instance variables of its class. In our example above, `aDog` (an individual instance) does not have direct access to the `count` variable of the `Dog` class (except, again, through an accessor method).

> **Important** A class does not have access to the instance variables of its own instances. An instance of a class does not have access to the class instance variables of its class.

For this reason, instance initialization methods must always be defined on the instance side, the class side has no access to instance variables, and so cannot initialize them! All that the class can do is to send initialization messages, using accessors, to newly created instances.

Java has nothing equivalent to class instance variables. Java and C++ static variables are more like Pharo class variables (discussed in Section 10.23), since in those languages all of the subclasses and all of their instances share the same static variable.

10.20 Example: Defining a Singleton

Singleton is the most misunderstood design pattern. When wrongly applied, it favors procedural style promoting single global access. However, the Singleton pattern provides a typical example of the use of class instance variables and class methods.

Listing 10-31 New state for classes.

```
WebServer class allInstVarNames
>>>   "#(#superclass #methodDict #format #layout #organization
      #subclasses #name #classPool #sharedPools #environment #category
      #uniqueInstance)"
```

Listing 10-32 Class-side accessor method uniqueInstance.

```
WebServer class >> uniqueInstance
    uniqueInstance ifNil: [ uniqueInstance := self new ].
    ^ uniqueInstance
```

Imagine that we would like to implement a class WebServer, and to use the Singleton pattern to ensure that it has only one instance.

We define the class WebServer as follow.

```
Object subclass: #WebServer
    instanceVariableNames: 'sessions'
    classVariableNames: ''
    package: 'Web'
```

Then, clicking on the **Class side** button, we add the (class) instance variable uniqueInstance.

```
WebServer class
    instanceVariableNames: 'uniqueInstance'
```

As a result, the class WebServer class will have a new instance variable (in addition to the variables that it inherits from Behavior, such as superclass and methodDict). It means that the value of this extra instance variable will describe the instance of the class WebServer class i.e., the class WebServer.

```
Point class allInstVarNames
>>>    "#(#superclass #methodDict #format #layout #organization
       #subclasses #name #classPool #sharedPools #environment #category)"
```

We can now define a class method named uniqueInstance, as shown below. This method first checks whether uniqueInstance has been initialized. If it has not, the method creates an instance and assigns it to the class instance variable uniqueInstance. Finally the value of uniqueInstance is returned. Since uniqueInstance is a class instance variable, this method can directly access it.

The first time that WebServer uniqueInstance is executed, an instance of the class WebServer will be created and assigned to the uniqueInstance variable. The next time, the previously created instance will be returned instead of creating a new one. (This pattern, checking if a variable is nil in an accessor method, and initializing its value if it is nil, is called *lazy initialization*).

Note that the instance creation code in the code above. Script 10-32 is written as `self new` and not as `WebServer new`. What is the difference? Since the `uniqueInstance` method is defined in `WebServer class`, you might think that there is no difference. And indeed, until someone creates a subclass of `WebServer`, they are the same. But suppose that `ReliableWebServer` is a subclass of `WebServer`, and inherits the `uniqueInstance` method. We would clearly expect `ReliableWebServer uniqueInstance` to answer a `ReliableWebServer`.

Using `self` ensures that this will happen, since `self` will be bound to the respective receiver, here the classes `WebServer` and `ReliableWebServer`. Note also that `WebServer` and `ReliableWebServer` will each have a different value for their `uniqueInstance` instance variable.

10.21 A note on lazy initialization

The setting of initial values for instances of objects generally belongs in the `initialize` method. Putting initialization calls only in `initialize` helps from a readability perspective – you don't have to hunt through all the accessor methods to see what the initial values are. Although it may be tempting to instead initialize instance variables in their respective accessor methods (using `ifNil:` checks), avoid this unless you have a good reason.

Do not over-use the lazy initialization pattern.

For example, in our `uniqueInstance` method above, we used lazy initialization because users won't typically expect to call `WebServer initialize`. Instead, they expect the class to be "ready" to return new unique instances. Because of this, lazy initialization makes sense. Similarly, if a variable is expensive to initialize (opening a database connection or a network socket, for example), you will sometimes choose to delay that initialization until you actually need it.

10.22 Shared variables

Now we will look at an aspect of Pharo that is not so easily covered by our five rules: shared variables.

Pharo provides three kinds of shared variables:

1. *Globally* shared variables.

2. *Class variables*: variables shared between instances and classes. (Not to be confused with class instance variables, discussed earlier).

3. *Pool variables*: variables shared amongst a group of classes,

The names of all of these shared variables start with a capital letter, to warn us that they are indeed shared between multiple objects.

Global variables

In Pharo, all global variables are stored in a namespace called `Smalltalk globals`, which is implemented as an instance of the class `SystemDictionary`. Global variables are accessible everywhere. Every class is named by a global variable. In addition, a few globals are used to name special or commonly useful objects.

The variable `Processor` names an instance of `ProcessScheduler`, the main process scheduler of Pharo.

```
Processor class
>>> ProcessorScheduler
```

Other useful global variables

Smalltalk is the instance of `SmalltalkImage`. It contains many functionality to manage the system. In particular it holds a reference to the main namespace `Smalltalk globals`. This namespace includes `Smalltalk` itself since it is a global variable. The keys to this namespace are the symbols that name the global objects in Pharo code. So, for example:

```
Smalltalk globals at: #Boolean
>>> Boolean
```

Since `Smalltalk` is itself a global variable:

```
Smalltalk globals at: #Smalltalk
>>> Smalltalk
```

```
(Smalltalk globals at: #Smalltalk) == Smalltalk
>>> true
```

World is an instance of `PasteUpMorph` that represents the screen. `World bounds` answers a rectangle that defines the whole screen space; all Morphs on the screen are submorphs of `World`.

Undeclared is another dictionary, which contains all the undeclared variables. If you write a method that references an undeclared variable, the browser will normally prompt you to declare it, for example as a global or as an instance variable of the class. However, if you later delete the declaration, the code will then reference an undeclared variable. Inspecting `Undeclared` can sometimes help explain strange behaviour!

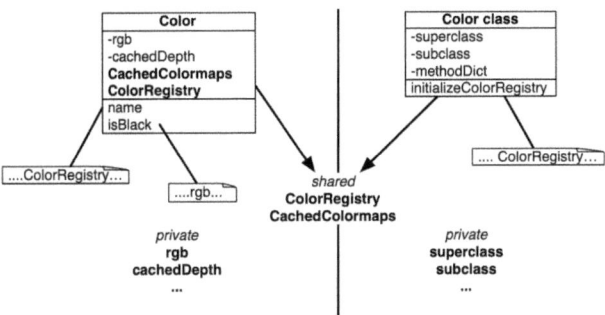

Figure 10-33 Instance and class methods accessing different variables.

Using globals in your code

The recommended practice is to strictly limit the use of global variables. It is usually better to use class instance variables or class variables, and to provide class methods to access them. Indeed, if Pharo were to be implemented from scratch today, most of the global variables that are not classes would be replaced by singletons or others.

The usual way to define a global is just to perform Do it on an assignment to a capitalized but undeclared identifier. The parser will then offer to declare the global for you. If you want to define a global programmatically, just execute Smalltalk globals at: #AGlobalName put: nil. To remove it, execute Smalltalk globals removeKey: #AGlobalName.

10.23 Class variables: Shared variables

Sometimes we need to share some data amongst all the instances of a class and the class itself. This is possible using *class variables*. The term *class variable* indicates that the lifetime of the variable is the same as that of the class. However, what the term does not convey is that these variables are shared amongst all the instances of a class as well as the class itself, as shown in Figure 10-33. Indeed, a better name would have been *shared variables* since this expresses more clearly their role, and also warns of the danger of using them, particularly if they are modified.

In Figure 10-33 we see that rgb and cachedDepth are instance variables of Color, hence only accessible to instances of Color. We also see that super-

Listing 10-34 Color and its class variables.
```
Object subclass: #Color
  instanceVariableNames: 'rgb cachedDepth cachedBitPattern alpha'
  classVariableNames: 'BlueShift CachedColormaps ColorRegistry
    ComponentMask ComponentMax GrayToIndexMap GreenShift
    HalfComponentMask IndexedColors MaskingMap RedShift'
  package: 'Colors-Base'
```

Listing 10-35 Using Lazy initialization.
```
    ColorNames ifNil: [ self initializeNames ].
    ^ ColorNames
```

class, subclass, methodDict and so on are *class instance variables*, i.e., instance variables only accessible to the Color class.

But we can also see something new: ColorRegistry and CachedColormaps are *class variables* defined for Color. The capitalization of these variables gives us a hint that they are shared. In fact, not only may all instances of Color access these shared variables, but also the Color class itself, *and any of its subclasses*. Both instance methods and class methods can access these shared variables.

A class variable is declared in the class definition template. For example, the class Color defines a large number of class variables to speed up color creation; its definition is show in the Script 10-34.

The class variable ColorRegistry is an instance of IdentityDictionary containing the frequently-used colors, referenced by name. This dictionary is shared by all the instances of Color, as well as the class itself. It is accessible from all the instance and class methods.

Class initialization

The presence of class variables raises the question: how do we initialize them?

One solution is lazy initialization (discussed earlier in this chapter). This can be done by introducing an accessor method which, when executed, initializes the variable if it has not yet been initialized. This implies that we must use the accessor all the time and never use the class variable directly. This furthermore imposes the cost of the accessor send and the initialization test.

Another solution is to override the class method initialize (we've seen this before in the Dog example).

If you adopt this solution, you will need to remember to invoke the initialize method after you define it (by evaluating Color initialize). Although class side initialize methods are executed automatically when code is loaded

10.24 Pool variables

Listing 10-36 Initializing the `Color` class.
```
Color class >> initialize
    ...
    self initializeColorRegistry.
    ...
```

Listing 10-37 Pool dictionaries in the `Text` class.
```
ArrayedCollection subclass: #Text
        instanceVariableNames: 'string runs'
        classVariableNames: ''
        poolDictionaries: 'TextConstants'
        package: 'Collections-Text'
```

Listing 10-38 Text>>testCR.
```
Text >> testCR
    ^ CR == Character cr
```

into memory (from a Monticello repository, for example), they are *not* executed automatically when they are first typed into the browser and compiled, or when they are edited and re-compiled.

10.24 Pool variables

Pool variables are variables that are shared between several classes that may not be related by inheritance. Pool variables should be defined as class variables of dedicated classes (subclasses of `SharedPool` as shown below). Our advice is to avoid them; you will need them only in rare and specific circumstances. Our goal here is therefore to explain pool variables just enough so that you can understand them when you are reading code.

A class that accesses a pool variable must mention the pool in its class definition. For example, the class `Text` indicates that it is using the pool `TextConstants`, which contains all the text constants such as `CR` and `LF`. `TextConstants` defines the variables `CR` that is bound to the value `Character cr`, i.e., the carriage return character.

This allows methods of the class `Text` to access the variables of the shared pool in the method body *directly*. For example, we can write the following method. We see that eventhough `Text` does not define a variable `CR`, since it declared that it uses the shared pool `TextConstants`, it can directly access it.

Here is how `TextConstants` is created. `TextConstants` is a special class subclass of `SharedPool` and it holds class variables.

```
SharedPool subclass: #TextConstants
  instanceVariableNames: ''
  classVariableNames: 'BS BS2 Basal Bold CR Centered Clear CrossedX
    CtrlA CtrlB CtrlC
  CtrlD CtrlDigits CtrlE CtrlF CtrlG CtrlH
  CtrlI CtrlJ CtrlK CtrlL CtrlM CtrlN CtrlO CtrlOpenBrackets CtrlP
    CtrlQ CtrlR CtrlS CtrlT
  CtrlU CtrlV CtrlW CtrlX CtrlY CtrlZ Ctrla Ctrlb Ctrlc Ctrld Ctrle
    Ctrlf Ctrlg Ctrlh Ctrli
  Ctrlj Ctrlk Ctrll Ctrlm Ctrln Ctrlo Ctrlp Ctrlq Ctrlr Ctrls Ctrlt
    Ctrlu Ctrlv Ctrlw
  Ctrlx Ctrly Ctrlz DefaultBaseline DefaultFontFamilySize
    DefaultLineGrid DefaultMarginTabsArray
  DefaultMask DefaultRule DefaultSpace DefaultTab DefaultTabsArray ESC
    EndOfRun Enter Italic
  Justified LeftFlush LeftMarginTab RightFlush RightMarginTab Space
    Tab TextSharedInformation'
  package: 'Text-Core-Base'
```

Once again, we recommend that you avoid the use of pool variables and pool dictionaries.

10.25 Abstract methods and abstract classes

An abstract class is a class that exists to be subclassed, rather than to be instantiated. An abstract class is usually incomplete, in the sense that it does not define all of the methods that it uses. The "placeholder" methods, those that the other methods assume to be (re)defined are called abstract methods.

Pharo has no dedicated syntax to specify that a method or a class is abstract. Instead, by convention, the body of an abstract method consists of the expression `self subclassResponsibility`. This indicates that subclasses have the responsibility to define a concrete version of the method. `self subclassResponsibility` methods should always be overridden, and thus should never be executed. If you forget to override one, and it is executed, an exception will be raised.

Similarly, a class is considered abstract if one of its methods is abstract. Nothing actually prevents you from creating an instance of an abstract class; everything will work until an abstract method is invoked.

10.26 Example: the abstract class `Magnitude`

`Magnitude` is an abstract class that helps us to define objects that can be compared to each other. Subclasses of `Magnitude` should implement the methods

Listing 10-39 Magnitude>> <.
```
Magnitude >> < aMagnitude
    "Answer whether the receiver is less than the argument."

    ^self subclassResponsibility
```

Listing 10-40 Magnitude>> >=.
```
Magnitude >> >= aMagnitude
    "Answer whether the receiver is greater than or equal to the
    argument."

    ^(self < aMagnitude) not
```

Listing 10-41 Character>> <=.
```
Character >> < aCharacter
    "Answer true if the receiver's value < aCharacter's value."

    ^self asciiValue < aCharacter asciiValue
```

<, = and hash. Using such messages, Magnitude defines other methods such as >, >=, <=, max:, min: between:and: and others for comparing objects. Such methods are inherited by subclasses. The method Magnitude>>< is abstract, and defined as shown in the following script.

By contrast, the method >= is concrete, and is defined in terms of <.

The same is true of the other comparison methods (they are all defined in terms of the abstract method <).

Character is a subclass of Magnitude; it overrides the < method (which, if you recall, is marked as abstract in Magnitude by the use of self subclass-Responsibility) with its own version (see the method definition below). %Script 10-41). Character also explicitly defines methods = and hash; it inherits from Magnitude the methods >=, <=, ~= and others.

10.27 Chapter summary

The object model of Pharo is both simple and uniform. Everything is an object, and pretty much everything happens by sending messages.

- Everything is an object. Primitive entities like integers are objects, but also classes are first-class objects.
- Every object is an instance of a class. Classes define the structure of their instances via *private* instance variables and the behaviour of their instances via *public* methods. Each class is the unique instance of its meta-

class. Class variables are private variables shared by the class and all the instances of the class. Classes cannot directly access instance variables of their instances, and instances cannot access instance variables of their class. Accessors must be defined if this is needed.

- Every class has a superclass. The root of the single inheritance hierarchy is `ProtoObject`. Classes you define, however, should normally inherit from `Object` or its subclasses. There is no syntax for defining abstract classes. An abstract class is simply a class with an abstract method (one whose implementation consists of the expression `self subclassResponsibility`). Although Pharo supports only single inheritance, it is easy to share implementations of methods by packaging them as *traits*.

- Everything happens by sending messages. We do not *call methods*, we *send messages*. The receiver then chooses its own method for responding to the message.

- Method lookup follows the inheritance chain; `self` sends are dynamic and start the method lookup in the class of the receiver, whereas `super` sends start the method lookup in the superclass of class in which the super send is written. From this perspective `super` sends are more static than `self` sends.

- There are three kinds of shared variables. Global variables are accessible everywhere in the system. Class variables are shared between a class, its subclasses and its instances. Pool variables are shared between a selected set of classes. You should avoid shared variables as much as possible.

CHAPTER 11

Traits: reusable class fragments

Although Pharo offers single inheritance between classes, it supports a mechanism called Traits for sharing class fragments (behavior and state) across unrelated classes. Traits are collections of methods that can be reused by multiple classes that are not constrained in an inheritance relation. Since Pharo 7.0, traits can also hold state.

Using traits allows one to share code between different classes without duplicating code. This makes it easy for classes to *reuse* useful behavior across classes.

As we will show later, traits propose a way to compose and resolve conflicts in disciplined manner. With traits this is not the latest loaded method that wins as this happens with other languages. In Pharo, the composer (be it a class or a trait) always takes precedence and can decide in its context how to resolve a conflict: Methods can be excluded but still accessible under a new name at composition time.

11.1 A simple trait

The following code defines a trait. The `uses:` clause is an empty array indicating that this trait is not composed of other traits.

Traits can define methods. The trait `TFlyingAbility` defines a single method `fly`.

```
TFlyingAbility >> fly
    ^ 'I''m flying!'
```

Traits: reusable class fragments

Listing 11-1 A simple trait.

```
Trait named: #TFlyingAbility
    uses: {}
    package: 'Traits-Example'
```

Now we define a class called `Bird`. It uses the trait `TFlyingAbility`, as a result the class contains then the `fly` method.

```
Object subclass: #Bird
    uses: TFlyingAbility
    instanceVariableNames: ''
    classVariableNames: ''
    package: 'Traits-Example'
```

Instances of the class `Bird` can execute the message `fly`.

```
Bird new fly
>>> 'I''m flying!'
```

11.2 Using a required method

The trait methods do not have to define a complete behavior. A trait method can invoke methods that will be available on the class using it.

Here the method `greeting` of the trait `TGreetable` in invoking the method `name` that is not defined in the trait itself. In such a case the class using the trait will have to implement such a *required* method.

```
Trait named: #TGreetable
    uses: {}
    package: 'Traits-Example'
```

```
TGreetable >> greeting
    ^ 'Hello ', self name
```

Notice that `self` in a trait represents the receiver of the message. Nothing changes compared to classes and default methods.

```
Object subclass: #Person
    uses: TGreetable
    instanceVariableNames: ''
    classVariableNames: ''
    package: 'Traits-Example'
```

We define the class `Person` which uses the trait `TGreetable`. In the class `Person`, we define the method `name`. The `greeting` method will invoke it.

```
Person >> name
    ^ 'Bob'
```
```
Person new greeting
>>> 'Hello Bob'
```

11.3 Self in a trait is the message receiver

One may wonder what self refers to in a trait. However, there is no difference between self used in a method defined in a class or defined in a trait. self always represents the receiver. The fact that the method is defined in a class or a trait has no influence on self.

We define a little Trait to expose this: the method whoAmI just return self.

```
Trait named: #TInspector
    uses: {}
    package: 'Traits-Example'
```
```
TInspector >> whoAmI
    ^ self
```
```
Object subclass: #Foo
    uses: TInspector
    instanceVariableNames: ''
    classVariableNames: ''
    package: 'Traits-Example'
```

The following snippet shows that self is the receiver, even when returned from a trait method.

```
| foo |
foo := Foo new.
foo whoAmI == foo
>>> true
```

11.4 Trait state

Since Pharo 7.0 traits can also define instance variables. Here the trait TCounting defines an instance variable named #count.

```
Trait named: #TCounting
    instanceVariableNames: 'count'
    package: 'Traits-Example'
```

The trait can initialize its state by defining a method initialize followed by the class named. Note that this is a coding convention. Here the trait TCounting defines the method initializeTCounting.

```
TCounting >> initializeTCounting
    count := 0
```

```
TCounting >> increment
    count := count + 1.
    ^ count
```

The class Counter uses the trait TCounting: its instances will have an instance variable named count.

```
Object subclass: #Counter
    uses: TCounting
    instanceVariableNames: ''
    classVariableNames: ''
    package: 'Traits-Example'
```

To initialize correctly Counter instances, the initialize method of the class Counter should invoke the previously defined trait method initializeTCounting.

```
Counter >> initialize
    self initializeTCounting
```

The following code shows that we created a counter and it has a well initialized instance variable.

```
Counter new increment; increment
>>> 2
```

11.5 A class can use two traits

A class is not limited to the use only one trait. It can use several traits. Imagine that we define another trait called TSpeakingAbility.

```
Trait named: #TSpeakingAbility
    uses: {}
    package: 'Traits-Example'
```

This trait defines a method named speak.

```
TSpeakingAbility >> speak
    ^ 'I''m speaking!'
```

Now we define a second trait TFlyingAbility.

```
Trait named: #TFlyingAbility
    instanceVariableNames: ''
    package: 'Traits-Example'
```

This trait defines a method flying.

11.6 Overriding method takes precedence over trait methods

```
TFlyingAbility >> fly
    ^ 'I''m flying'
```

Now the class Duck can use both traits TFlyingAbility and TSpeakingAbility as follows:

```
Object subclass: #Duck
    uses: TFlyingAbility + TSpeakingAbility
    instanceVariableNames: ''
    classVariableNames: ''
    package: 'Traits-Example'
```

Instances of the class Duck get all the behavior from the two traits.

```
| d |
d := Duck new.
d speak
>>> 'I''m speaking!'
d fly
>>> 'I''m flying!'
```

11.6 Overriding method takes precedence over trait methods

A method originating from a trait acts as if it would have been defined in the class (or trait) using that trait. Now the user of a trait (be it a class or another trait) can always redefine the method originating from the trait and the redefinition takes precedence in the user over the method of trait.

Let us illustrate it. In the class Duck we can redefine the method speak to do something else and for example send the message quack.

```
Duck >> quack
    ^ 'QUACK'
```

```
Duck >> speak
    ^ self quack
```

It means that

- the trait method speak is not accessible from the class anymore, and
- the new method is used instead, even by methods using the message speak.

```
Duck new speak
>>> 'QUACK'
```

We define a new method call doubleSpeak as follows:

```
TSpeakingAbility >> doubleSpeak
    ^ 'I double: ', self speak, ' ', self speak
```

The following example shows that the locally redefined version of the method speak of the class Duck takes precedence over the one of the trait TSqueakingAbility.

```
Duck new doubleSpeak
>>> 'I double: QUACK QUACK'
```

11.7 Accessing overridden trait methods

Sometimes you want to override a method from a trait and at the same time still be able to access the overridden method. This is possible by creating an alias to that overridden method in the class trait composition clause using the @ and -> operators as follows:

```
Object subclass: #Duck
   uses: TFlyingAbility + TSpeakingAbility @{#originalSpeak -> #speak}
   instanceVariableNames: ''
   classVariableNames: ''
   package: 'Traits-Example'
```

Note that the arrow means that the new method is the same as the old one: it just has a new name. Here we say that originalSpeak is the new name of speak.

The overridden method can be accessed sending a message with its new name as with any method. Here we define the method differentSpeak and it is sending the message originalSpeak.

```
Duck >> differentSpeak
    ^ self originalSpeak, ' ', self speak
```

```
Duck new differentSpeak
>>> 'I''m speaking! QUACK'
```

Pay attention that an alias is not a full method rename. Indeed if the overridden method is recursive, it will not call the new name, but the old one. An alias just gives a new name to an existing method, it does not change its definition: nothing in the method body is changed.

11.8 Handling conflict

It may happen that two traits used in the same class define the same method. This situation is a conflict. To solve such a conflict, there are two strategies:

1. Using the exclude operator (-), you can exclude the conflicting method from the trait defining the method. In this case the other method will be the one available in the class,
2. or redefine the conflicting method locally in the class. In such a case, the conflicting methods are overridden and the new redefined behavior is the one that will be available in the class. Note that overriddent methods can be made accessible as previously explained with the @ operator.

Here is an example. Let us define another trait named THighFlyingAbility.

```
Trait named: #THighFlyingAbility
    instanceVariableNames: ''
    package: 'Traits-Example'
```

This trait defines a fly method.

```
THighFlyingAbility >> fly
    ^ 'I''m flying high'
```

When we define the class Eagle that uses the two traits THighFlyingAbility and TFlyingAbility, we have a conflict when sending the message fly because the runtime does not know which method to execute.

```
Object subclass: #Eagle
    uses: THighFlyingAbility + TFlyingAbility
    instanceVariableNames: ''
    classVariableNames: ''
    package: 'Traits-Example'
```

```
Eagle new fly
>>> 'A class or trait does not properly resolve a conflict between
      multiple traits it uses.'
```

11.9 Conflict resolution: excluding a method

To solve the conflict, during the composition, we can simply exclude the fly method from the trait TFlyingAbility as follows:

```
Object subclass: #Eagle
    uses: THighFlyingAbility + (TFlyingAbility - #fly)
    instanceVariableNames: ''
    classVariableNames: ''
    package: 'Traits-Example'
```

Now there is only one fly method, the one from THighFlyingAbility.

```
Eagle new fly
>>> 'I''m flying high'
```

11.10 Conflict resolution: redefining the method

Another way to solve the conflict is to simply redefine the conflicting method in the class using the traits.

```
Object subclass: #Eagle
    uses: THighFlyingAbility + TFlyingAbility
    instanceVariableNames: ''
    classVariableNames: ''
    package: 'Traits-Example'
```

```
Eagle >> fly
    ^ 'Flying and flying high'
```

Now there is only one `fly` method: the one defined in the class `Eagle`.

```
Eagle new fly
>>> 'Flying and flying high'
```

You can also access the overridden methods by creating an alias associated with the trait as explained before.

11.11 Conclusion

Traits are groups of methods and state that can be reused in different users (classes or traits), supporting this way a kind of multiple inheritance in the context of a single inheritance language. A class or trait can be composed of several traits. Traits can define instance variables and methods. When the traits used in a class define method having the same name, this leads to a conflict.

There are two ways to resolve a conflict:

- The user (class or trait) can redefine the conflicting method locally: local methods take precedence over trait ones.
- The user can exclude a conflicting method.

In addition an overridden method can be accessed via an alias defined in the trait composition clause.

CHAPTER **12**

SUnit: Tests in Pharo

SUnit is a minimal yet powerful framework that supports the creation and validation of tests. As might be guessed from its name, the design of SUnit focussed on *Unit Tests*, but in fact it can be used for integration tests and functional tests as well. SUnit was originally developed by Kent Beck and subsequently extended by Joseph Pelrine and many contributors. SUnit is the mother of all the other xUnit frameworks.

This chapter is as short as possible to show you that tests are simple. For a more in depth description of SUnit and different approaches of testing you can read the book: *Testing in Pharo* available at http://books.pharo.org.

In this chapter we start by discussing why we test, and what makes a good test. We then present a series of small examples showing how to use SUnit. Finally, we look at the implementation of SUnit, so that you can understand how Pharo uses the power of reflection in supporting its tools. Note that the version documented in this chapter and used in Pharo is a modified version of SUnit3.3.

12.1 Introduction

The interest in testing and Test-Driven Development is not limited to Pharo. Automated testing has become a hallmark of the *Agile software development* movement, and any software developer concerned with improving software quality would do well to adopt it. Indeed, developers in many languages have come to appreciate the power of unit testing, and versions of *xUnit* now exist for every programming language.

Neither testing, nor the building of test suites, is new. By now, everybody knows that tests are a good way to catch errors. eXtreme Programming, by making testing a core practice and by emphasizing *automated* tests, has helped to make testing productive and fun, rather than a chore that programmers dislike.

SUnit is valuable because it allows us to write *executable* tests that are self-checking: the test itself defines what the correct result should be. It also helps us to organize tests into groups, to describe the context in which the tests must run, and to run a group of tests automatically. In less than two minutes you can write tests using SUnit, so instead of writing small code snippets in a playground, we encourage you to use SUnit and get all the advantages of stored and automatically executable tests.

12.2 Why testing is important

Unfortunately, many developers believe that tests are a waste of their time. After all, *they* do not write bugs, only *other* programmers do that. Most of us have said, at some time or other: *I would write tests if I had more time.* If you never write a bug, and if your code will never be changed in the future, then indeed tests are a waste of your time. However, this most likely also means that your application is trivial, or that it is not used by you or anyone else. Think of tests as an investment for the future: having a suite of tests is quite useful now, but it will be *extremely* useful when your application, or the environment in which it runs, changes in the future.

Tests play several roles. First, they provide documentation of the functionality that they cover. This documentation is active: watching the tests pass tells you that the documentation is up to date. Second, tests help developers to confirm that some changes that they have just made to a package have not broken anything else in the system, and to find the parts that break when that confidence turns out to be misplaced. Finally, writing tests during, or even before, programming forces you to think about the functionality that you want to design, *and how it should appear to the client code*, rather than about how to implement it.

By writing the tests first, i.e., before the code, you are compelled to state the context in which your functionality will run, the way it will interact with the client code, and the expected results. Your code will improve. Try it.

We cannot test all aspects of any realistic application. Covering a complete application is simply impossible and should not be the goal of testing. Even with a good test suite some bugs will still creep into the application, where they can lay dormant waiting for an opportunity to damage your system. If you find that this has happened, take advantage of it! As soon as you uncover the bug, write a test that exposes it, run the test, and watch it fail. Now you can start to fix the bug: the tests will tell you when you are done.

12.3 What makes a good test?

Writing good tests is a skill that can be learned by practicing. Let us look at the properties that tests should have to get the maximum benefit.

- *Tests should be repeatable.* You should be able to run a test as often as you want, and always get the same answer.

- *Tests should run without human intervention.* You should be able to run them unattended.

- *Tests should tell a story.* Each test should cover one aspect of a piece of code. A test should act as a scenario that you or someone else can read to understand a piece of functionality.

- *Tests should be validate one aspect.* When a test fails it should show that a single aspect is broken. Indeed if a test covers multiple aspects, first it will break more often and second it will force developer to understand a larger set of options when fixing.

One consequence of such properties is that the number of tests should be somewhat proportional to the number of aspects to be tested: changing one aspect of the system should not break all the tests but only a limited number. This is important because having 100 tests fail should send a much stronger message than having 10 tests fail. However, it is not always possible to achieve this ideal: in particular, if a change breaks the initialization of an object, or the set-up of a test, it is likely to cause all of the tests to fail.

12.4 SUnit step by step

Writing tests is not difficult in itself. Now let's write our first test, and show you the benefits of using SUnit. We use an example that tests the class Set.

We will:

- Define a class to group of tests and benefit from SUnit behavior.
- Define test methods.
- Use assertions to verify expected results.
- Execute the tests.

Write the code and execute the tests as we go along.

Listing 12-1 An Example Set Test class

```
TestCase subclass: #MyExampleSetTest
    instanceVariableNames: 'full empty'
    classVariableNames: ''
    package: 'MySetTest'
```

12.5 Step 1: Create the test class

First you should create a new subclass of `TestCase` called `MyExampleSetTest`. Add two instance variables so that your new class looks like this:

We will use the class `MyExampleSetTest` to group all the tests related to the class `Set`. It defines the context in which the tests will run. Here the context is described by the two instance variables `full` and `empty` that we will use to represent a full and an empty set.

The name of the class is not critical, but by convention it should end in `Test`. If you define a class called `Pattern` and call the corresponding test class `PatternTest`, the two classes will be alphabetized together in the browser (assuming that they are in the same package). It *is* critical that your class is a subclass of `TestCase`.

12.6 Step 2: Initialize the test context

The message `TestCase >> setUp` defines the context in which the tests will run, a bit like an initialize method. `setUp` is invoked before the execution of each test method defined in the test class.

Define the `setUp` method as follows, to initialize the `empty` variable to refer to an empty set and the `full` variable to refer to a set containing two elements.

```
MyExampleSetTest >> setUp
    empty := Set new.
    full := Set with: 5 with: 6
```

In testing jargon the context is called the *fixture* for the test.

12.7 Step 3: Write some test methods

Let's create some tests by defining some methods in the class `MyExampleSetTest`. Each method represents one test. The names of the methods should start with the string `'test'` so that SUnit will collect them into test suites. Test methods take no arguments.

Define the following test methods. The first test, named `testIncludes`, tests the `includes:` method of `Set`. The test says that sending the message includes: 5 to a set containing 5 should return true. Clearly, this test relies on the fact that the setUp method has already run.

```
MyExampleSetTest >> testIncludes
  self assert: (full includes: 5).
  self assert: (full includes: 6)
```

The second test, named testOccurrences, verifies that the number of occurrences of 5 in full set is equal to one, even if we add another element 5 to the set.

```
MyExampleSetTest >> testOccurrences
  self assert: (empty occurrencesOf: 0) equals: 0.
  self assert: (full occurrencesOf: 5) equals: 1.
  full add: 5.
  self assert: (full occurrencesOf: 5) equals: 1
```

Finally, we test that the set no longer contains the element 5 after we have removed it.

```
MyExampleSetTest >> testRemove
  full remove: 5.
  self assert: (full includes: 6).
  self deny: (full includes: 5)
```

Note the use of the method TestCase >> deny: to assert something that should not be true. aTest deny: anExpression is equivalent to aTest assert: anExpression not, but is much more readable.

12.8 Step 4: Run the tests

The easiest way to run the tests is directly from the browser. Simply click on the icon of the class name, or on an individual test method, and select *Run tests (t)* or press the icon. The test methods will be flagged green or red, depending on whether they pass or not (as shown in Figure 12-2).

You can also select sets of test suites to run, and obtain a more detailed log of the results using the SUnit Test Runner, which you can open by selecting World > Test Runner.

Open a Test Runner, select the package *MySetTest*, and click the Run Selected button.

You can also run a single test (and print the usual pass/fail result summary) by executing a *Print it* on the following code: MyExampleSetTest run: #testRemove.

Some people include an executable comment in their test methods that allows running a test method with a *Do it* from the browser, as shown below.

SUnit: Tests in Pharo

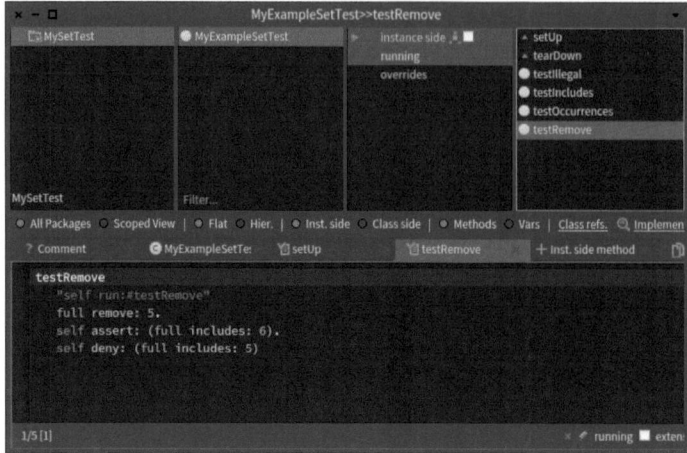

Figure 12-2 Running SUnit tests from the System Browser.

```
MyExampleSetTest >> testRemove
    full remove: 5.
    self assert: (full includes: 6).
    self deny: (full includes: 5)
```

Introduce a bug in `MyExampleSetTest >> testRemove` and run the tests again. For example, change 6 to 7, as in:

```
MyExampleSetTest >> testRemove
    full remove: 5.
    self assert: (full includes: 7).
    self deny: (full includes: 5)
```

The tests that did not pass (if any) are listed in the right-hand panes of the *Test Runner*. If you want to debug one, to see why it failed, just click on the name. Alternatively, you can execute one of the following expressions:

```
(MyExampleSetTest selector: #testRemove) debug
```

```
MyExampleSetTest debug: #testRemove
```

12.9 Step 5: Interpret the results

The method `assert:` is defined in the class `TestAsserter`. This is a superclass of `TestCase` and therefore all other `TestCase` subclasses and is responsible for all kind of test result assertions. The `assert:` method expects a boolean argument, usually the value of a tested expression. When the argument is true, the test passes; when the argument is false, the test fails.

There are actually three possible outcomes of a test: *passing, failing,* and *raising an error*.

- **Passing**. The outcome that we hope for is that all of the assertions in the test are true, in which case the test passes. Visually test runner tools, use green to indicate that a test passes.

- **Failing**. The obvious way is that one of the assertions can be false, causing the test to *fail*. Failing tests are associated with the yellow color.

- **Error**. The other possibility is that some kind of error occurs during the execution of the test, such as a *message not understood* error or an *index out of bounds* error. If an error occurs, the assertions in the test method may not have been executed at all, so we can't say that the test has failed; nevertheless, something is clearly wrong! Errors are usually colored in red.

You can try and modify your tests to provoke both errors and failures.

12.10 Using `assert:equals:`

The message `assert:equals:` offers a better report than `assert:` in case of error. For example, the two following tests are equivalent. However, the second one will report the value that the test is expecting: this makes easier to understand the failure. In this example, we suppose that aDateAndTime is an instance variable of the test class.

```
testAsDate
  self assert: aDateAndTime asDate = ('February 29, 2004' asDate
    translateTo: 2 hours).
```

```
testAsDate
  self
    assert: aDateAndTime asDate
    equals: ('February 29, 2004' asDate translateTo: 2 hours).
```

12.11 Skipping a test

Sometimes in the middle of a development, you may want to skip a test instead of removing it or renaming it to prevent it from running. You can simply invoke the `TestAsserter` message `skip` on your test case instance. For example, the following test uses it to define a conditional test.

Listing 12-3 Testing error raising

```
MyExampleSetTest >> testIllegal
    self should: [ empty at: 5 ] raise: Error.
    self should: [ empty at: 5 put: #zork ] raise: Error
```

```
OCCompiledMethodIntegrityTest >> testPragmas

    | newCompiledMethod originalCompiledMethod |
    (Smalltalk globals hasClassNamed: #Compiler) ifFalse: [ ^ self skip
        ].
    ...
```

This is handy to make sure that your automated execution of tests is reporting success.

12.12 Asserting exceptions

SUnit provides two additional important methods, `TestAsserter >> should:raise:` and `TestAsserter >> shouldnt:raise:` for testing exception raising.

For example, you would use `self should: aBlock raise: anException` to test that a particular exception is raised during the execution of `aBlock`. The method below illustrates the use of `should:raise:`.

Try running this test. Note that the first argument of the `should:` and `shouldnt:` methods is a block that contains the expression to be executed.

12.13 Programmatically running tests

Normally, you will run your tests using the Test Runner or using your code browser.

Running a single test

If you don't want to launch the Test Runner UI from the World menu, you can execute `TestRunner open`. You can also run a single test as follows:

```
MyExampleSetTest run: #testRemove
>>> 1 run, 1 passed, 0 failed, 0 errors
```

Running all the tests in a test class

Any subclass of `TestCase` responds to the message `suite`, which will build a test suite that contains all the methods in the class whose names start with the string *test*.

To run the tests in the suite, send it the message run. For example:

```
MyExampleSetTest suite run
>>> 4 run, 4 passed, 0 failed, 0 errors
```

12.14 Conclusion

This chapter explained why tests are an important investment in the future of your code. We explained in a step-by-step fashion how to define a few tests for the class Set.

- To maximize their potential, unit tests should be fast, repeatable, independent of any direct human interaction and cover a single unit of functionality.

- Tests for a class called MyClass belong in a class named MyClassTest, which should be introduced as a subclass of TestCase.

- Initialize your test data in a setUp method.

- Each test method should start with the word *test*.

- Use the TestCase methods assert:, deny: and others to make assertions.

- Run tests!

Several software development methodologies such as *eXtreme Programming* and Test-Driven Development (TDD) advocate writing tests before writing code. This may seem to go against our deep instincts as software developers. All we can say is: go ahead and try it. We have found that writing the tests before the code helps us to know what we want to code, helps us know when we are done, and helps us conceptualize the functionality of a class and to design its interface. Moreover, test-first development gives us the courage to go fast, because we are not afraid that we will forget something important.

CHAPTER 13

Basic classes

Pharo is a really simple language but powerful language. Part of its power is not in the language but in its class libraries. To program effectively in it, you will need to learn how the class libraries support the language and environment. The class libraries are entirely written in Pharo, and can easily be extended. (Recall that a package may add new functionality to a class even if it does not define this class.)

Our goal here is not to present in tedious detail the whole of the Pharo class library, but rather to point out the key classes and methods that you will need to use (or subclass/override) to program effectively. In this chapter, we will cover the basic classes that you will need for nearly every application: Object, Number and its subclasses, Character, String, Symbol, and Boolean.

13.1 Object

For all intents and purposes, Object is the root of the inheritance hierarchy. Actually, in Pharo the true root of the hierarchy is ProtoObject, which is used to define minimal entities that masquerade as objects, but we can ignore this point for the time being.

Object defines almost 400 methods (in other words, every class that you define will automatically provide all those methods). *Note:* You can count the number of methods in a class like so:

```
Object selectors size          "Count the instance methods in Object"
Object class selectors size    "Count the class methods"
```

Class `Object` provides default behaviour common to all normal objects, such as access, copying, comparison, error handling, message sending, and reflection. Also utility messages that all objects should respond to are defined here. `Object` has no instance variables, nor should any be added. This is due to several classes of objects that inherit from `Object` that have special implementations (`SmallInteger` and `UndefinedObject` for example) that the VM knows about and depends on the structure and layout of certain standard classes.

If we begin to browse the method protocols on the instance side of `Object` we will start to see some of the key behaviour it provides.

13.2 Object printing

Every object can return a printed form of itself. You can select any expression in a textpane and select the `Print it` menu item: this executes the expression and asks the returned object to print itself. In fact this sends the message `printString` to the returned object. The method `printString`, which is a template method, at its core sends the message `printOn:` to its receiver. The message `printOn:` is a hook that can be specialized.

Method `Object>>printOn:` is very likely one of the methods that you will most frequently override. This method takes as its argument a `Stream` on which a `String` representation of the object will be written. The default implementation simply writes the class name preceded by a or an. `Object>>printString` returns the `String` that is written.

For example, the class `OpalCompiler` does not redefine the method `printOn:` and sending the message `printString` to an instance executes the methods defined in `Object`.

```
OpalCompiler new printString
>>> 'an OpalCompiler'
```

The class `Color` shows an example of `printOn:` specialization. It prints the name of the class followed by the name of the class method used to generate that color.

```
Color red printString
>>> 'Color red'
```

printOn: vs. displayStringOn:

You should consider that the message `printOn:` is to better describe your objects when you are developing. Indeed when you are using the inspector or the debugger, it is a lot more efficient to see a precise description of your object instead of the generic one. Now `printOn:` is not done to be used to

13.3 Representation and self-evaluating representation

Listing 13-1 printOn: redefinition.

```
Color >> printOn: aStream
    | name |
    (name := self name).
    name = #unnamed
        ifFalse: [
            ^ aStream
                nextPutAll: 'Color ';
                nextPutAll: name ].
    self storeOn: aStream
```

nicely display objects in UI lists for example, because you usually want to display a different kind of information. For this purpose you should use `displayStringOn:`. The default implementation of `displayStringOn:` is to invoke `printOn:`.

Note that the introduction of `displayStringOn:` is recent so many libraries are still not making this distinction. It is not really a problem but when you write new code, you should be aware of this.

printOn: vs. storeOn:

Note that the message `printOn:` is not the same as `storeOn:`. The message `storeOn:` writes to its argument stream an expression that can be used to recreate the receiver. This expression is executed when the stream is read using the message `readFrom:`. On the other hand, the message `printOn:` just returns a textual version of the receiver. Of course, it may happen that this textual representation may represent the receiver as a self-evaluating expression.

13.3 Representation and self-evaluating representation

In functional programming, expressions return values when executed. In Pharo, message sends (expressions) return objects (values). Some objects have the nice property that their value is themselves. For example, the value of the object `true` is itself i.e., the object `true`. We call such objects *self-evaluating objects*. You can see a *printed* version of an object value when you print the object in a playground. Here are some examples of such self-evaluating expressions.

```
true
>>> true
```

```
3@4
>>> (3@4)
```

Listing 13-2 Self-evaluation of Point
```
Point >> printOn: aStream
    "The receiver prints on aStream in terms of infix notation."

    aStream nextPut: $(.
    x printOn: aStream.
    aStream nextPut: $@.
    (y notNil and: [y negative])
        ifTrue: [
            "Avoid ambiguous @- construct"
            aStream space ].
    y printOn: aStream.
    aStream nextPut: $).
```

```
$a
>>> $a
```
```
#(1 2 3)
>>> #(1 2 3)
```
```
Color red
>>> Color red
```

Note that some objects such as arrays are self-evaluating or not depending on the objects they contain. For example, an array of booleans is self-evaluating, whereas an array of persons is not. The following example shows that a dynamic array is self-evaluating only if its elements are:

```
{10@10. 100@100}
>>> {(10@10). (100@100)}
```
```
{OpalCompiler new . 100@100}
>>> an Array(an OpalCompiler (100@100))
```

Remember that literal arrays can only contain literals. Hence the following array does not contain two points but rather six literal elements.

```
#(10@10 100@100)
>>> #(10 #@ 10 100 #@ 100)
```

Lots of `printOn:` method specializations implement self-evaluating behavior. The implementations of `Point>>printOn:` and `Interval>>printOn:` are self-evaluating.

```
1 to: 10
>>> (1 to: 10)    "intervals are self-evaluating"
```

13.4 Identity and equality

Listing 13-3 Self-evaluation of `Interval`
```
Interval >> printOn: aStream
    aStream nextPut: $( ;
        print: start;
        nextPutAll: ' to: ';
        print: stop.
    step ~= 1 ifTrue: [aStream nextPutAll: ' by: '; print: step].
    aStream nextPut: $)
```

Listing 13-4 Object equality
```
Object >> = anObject
    "Answer whether the receiver and the argument represent the same
    object.
    If = is redefined in any subclass, consider also redefining the
    message hash."

    ^ self == anObject
```

13.4 Identity and equality

In Pharo, the message = tests object *equality* while the message == tests object *identity*. The former is used to check whether two objects represent the same value, while the latter is used to check whether two expressions represent the same object.

The default implementation of object equality is to test for object identity:

If you override =, you should consider overriding hash. If instances of your class are ever used as keys in a Dictionary, then you should make sure that instances that are considered to be equal have the same hash value.

Although you should override = and hash together, you should *never* override ==. The semantics of object identity is the same for all classes. Message == is a primitive method of ProtoObject.

Note that Pharo has some strange equality behaviour compared to other Smalltalks. For example a symbol and a string can be equal. (We consider this to be a bug, not a feature.)

```
#'lulu' = 'lulu'
>>> true
```

```
'lulu' = #'lulu'
>>> true
```

13.5 Class membership

Several methods allow you to query the class of an object.

class

You can ask any object about its class using the message `class`.

```
1 class
>>> SmallInteger
```

isKindOf:

`Object>>isKindOf:` answers whether the receiver's class is either the same as, or a subclass of the argument class.

```
1 isKindOf: SmallInteger
>>> true
```

```
1 isKindOf: Integer
>>> true
```

```
1 isKindOf: Number
>>> true
```

```
1 isKindOf: Object
>>> true
```

```
1 isKindOf: String
>>> false
```

```
1/3 isKindOf: Number
>>> true
```

```
1/3 isKindOf: Integer
>>> false
```

1/3 which is a `Fraction` is a kind of `Number`, since the class `Number` is a superclass of the class `Fraction`, but 1/3 is not an `Integer`.

respondsTo:

`Object>>respondsTo:` answers whether the receiver understands the message selector given as an argument.

```
1 respondsTo: #,
>>> false
```

13.6 About `isKindOf:` and `respondTo:`

A note on the usage of `isKindOf:` and `respondsTo:`. Normally it is a bad idea to query an object for its class, or to ask it which messages it understands. Instead of making decisions based on the class of object, you should simply send a message to the object and let it decide (on the basis of its class) how it should behave. Client of an object should not query the object to decide with messages to send it. The "Don't Ask, Tell" is an important cornerstone of good object-oriented design. So watch out if you need to use these messages.

13.7 Shallow copying objects

Copying objects introduces some subtle issues. Since instance variables are accessed by reference, a *shallow copy* of an object shares its references to instance variables with the original object:

```
a1 := { { 'harry' } }.
a1
>>> #(#('harry'))
```

```
a2 := a1 shallowCopy.
a2
>>> #(#('harry'))
```

```
(a1 at: 1) at: 1 put: 'sally'.
a1
>>> #(#('sally'))
```

```
a2
>>> #(#('sally'))     "the subarray is shared!"
```

`Object>>shallowCopy` is a primitive method that creates a shallow copy of an object. Since a2 is only a shallow copy of a1, the two arrays share a reference to the nested `Array` that they contain.

13.8 Deep copying objects

There are two ways to address the problems of sharing raised by shallow copy: (1) using `deepCopy`, (2) specializing `postCopy` and using `copy`.

deepCopy

`Object>>deepCopy` makes an arbitrarily deep copy of an object.

Listing 13-5 Copying objects as a template method
```
Object >> copy
    "Answer another instance just like the receiver.
    Subclasses typically override postCopy;
    they typically do not override shallowCopy."

    ^ self shallowCopy postCopy
```

```
a1 := { { { 'harry' } } } .
a2 := a1 deepCopy.
(a1 at: 1) at: 1 put: 'sally'.
a1
>>> #(#('sally'))
```
```
a2
>>> #(#(#('harry')))
```

The problem with `deepCopy` is that it will not terminate when applied to a mutually recursive structure:

```
a1 := { 'harry' }.
a2 := { a1 }.
a1 at: 1 put: a2.
a1 deepCopy
>>> !''... does not terminate!''!
```

copy

The other solution is to use message `copy`. It is implemented on `Object` as follows: the method `postCopy` is sent to the result of the message `shallowCopy`.

```
Object >> postCopy
    ^ self
```

By default `postCopy` returns self. It means that by default `copy` is doing the same as `shallowCopy` but each subclass can decide to customise the `postCopy` method which acts as a hook. You should override `postCopy` to copy any instance variables that should not be shared. In addition there is a good chance that `postCopy` should always do a `super postCopy` to ensure that state of the superclass is also copied.

13.9 Debugging

`Object` defines also some methods related to debugging.

13.10 Error handling

Listing 13-6 Checking a pre-condition
```
Stack >> pop
    "Return the first element and remove it from the stack."

    self assert: [ self isNotEmpty ].
    ^ self linkedList removeFirst element
```

halt

The most important method here is `halt`. To set a breakpoint in a method, simply insert the expression `self halt` at some point in the body of the method. Note that since `halt` is defined on `Object` you can also write `1 halt`.

When this message is sent, execution will be interrupted and a debugger will open to this point in your program.

You can also use `Halt once` or `Halt if: aCondition`. Have a look at the class `Halt` which is an exception dedicated to debugging.

assert:

The next most important message is `assert:`, which expects a block as its argument. If the block evaluates to `true`, execution continues. Otherwise an `AssertionFailure` exception will be raised. If this exception is not otherwise caught, the debugger will open to this point in the execution. `assert:` is especially useful to support *design by contract*. The most typical usage is to check non-trivial pre-conditions to public methods of objects. `Stack>>pop` could easily have been implemented as follows (note that this definition is anhypothetical example and not in the Pharo 8.0 system):

Do not confuse `Object>>assert:` with `TestCase>>assert:`, which occurs in the SUnit testing framework (see Chapter : SUnit). While the former expects a block as its argument (actually, it will take any argument that understands `value`, including a `Boolean`), the latter expects a `Boolean`. Although both are useful for debugging, they each serve a very different purpose.

13.10 Error handling

This protocol contains several methods useful for signaling run-time errors.

doesNotUnderstand:

The message `doesNotUnderstand:` (commonly abbreviated in discussions as DNU or MNU) is sent whenever message lookup fails. The default implementation, i.e., `Object>>doesNotUnderstand:` will trigger the debugger at

Listing 13-7 Signaling that a method is abstract
```
Object >> subclassResponsibility
    "This message sets up a framework for the behavior of the class'
    subclasses.
    Announce that the subclass should have implemented this message."

    SubclassResponsibility signalFor: thisContext sender selector
```

this point. It may be useful to override `doesNotUnderstand:` to provide some other behaviour.

error

`Object>>error` and `Object>>error:` are generic methods that can be used to raise exceptions. Generally it is better to raise your own custom exceptions, so you can distinguish errors arising from your code from those coming from kernel classes.

subclassResponsibility

Abstract methods are implemented by convention with the body `self subclassResponsibility`. Should an abstract class be instantiated by accident, then calls to abstract methods will result in `Object>>subclassResponsibility` being executed.

`Magnitude`, `Number`, and `Boolean` are classical examples of abstract classes that we shall see shortly in this chapter.

```
Number new + 1
>>> !''Error: Number is an abstract class. Make a concrete subclass.''!
```

shouldNotImplement

`self shouldNotImplement` is sent by convention to signal that an inherited method is not appropriate for this subclass. This is generally a sign that something is not quite right with the design of the class hierarchy. Due to the limitations of single inheritance, however, sometimes it is very hard to avoid such workarounds.

A typical example is `Collection>>remove:` which is inherited by `Dictionary` but flagged as not implemented. A `Dictionary` provides `removeKey:` instead.

13.11 Testing

Listing 13-8 initialize as an empty hook method

```
ProtoObject >> initialize
    "Subclasses should redefine this method to perform initializations
    on instance creation"
```

deprecated: and related

Sending self deprecated: signals that the current method should no longer be used, if deprecation has been turned on. You can turn it on/off in the Debugging section using the Settings browser. The argument should describe an alternative. Look for senders of the message deprecated: and other related messages to get an idea.

13.11 Testing

Testing methods have nothing to do with SUnit testing! A testing method is one that lets you ask a question about the state of the receiver and returns a Boolean.

Numerous testing methods are provided by Object. There are isArray, isBoolean, isBlock, isCollection and so on. Generally such methods are to be avoided since querying an object for its class is a form of violation of encapsulation. They are often used as an alternative to isKindOf: but they show the same limit in the design. Instead of testing an object for its class, one should simply send a message and let the object decide how to handle it.

Nevertheless some of these testing methods are undeniably useful. The most useful are probably ProtoObject>>isNil and Object>>notNil. The Null Object design pattern can obviate the need for even these methods but it is often not possible and not the right choice.

13.12 Initialize

A final key method that occurs not in Object but in ProtoObject is initialize.

The reason this is important is that in Pharo, the default new method defined for every class in the system will send initialize to newly created instances.

This means that simply by overriding the initialize hook method, new instances of your class will automatically be initialized. The initialize method should normally perform a super initialize to establish the class invariant for any inherited instance variables.

Basic classes

Listing 13-9 new as a class-side template method

```
Behavior >> new
    "Answer a new initialized instance of the receiver (which is a
    class) with no indexable
    variables. Fail if the class is indexable."
    ^ self basicNew initialize
```

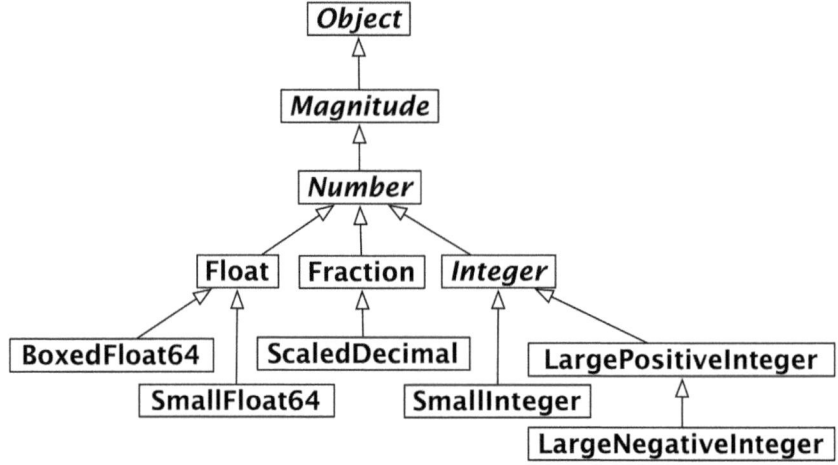

Figure 13-10 The number hierarchy.

13.13 Numbers

Numbers in Pharo are not primitive data values but true objects. Of course numbers are implemented efficiently in the virtual machine, but the Number hierarchy is as perfectly accessible and extensible as any other portion of the class hierarchy.

The abstract root of this hierarchy is Magnitude, which represents all kinds of classes supporting comparison operators. Number adds various arithmetic and other operators as mostly abstract methods. Float and Fraction represent, respectively, floating point numbers and fractional values. Float subclasses (BoxedFloat64 and SmallFloat64) represent Floats on certain architectures. For example BoxedFloat64 is only available for 64 bit systems. Integer is also abstract, thus distinguishing between subclasses SmallInteger, LargePositiveInteger and LargeNegativeInteger. For the most part, users do not need to be aware of the difference between the three Integer classes, as values are automatically converted as needed.

13.14 Magnitude

Listing 13-11 Abstract comparison methods

```
Magnitude >> < aMagnitude
    "Answer whether the receiver is less than the argument."

    ^ self subclassResponsibility

Magnitude >> > aMagnitude
    "Answer whether the receiver is greater than the argument."

    ^ aMagnitude < self
```

13.14 Magnitude

Magnitude is the parent not only of the Number classes, but also of other classes supporting comparison operations, such as Character, Duration and Timespan.

Methods < and = are abstract. The remaining operators are generically defined. For example:

13.15 Numbers

Similarly, Number defines +, -, * and / to be abstract, but all other arithmetic operators are generically defined.

All Number objects support various *converting* operators, such as asFloat and asInteger. There are also numerous *shortcut constructor methods* which generate Durations, such as hour, day and week.

Numbers directly support common *math functions* such as sin, log, raiseTo:, squared, sqrt and so on.

The method Number>>printOn: is implemented in terms of the abstract method Number>>printOn:base:. (The default base is 10.)

Testing methods include even, odd, positive and negative. Unsurprisingly Number overrides isNumber. More interestingly, isInfinite is defined to return false.

Truncation methods include floor, ceiling, integerPart, fractionPart and so on.

```
1 + 2.5
>>> 3.5              "Addition of two numbers"
```

```
3.4 * 5
>>> 17.0             "Multiplication of two numbers"
```

```
8 / 2
>>> 4                    "Division of two numbers"
```

```
10 - 8.3
>>> 1.7                  "Subtraction of two numbers"
```

```
12 = 11
>>> false                "Equality between two numbers"
```

```
12 ~= 11
>>> true                 "Test if two numbers are different"
```

```
12 > 9
>>> true                 "Greater than"
```

```
12 >= 10
>>> true                 "Greater or equal  than"
```

```
12 < 10
>>> false                "Smaller than"
```

```
100@10
>>> 100@10     "Point creation"
```

The following example works surprisingly well in Pharo:

```
1000 factorial / 999 factorial
>>> 1000
```

Note that `1000 factorial` is really calculated, which in many other languages can be quite difficult to compute. This is an excellent example of automatic coercion and exact handling of a number.

> **To do** Try to display the result of `1000 factorial`. It takes more time to display it than to calculate it!

13.16 Floats

`Float` implements the abstract `Number` methods for floating point numbers.

More interestingly, `Float class` (i.e., the class-side of `Float`) provides methods to return the following *constants*: e, infinity, nan and pi.

```
Float pi
>>> 3.141592653589793
```

```
Float infinity
>>> Float infinity
```

```
Float infinity isInfinite
>>> true
```

13.17 Fractions

Fractions are represented by instance variables for the numerator and denominator, which should be Integers. Fractions are normally created by Integer division (rather than using the constructor method Fraction>>numerator:denominator:):

```
6/8
>>> (3/4)
```

```
(6/8) class
>>> Fraction
```

Multiplying a Fraction by an Integer or another Fraction may yield an Integer:

```
6/8 * 4
>>> 3
```

13.18 Integers

Integer is the abstract parent of three concrete integer implementations. In addition to providing concrete implementations of many abstract Number methods, it also adds a few methods specific to integers, such as factorial, atRandom, isPrime, gcd: and many others.

SmallInteger is special in that its instances are represented compactly – instead of being stored as a reference, a SmallInteger is represented directly using the bits that would otherwise be used to hold a reference. The first bit of an object reference indicates whether the object is a SmallInteger or not. The virtual machine abstracts that from you, therefore you cannot see this directly when inspecting the object.

The class methods minVal and maxVal tell us the range of a SmallInteger, note that it varies depending on the size of your image from either (2 raisedTo: 30) - 1 for a 32-bits image or (2 raisedTo: 60) - 1 for a 64-bits one.

```
SmallInteger maxVal = ((2 raisedTo: 30) - 1)
>>> true
```

```
SmallInteger minVal = (2 raisedTo: 30) negated
>>> true
```

When a SmallInteger goes out of this range, it is automatically converted to a LargePositiveInteger or a LargeNegativeInteger, as needed:

```
(SmallInteger maxVal + 1) class
>>> LargePositiveInteger
```

```
(SmallInteger minVal - 1) class
>>> LargeNegativeInteger
```

Large integers are similarly converted back to small integers when appropriate.

As in most programming languages, integers can be useful for specifying iterative behaviour. There is a dedicated method `timesRepeat:` for evaluating a block repeatedly. We have already seen a similar example in Chapter : Syntax in a Nutshell.

```
| n |
n := 2.
3 timesRepeat: [ n := n * n ].
n
>>> 256
```

13.19 Characters

`Character` is defined a subclass of `Magnitude`. Printable characters are represented in Pharo as `$<char>`. For example:

```
$a < $b
>>> true
```

Non-printing characters can be generated by various class methods. `Character class>>value:` takes the Unicode (or ASCII) integer value as argument and returns the corresponding character. The protocol `accessing untypeable characters` contains a number of convenience constructor methods such as `backspace`, `cr`, `escape`, `euro`, `space`, `tab`, and so on.

```
Character space = (Character value: Character space asciiValue)
>>> true
```

The `printOn:` method is clever enough to know which of the three ways to generate characters offers the most appropriate representation:

```
Character value: 1
>>> Character home
```

```
Character value: 2
>>> Character value: 2
```

```
Character value: 32
>>> Character space
```

```
Character value: 97
>>> $a
```

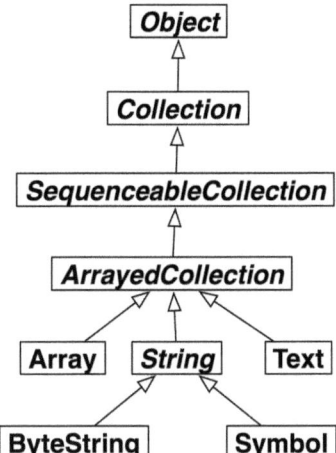

Figure 13-12 The String Hierarchy.

Various convenient *testing* methods are built in: isAlphaNumeric, isCharacter, isDigit, isLowercase, isVowel, and so on.

To convert a Character to the string containing just that character, send asString. In this case asString and printString yield different results:

```
$a asString
>>> 'a'
```

```
$a
>>> $a
```

```
$a printString
>>> '$a'
```

Like SmallInteger, a Character is a immediate value not a object reference. Most of the time you won't see any difference and can use objects of class Character like any other too. But this means, equal value characters are always *identical*:

```
(Character value: 97) == $a
>>> true
```

13.20 Strings

A String is an indexed Collection that holds only Characters.

In fact, String is abstract and Pharo strings are actually instances of the concrete class ByteString.

```
'hello world' class
>>> ByteString
```

The other important subclass of String is Symbol. The key difference is that there is only ever one single instance of Symbol with a given value. (This is sometimes called *the unique instance property*). In contrast, two separately constructed Strings that happen to contain the same sequence of characters will often be different objects.

```
'hel','lo' == 'hello'
>>> false
```

```
('hel','lo') asSymbol == #hello
>>> true
```

Another important difference is that a String is mutable, whereas a Symbol is immutable. Note that it is a bad idea to mutate literal strings because they can be shared between multiple method execution.

```
'hello' at: 2 put: $u; yourself
>>> 'hullo'
```

```
#hello at: 2 put: $u
>>> Error: symbols can not be modified.
```

It is easy to forget that since strings are collections, they understand the same messages that other collections do:

```
#hello indexOf: $o
>>> 5
```

Although String does not inherit from Magnitude, it does support the usual comparing methods, <, = and so on. In addition, String>>match: is useful for some basic glob-style pattern-matching:

```
'*or*' match: 'zorro'
>>> true
```

Strings support a rather large number of conversion methods. Many of these are shortcut constructor methods for other classes, such as asDate, asInteger and so on. There are also a number of useful methods for converting a string to another string, such as capitalized and translateToLowercase.

For more on strings and collections, see Chapter : Collections.

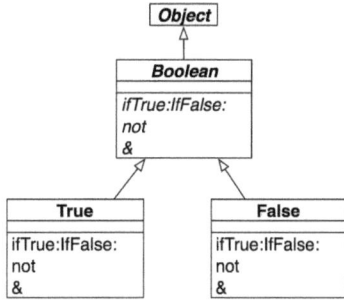

Figure 13-13 The Boolean Hierarchy.

Listing 13-14 Implementations of ifTrue:ifFalse:
```
True >> ifTrue: trueAlternativeBlock ifFalse: falseAlternativeBlock
    ^ trueAlternativeBlock value

False >> ifTrue: trueAlternativeBlock ifFalse: falseAlternativeBlock
    ^ falseAlternativeBlock value
```

13.21 Booleans

The class Boolean offers a fascinating insight into how much of the Pharo language has been pushed into the class library. Boolean is the abstract superclass of the singleton classes True and False.

Most of the behaviour of Booleans can be understood by considering the method ifTrue:ifFalse:, which takes two Blocks as arguments.

```
4 factorial > 20
  ifTrue: [ 'bigger' ]
  ifFalse: [ 'smaller' ]
>>> 'bigger'
```

The method ifTrue:ifFalse: is abstract in class Boolean. The implementations in its concrete subclasses are both trivial:

Each of them execute the correct block depending on the receiver of the message. In fact, this is the essence of OOP: when a message is sent to an object, the object itself determines which method will be used to respond. In this case an instance of True simply executes the *true* alternative, while an instance of False executes the *false* alternative. All the abstract Boolean methods are implemented in this way for True and False. For example the implementation of negation (message not) is defined the same way:

Booleans offer several useful convenience methods, such as ifTrue:, ifFalse:, and ifFalse:ifTrue. You also have the choice between eager and

Listing 13-15 Implementing negation

```
True >> not
    "Negation--answer false since the receiver is true."
    ^ false

False >> not
    "Negation--answer true since the receiver is false."
    ^ true
```

lazy conjunctions and disjunctions.

In the first example below, both Boolean subexpressions are executed, since & takes a Boolean argument. Even if (1 > 2) is obviously false and there is no need to check (3 < 4), & execute its arguments.

```
( 1 > 2 ) & ( 3 < 4 )
>>> false    "Eager, must evaluate both sides"
```

In the second and third examples, only the receiver expression 1 > 2 is executed and false – the argument closure is not executed. Notice that the message and: expects a closure as argument. In the third example, the expression [1 / 0] is not executed and does not raise an error, because and: only execute is argument if the receiver true.

```
( 1 > 2 ) and: [ 3 < 4 ]
>>> false    "Lazy, only evaluate receiver"
```

```
( 1 > 2 ) and: [ 1 / 0 ]
>>> false    "argument block is never executed, so no exception"
```

A lazy or: is also offering the similar behavior. It only executes the argument in this case, when the receiver is false.

Try to imagine how and: and or: are implemented. Check the implementations in Boolean, True and False.

13.22 Chapter summary

- If you override = then you should override hash as well.
- Override postCopy to correctly implement copying for your objects.
- Use self halt. to set a breakpoint.
- Return self subclassResponsibility to make a method abstract.
- To give an object a String representation you should override printOn:.
- Override the hook method initialize to properly initialize instances.

13.22 Chapter summary

- Number methods automatically convert between `Floats`, `Fractions` and `Integers`.
- `Fractions` truly represent rational numbers rather than floats.
- All `Characters` are like unique instances.
- `Strings` are mutable; `Symbols` are not. Take care not to mutate string literals, however!
- `Symbols` are unique; `Strings` are not.
- `Strings` and `Symbols` are `Collections` and therefore support the usual `Collection` methods.

CHAPTER 14

Collections

To make good use of the collection classes, the reader needs at least a superficial knowledge of the wide variety of collections that exist, and their commonalities and differences. This is what this chapter is about.

The collection classes form a loosely-defined group of general-purpose subclasses of `Collection` and `Stream`. Some of these subclasses such as `Bitmap`, or `CompiledMethod` are special-purpose classes crafted for use in other parts of the system or in applications, and hence not categorized as *Collections* by the system organization.

In this chapter, we use the term *Collection Hierarchy* to mean `Collection` and its subclasses that are *also* in the packages labelled `Collections-*`. We use the term *Stream Hierarchy* to mean `Stream` and its subclasses that are *also* in the `Collections-Streams` packages.

In this chapter we focus mainly on the subset of collection classes shown in Figure 14-1. Streams will be discussed separately in Chapter : Streams.

Pharo by default provide a good set of collections. In addition, the project "Containers" available at http://www.github.com/Pharo-Containers/ proposes alternate implementations or new collections and data structures.

Let us start with an important point about the design of the collections in Pharo. Their APIs heavily use high-order functions: so while we can use for loops like in old Java, most of the time Pharo developers will use iterator style based on high-order functions.

Collections

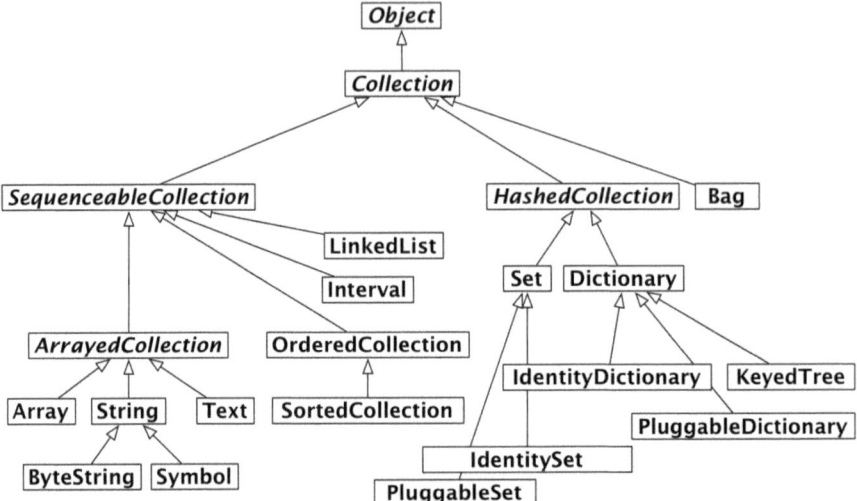

Figure 14-1 Some of the key collection classes in Pharo.

14.1 High-order functions

Programming with collections using high-order functions rather than individual elements is an important way to raise the level of abstraction of a program. The Lisp function map, which applies an argument function to every element of a list and returns a new list containing the results is an early example of this style. Following its Smalltalk root, Pharo adopts this collection-based high-order programming as a central tenet. Modern functional programming languages such as ML and Haskell have followed Smalltalk's lead.

Why is this a good idea? Let us suppose you have a data structure containing a collection of student records, and wish to perform some action on all of the students that meet some criteria. Programmers raised to use an imperative language will immediately reach for a loop, but the Pharo programmer will write:

```
students
  select: [ :each | each gpa < threshold ]
```

This expression returns a new collection containing precisely those elements of students for which the block (the bracketed function) returns true. The block can be thought of as a lambda-expression defining an anonymous function x. x gpa < threshold. This code has the simplicity and elegance of a domain-specific query language.

The message select: is understood by *all* collections in Pharo. There is no

need to find out if the student data structure is an array or a linked list: the
select: message is understood by both. Note that this it's quite different
from using a loop, where one must know whether students is an array or a
linked list before the loop can be set up.

In Pharo, when one speaks of a collection without being more specific about
the kind of collection, one means an object that supports well-defined protocols for testing membership and enumerating the elements. *All* collections
understand the testing messages includes:, isEmpty and occurrencesOf:.
All collections understand the enumeration messages do:, select:, reject:
(which is the opposite of select:), collect: (which is like Lisp's map), detect:ifNone:, inject:into: (which performs a left fold) and many more. It
is the ubiquity of this protocol, as well as its variety, that makes it so powerful.

The table below summarizes the standard protocols supported by most of the
classes in the collection hierarchy. These methods are defined, redefined, optimized or occasionally even forbidden by subclasses of Collection.

Protocol	Methods
accessing	size, capacity, at:, at:put:
testing	isEmpty, includes:, contains:, occurrencesOf:
adding	add:, addAll:
removing	remove:, remove:ifAbsent:, removeAll:
enumerating	do:, collect:, select:, reject:
	detect:, detect:ifNone:, inject:into:
converting	asBag, asSet, asOrderedCollection, asSortedCollection, asArray, asSortedCollection:
creation	with:, with:with:, with:with:with:, with:with:with:with:, withAll:

14.2 The varieties of collections

Beyond this basic uniformity, there are many different kinds of collections
either supporting different protocols or providing different behaviour for the
same requests. Let us briefly observe some of the key differences:

Sequenceable: Instances of all subclasses of SequenceableCollection start
from a first element and proceed in a well-defined order to a last element. Instances of Set, Bag and Dictionary, on the other hand, are not
sequenceable.

Sortable: A SortedCollection maintains its elements in sort order.

Indexable: Most sequenceable collections are also indexable, that is, elements can be retrieved with message at: anIndex. Array is the familiar
indexable data structure with a fixed size; anArray at: n retrieves the

n^{th} element of anArray, and anArray at: n put: v changes the nth element to v. LinkedLists is sequenceable but not indexable, that is, they understand first and last, but not the message at:.

Keyed: Instances of Dictionary and its subclasses are accessed by keys instead of indices.

Mutable: Most collections are mutable, but Intervals and Symbols are not. An Interval is an immutable collection representing a range of Integers. For example, 5 to: 16 by: 2 is an interval that contains the elements 5, 7, 9, 11, 13 and 15. It is indexable with message at: anIndex, but cannot be changed with message at: anIndex put: aValue.

Growable: Instances of Interval and Array are always of a fixed size. Other kinds of collections (sorted collections, ordered collections, and linked lists) can grow after creation. The class OrderedCollection is more general than Array; the size of an OrderedCollection grows on demand, and it defines messages addFirst: anElement and addLast: anElement as well as messages at: anIndex and at: anIndex put: aValue.

Accepts duplicates: A Set filters out duplicates, but a Bag does not. Classes Dictionary, Set and Bag use the = method provided by the elements; the Identity variants of these classes use the == method, which tests whether the arguments are the same object, and the Pluggable variants use an arbitrary equivalence relation supplied by the creator of the collection.

Heterogeneous: Most collections will hold any kind of element. A String, CharacterArray or Symbol, however, only holds Characters. An Array will hold any mix of objects, but a ByteArray only holds Bytes. A LinkedList is constrained to hold elements that conform to the Link accessing protocol.

14.3 Collection implementations

These categorizations by functionality are not our only concern; we must also consider how the collection classes are implemented. As shown in Figure 14-2, five main implementation techniques are employed.

- Arrays store their elements in the (indexable) instance variables of the collection object itself; as a consequence, arrays must be of a fixed size, but can be created with a single memory allocation.

- OrderedCollections and SortedCollections store their elements in an array that is referenced by one of the instance variables of the collec-

14.4 Examples of key classes

Arrayed Implementation	Ordered Implementation	Hashed Implementation	Linked Implementation	Interval Implementation
Array String Symbol	OrderedCollection SortedCollection Text Heap	Set IdentitySet PluggableSet Bag IdentityBag Dictionary IdentityDictionary PluggableDictionary	LinkedList SkipList	Interval

Figure 14-2 Some collection classes categorized by implementation technique.

tion. Consequently, the internal array can be replaced with a larger one if the collection grows beyond its storage capacity.

- The various kinds of set and dictionary also reference a subsidiary array for storage, but use the array as a hash table. Bags use a subsidiary Dictionary, with the elements of the bag as keys and the number of occurrences as values.
- LinkedLists use a standard singly-linked representation.
- Intervals are represented by three integers that record the two endpoints and the step size.

In addition to these classes, there are also *weak* variants of Array, Set and of the various kinds of dictionary. These collections hold onto their elements weakly, i.e., in a way that does not prevent the elements from being garbage collected. The Pharo virtual machine is aware of these classes and handles them specially.

14.4 Examples of key classes

We present now the most common or important collection classes using simple code examples. The main protocols of collections are:

- messages at:, at:put: — to access an element,
- messages add:, remove: — to add or remove an element,
- messages size, isEmpty, include: — to get some information about the collection,
- messages do:, collect:, select: — to iterate over the collection.

Each collection may implement (or not) such protocols, and when they do, they interpret them to fit with their semantics. We suggest you to browse the classes themselves in order to identify specific and more advanced protocols.

We will focus on the most common collection classes: `OrderedCollection`, `Set`, `SortedCollection`, `Dictionary`, `Interval`, and `Array`.

14.5 Common creation protocol

There are several ways to create instances of collections. The most generic ones use the message `new: aSize` and `with: anElement`.

- `new: anInteger` creates a collection of size `anInteger` whose elements will all be `nil`.
- `with: anObject` creates a collection and adds `anObject` to the created collection.

Different collections will realize this behaviour differently.

You can create collections with initial elements using the methods `with:`, `with:with:` etc. for up to six elements.

```
Array with: 1
>>> #(1)
```

```
Array with: 1 with: 2
>>> #(1 2)
```

```
Array with: 1 with: 2 with: 3
>>> #(1 2 3)
```

```
Array with: 1 with: 2 with: 3 with: 4
>>> #(1 2 3 4)
```

```
Array with: 1 with: 2 with: 3 with: 4 with: 5
>>> #(1 2 3 4 5)
```

```
Array with: 1 with: 2 with: 3 with: 4 with: 5 with: 6
>>> #(1 2 3 4 5 6)
```

You can also use message `addAll: aCollection` to add all elements of one kind of collection to another kind:

```
(1 to: 5) asOrderedCollection addAll: '678'; yourself
>>> an OrderedCollection(1 2 3 4 5 6 7 8)
```

Take care that `addAll:` returns its argument, and not the receiver!

You can also create many collections with `withAll: aCollection`.

```
Array withAll: #(7 3 1 3)
>>> #(7 3 1 3)
```

```
OrderedCollection withAll: #(7 3 1 3)
>>> an OrderedCollection(7 3 1 3)
```

```
SortedCollection withAll: #(7 3 1 3)
>>> a SortedCollection(1 3 3 7)
```

```
Set withAll: #(7 3 1 3)
>>> a Set(7 1 3)
```

```
Bag withAll: #(7 3 1 3)
>>> a Bag(7 1 3 3)
```

14.6 Array

An Array is a fixed-sized collection of elements accessed by integer indices. Contrary to the C convention in Pharo, the first element of an array is at position 1 and not 0. The main protocol to access array elements is the method at: and at:put:.

- at: anInteger returns the element at index anInteger.
- at: anInteger put: anObject puts anObject at index anInteger.

Arrays are fixed-size collections therefore we cannot add or remove elements at the end of an array. The following code creates an array of size 5, puts values in the first 3 locations and returns the first element.

```
| anArray |
anArray := Array new: 5.
anArray at: 1 put: 4.
anArray at: 2 put: 3/2.
anArray at: 3 put: 'ssss'.
anArray at: 1
>>> 4
```

There are several ways to create instances of the class Array. We can use

- new:, with:,
- #( ) construct - literal arrays and
- { . } dynamic compact syntax.

Creation with new:

The message new: anInteger creates an array of size anInteger. Array new: 5 creates an array of size 5.

❙ Note   The value of each element is initialized to nil.

Creation using with:

The with:* messages allow one to specify the value of the elements. The following code creates an array of three elements consisting of the number 4, the fraction 3/2 and the string 'lulu'.

```
Array with: 4 with: 3/2 with: 'lulu'
>>> {4. (3/2). 'lulu'}
```

Literal creation with #( )

The expression #( ) creates literal arrays with constants or *literal* elements that have to be known when the expression is compiled, and not when it is executed. The following code creates an array of size 2 where the first element is the (literal) number 1 and the second the (literal) string 'here'.

```
#(1 'here') size
>>> 2
```

Now, if you execute the expression #(1+2), you do not get an array with a single element 3 but instead you get the array #(1 #+ 2) i.e., with three elements: 1, the symbol #+ and the number 2.

```
#(1+2)
>>>   #(1 #+ 2)
```

This occurs because the construct #( ) does not execute the expressions it contains. The elements are only objects that are created when parsing the expression (called literal objects). The expression is scanned and the resulting elements are fed to a new array. Literal arrays contain numbers, nil, true, false, symbols, strings and other literal arrays. During the execution of #( ) expressions, there are no messages sent.

Dynamic creation with { . }

Finally, you can create a dynamic array using the construct { . }. The expression { a . b } is totally equivalent to Array with: a with: b. This means in particular that the expressions enclosed by { and } are executed (contrary to the case of #( )).

```
{ 1 + 2 }
>>> #(3)
```

```
{(1/2) asFloat} at: 1
>>> 0.5
```

```
{10 atRandom. 1/3} at: 2
>>> (1/3)
```

Element Access

Elements of all sequenceable collections can be accessed with messages `at: anIndex` and `at: anIndex put: anObject`.

```
| anArray |
anArray := #(1 2 3 4 5 6) copy.
anArray at: 3 >>> 3
anArray at: 3 put: 33.
anArray at: 3
>>> 33
```

Be careful: general principle is that literal arrays are not be modified! Literal arrays are kept in compiled method literal frames (a space where literals appearing in a method are stored), therefore unless you copy the array, the second time you execute the code your *literal* array may not have the value you expect. In the example, without copying the array, the second time around, the literal #(1 2 3 4 5 6) will actually be #(1 2 33 4 5 6)! Dynamic arrays do not have this problem because they are not stored in literal frames.

14.7 OrderedCollection

OrderedCollection is one of the collections that can grow, and to which elements can be added sequentially. It offers a variety of messages such as `add:`, `addFirst:`, `addLast:`, and `addAll:`.

```
| ordCol |
ordCol := OrderedCollection new.
ordCol add: 'Seaside'; add: 'SmalltalkHub'; addFirst: 'GitHub'.
ordCol
>>> an OrderedCollection('GitHub' 'Seaside' 'SmalltalkHub')
```

Removing Elements

The message `remove: anObject` removes the first occurrence of an object from the collection. If the collection does not include such an object, it raises an error.

```
ordCol add: 'GitHub'.
ordCol remove: 'GitHub'.
ordCol
>>> an OrderedCollection('Seaside' 'SmalltalkHub' 'GitHub')
```

There is a variant of `remove:` named `remove:ifAbsent:` that allows one to specify as second argument a block that is executed in case the element to be removed is not in the collection.

```
result := ordCol remove: 'zork' ifAbsent: [33].
result
>>> 33
```

Conversion

It is possible to get an OrderedCollection from an Array (or any other collection) by sending the message asOrderedCollection:

```
#(1 2 3) asOrderedCollection
>>> an OrderedCollection(1 2 3)
```

```
'hello' asOrderedCollection
>>> an OrderedCollection($h $e $l $l $o)
```

14.8 Interval

The class Interval represents ranges of numbers. For example, the interval of numbers from 1 to 100 is defined as follows:

```
Interval from: 1 to: 100
>>> (1 to: 100)
```

The result of printString reveals that the class Number provides us with a convenience method called to: to generate intervals:

```
(Interval from: 1 to: 100) = (1 to: 100)
>>> true
```

We can use Interval class>>from:to:by: or Number>>to:by: to specify the step between two numbers as follow:

```
(Interval from: 1 to: 100 by: 0.5) size
>>> 199
```

```
(1 to: 100 by: 0.5) at: 198
>>> 99.5
```

```
(1/2 to: 54/7 by: 1/3) last
>>> (15/2)
```

14.9 Dictionary

Dictionaries are important collections whose elements are accessed using keys. Among the most commonly used messages of dictionary you will find at: aKey, at: aKey put: aValue, at: aKey ifAbsent: aBlock, keys, and values.

```
| colors |
colors := Dictionary new.
colors at: #yellow put: Color yellow.
colors at: #blue put: Color blue.
colors at: #red put: Color red.
colors at: #yellow
>>> Color yellow
```

```
colors keys
>>> #(#red #blue #yellow)
```

```
colors values
>>> {Color red . Color blue . Color yellow}
```

Dictionaries compare keys by equality. Two keys are considered to be the same if they return true when compared using =. A common and difficult to spot bug is to use as key an object whose = method has been redefined but not its hash method. Both methods are used in the implementation of dictionary and when comparing objects.

In its implementation, a Dictionary can be seen as consisting of a set of (key value) associations created using the message ->. We can create a Dictionary from a collection of associations, or we may convert a dictionary to an array of associations.

```
| colors |
colors := Dictionary newFrom: { #blue->Color blue . #red->Color red .
    #yellow->Color yellow }.
colors removeKey: #blue.
colors associations
>>> {#yellow->Color yellow. #red->Color red}
```

14.10 **IdentityDictionary**

While a dictionary uses the result of the messages = and hash to determine if two keys are the same, the class IdentityDictionary uses the identity (message ==) of the key instead of its values, i.e., it considers two keys to be equal *only* if they are the same object.

Often Symbols are used as keys, in which case it is natural to use an IdentityDictionary, since a Symbol is guaranteed to be globally unique. If, on the other hand, your keys are Strings, it is better to use a plain Dictionary, or you may get into trouble:

```
a := 'foobar'.
b := a copy.
trouble := IdentityDictionary new.
trouble at: a put: 'a'; at: b put: 'b'.
```

```
trouble at: a
>>> 'a'
```
```
trouble at: b
>>> 'b'
```
```
trouble at: 'foobar'
>>> 'a'
```

Since a and b are different objects, they are treated as different objects. Interestingly, the literal 'foobar' is allocated just once, so is really the same object as a. You don't want your code to depend on behaviour like this! A plain Dictionary would give the same value for any key equal to 'foobar'.

Use only globally unique objects (like Symbols or SmallIntegers) as keys for an IdentityDictionary, and Strings (or other objects) as keys for a plain Dictionary.

IdentityDictionary example

The expression Smalltalk globals returns an instance of SystemDictionary, a subclass of IdentityDictionary, hence all its keys are ByteSymbols (ByteSymbol is a subclass of Symbol).

```
Smalltalk globals keys collect: [ :each | each class ] as: Set
>>> a Set(ByteSymbol)
```

Here we are using collect:as: to specify the result collection to be of class Set, that way we collect each kind of class used as a key only once.

14.11 Set

The class Set is a collection which behaves as a mathematical set, i.e., as a collection with no duplicate elements and without any order. In a Set, elements are added using the message add: and they cannot be accessed using the message at:. Objects put in a set should implement the methods hash and =.

```
s := Set new.
s add: 4/2; add: 4; add:2.
s size
>>> 2
```

You can also create sets using Set class>>newFrom: or the conversion message Collection>>asSet:

```
(Set newFrom: #( 1 2 3 1 4 )) = #(1 2 3 4 3 2 1) asSet
>>> true
```

asSet offers us a convenient way to eliminate duplicates from a collection:

```
{ Color black. Color white. (Color red + Color blue + Color green) }
    asSet size
>>> 2
```

> **Note** red + blue + green = white.

A Bag is much like a Set except that it does allow duplicates:

```
{ Color black. Color white. (Color red + Color blue + Color green) }
    asBag size
>>> 3
```

The set operations *union*, *intersection* and *membership test* are implemented by the Collection messages union:, intersection:, and includes:. The receiver is first converted to a Set, so these operations work for all kinds of collections!

```
(1 to: 6) union: (4 to: 10)
>>> a Set(1 2 3 4 5 6 7 8 9 10)
```

```
'hello' intersection: 'there'
>>> 'eh'
```

```
#Pharo includes: $a
>>> true
```

As we explain below, elements of a set are accessed using iterators (see Section 14.14).

14.12 SortedCollection

In contrast to an OrderedCollection, a SortedCollection maintains its elements in sort order. By default, a sorted collection uses the message <= to establish sort order, so it can sort instances of subclasses of the abstract class Magnitude, which defines the protocol of comparable objects (<, =, >, >=, between:and:...). (See Chapter : Basic Classes).

You can create a SortedCollection by creating a new instance and adding elements to it:

```
SortedCollection new add: 5; add: 2; add: 50; add: -10; yourself.
>>> a SortedCollection(-10 2 5 50)
```

More usually, though, one will send the conversion message asSortedCollection to an existing collection:

```
#(5 2 50 -10) asSortedCollection
>>> a SortedCollection(-10 2 5 50)
```

```
'hello' asSortedCollection
>>> a SortedCollection($e $h $l $l $o)
```

How do you get a String back from this result? asString unfortunately returns the printString representation, which is not what we want:

```
'hello' asSortedCollection asString
>>> 'a SortedCollection($e $h $l $l $o)'
```

The correct answer is to either use String class>>newFrom:, String class>>withAll: or Object>>as:.

```
'hello' asSortedCollection as: String
>>> 'ehllo'
```

```
String newFrom: 'hello' asSortedCollection
>>> 'ehllo'
```

```
String withAll: 'hello' asSortedCollection
>>> 'ehllo'
```

It is possible to have different kinds of elements in a SortedCollection as long as they are all comparable. For example, we can mix different kinds of numbers such as integers, floats and fractions:

```
{ 5 . 2/ -3 . 5.21 } asSortedCollection
>>> a SortedCollection((-2/3) 5 5.21)
```

Imagine that you want to sort objects that do not define the method <= or that you would like to have a different sorting criterion. You can do this by supplying a two argument block, called a sortblock, to the sorted collection. For example, the class Color is not a Magnitude and it does not implement the method <=, but we can specify a block stating that the colors should be sorted according to their luminance (a measure of brightness).

```
col := SortedCollection
        sortBlock: [ :c1 :c2 | c1 luminance <= c2 luminance ].
col addAll: { Color red . Color yellow . Color white . Color black }.
col
>>> a SortedCollection(Color black Color red Color yellow Color white)
```

14.13 Strings

In Pharo, a String is a collection of Characters. It is sequenceable, indexable, mutable and homogeneous, containing only Character instances. Like Arrays, Strings have a dedicated syntax, and are normally created by directly

14.13 Strings

specifying a String literal within single quotes, but the usual collection creation methods will work as well.

```
'Hello'
>>> 'Hello'
```

```
String with: $A
>>> 'A'
```

```
String with: $h with: $i with: $!
>>> 'hi!'
```

```
String newFrom: #($h $e $l $l $o)
>>> 'hello'
```

In actual fact, String is abstract. When we instantiate a String we actually get either an 8-bit ByteString or a 32-bit WideString. To keep things simple, we usually ignore the difference and just talk about instances of String.

While strings are delimited by single quotes, a string can contain a single quote: to define a string with a single quote we should type it twice. Note that the string will contain only one element and not two as shown below:

```
'l''idiot' at: 2
>>> $'
```

```
'l''idiot' at: 3
>>> $i
```

The message , concatenates two instances of String. Such messages can chained as follows:

```
s := 'no', ' ', 'worries'.
s
>>> 'no worries'
```

Since a string is a mutable collection we can also change it using the message at:put:. From a design point of view better avoid mutating strings since strings are often shared over method execution.

```
s at: 4 put: $h; at: 5 put: $u.
s
>>> 'no hurries'
```

Note that the comma method is defined by Collection, so it will work for any kind of collection!

```
(1 to: 3), '45'
>>> #(1 2 3 $4 $5)
```

211

We can also modify an existing string using `replaceAll:with:` or `replaceFrom:to:with:` as shown below. Note that the number of characters and the interval should have the same size.

```
s replaceAll: $n with: $N.
s
>>> 'No hurries'
```

```
s replaceFrom: 4 to: 5 with: 'wo'.
s
>>> 'No worries'
```

In contrast to the methods described above, the method `copyReplaceAll:` creates a new string. (Curiously, here the arguments are substrings rather than individual characters, and their sizes do not have to match.)

```
s copyReplaceAll: 'rries' with: 'mbats'
>>> 'No wombats'
```

A quick look at the implementation of these methods reveals that they are defined not only for `Strings`, but for any kind of `SequenceableCollection`, so the following also works:

```
(1 to: 6) copyReplaceAll: (3 to: 5) with: { 'three' . 'etc.' }
>>> #(1 2 'three' 'etc.' 6)
```

String matching

It is possible to ask whether a pattern matches a string by sending the `match:` message. The pattern can use `*` to match an arbitrary series of characters and `#` to match a single character. Note that `match:` is sent to the pattern and not the string to be matched.

```
'Linux *' match: 'Linux mag'
>>> true
```

```
'GNU#Linux #ag' match: 'GNU/Linux tag'
>>> true
```

More advanced pattern matching facilities are also available in the `Regex` package.

Substrings

For substring manipulation we can use messages like `first`, `first:`, `allButFirst:`, `copyFrom:to:` and others, defined in `SequenceableCollection`.

```
'alphabet' at: 6
>>> $b
```

14.13 Strings

```
'alphabet' first
>>> $a
```
```
'alphabet' first: 5
>>> 'alpha'
```
```
'alphabet' allButFirst: 3
>>> 'habet'
```
```
'alphabet' copyFrom: 5 to: 7
>>> 'abe'
```
```
'alphabet' copyFrom: 3 to: 3
>>> 'p' (not $p)
```

Be aware that result type can be different, depending on the method used. Most of the substring-related methods return String instances. But the messages that always return one element of the String collection, return a Character instance (for example, 'alphabet' at: 6 returns the character $b). For a complete list of substring-related messages, browse the SequenceableCollection class (especially the accessing protocol).

Some predicates on strings

The following examples illustrate the use of isEmpty, includes: and anySatisfy: which are also messages defined not only on Strings but more generally on collections.

```
'Hello' isEmpty
>>> false
```
```
'Hello' includes: $a
>>> false
```
```
'JOE' anySatisfy: [ :c | c isLowercase ]
>>> false
```
```
'Joe' anySatisfy: [ :c | c isLowercase ]
>>> true
```

String templating

There are three messages that are useful to manage string templating: format:, expandMacros, and expandMacrosWith:.

```
'{1} is {2}' format: {'Pharo' . 'cool'}
>>> 'Pharo is cool'
```

The messages of the expandMacros family offer variable substitution, using <n> for carriage return, <t> for tabulation, <1s>, <2s>, <3s> for arguments

(<1p>, <2p>, surrounds the string with single quotes), and <1?value1:value2> for conditional.

```
'look-<t>-here' expandMacros
>>> 'look-    -here'
```

```
'<1s> is <2s>' expandMacrosWith: 'Pharo' with: 'cool'
>>> 'Pharo is cool'
```

```
'<2s> is <1s>' expandMacrosWith: 'Pharo' with: 'cool'
>>> 'cool is Pharo'
```

```
'<1p> or <1s>' expandMacrosWith: 'Pharo' with: 'cool'
>>> '''Pharo'' or Pharo'
```

```
'<1?Quentin:Thibaut> plays' expandMacrosWith: true
>>> 'Quentin plays'
```

```
'<1?Quentin:Thibaut> plays' expandMacrosWith: false
>>> 'Thibaut plays'
```

Some other utility methods

The class `String` offers numerous other utilities including the messages `asLowercase`, `asUppercase` and `capitalized`.

```
'XYZ' asLowercase
>>> 'xyz'
```

```
'xyz' asUppercase
>>> 'XYZ'
```

```
'tintin' capitalized
>>> 'Tintin'
```

```
'Tintin' uncapitalized
>>> 'tintin'
```

```
'1.54' asNumber
>>> 1.54
```

```
'this sentence is without a doubt far too long' contractTo: 20
>>> 'this sent...too long'
```

asString vs. printString

Note that there is generally a difference between asking an object its string representation by sending the message `printString` and converting it to a string by sending the message `asString`. Here is an example of the difference.

```
#ASymbol printString
>>> '#ASymbol'
```

```
#ASymbol asString
>>> 'ASymbol'
```

A symbol is similar to a string but is guaranteed to be globally unique. For this reason symbols are preferred to strings as keys for dictionaries, in particular for instances of `IdentityDictionary`. See also Chapter : Basic Classes for more about `String` and `Symbol`.

14.14 Collection iterators

In Pharo loops and conditionals are simply messages sent to collections or other objects such as integers or blocks (see also Chapter : Understanding message syntax). In addition to low-level messages such as `to:do:` which evaluates a block with an argument ranging from an initial to a final number, the collection hierarchy offers various high-level iterators. Using such iterators will make your code more robust and compact.

Iterating (do:)

The method `do:` is the basic collection iterator. It applies its argument (a block taking a single argument) to each element of the receiver. The following example prints all the strings contained in the receiver to the transcript.

```
#('bob' 'joe' 'toto') do: [:each | Transcript show: each; cr].
```

Variants

There are a lot of variants of `do:`, such as `do:without:`, `doWithIndex:` and `reverseDo:`.

For the indexed collections (`Array`, `OrderedCollection`, `SortedCollection`) the message `doWithIndex:` also gives access to the current index. This message is related to `to:do:` which is defined in class `Number`.

```
#('bob' 'joe' 'toto')
    doWithIndex: [ :each :i | (each = 'joe') ifTrue: [ ^ i ] ]
>>> 2
```

For ordered collections, the message `reverseDo:` walks the collection in the reverse order.

The following code shows an interesting message: `do:separatedBy:` which executes the second block only in between two elements.

```
| res |
res := ''.
#('bob' 'joe' 'toto')
    do: [ :e | res := res, e ]
    separatedBy: [ res := res, '.' ].
res
>>> 'bob.joe.toto'
```

Note that this code is not especially efficient since it creates intermediate strings and it would be better to use a write stream to buffer the result (see Chapter : Streams):

```
String streamContents: [ :stream |
    #('bob' 'joe' 'toto') asStringOn: stream delimiter: '.' ]
>>> 'bob.joe.toto'
```

Dictionaries

When the message do: is sent to a dictionary, the elements taken into account are the values, not the associations. The proper messages to use are keysDo:, valuesDo:, and associationsDo:, which iterate respectively on keys, values or associations.

```
colors := Dictionary newFrom: { #yellow -> Color yellow. #blue ->
    Color blue. #red -> Color red }.
colors keysDo: [ :key | Transcript show: key; cr ].
colors valuesDo: [ :value | Transcript show: value; cr ].
colors associationsDo: [:value | Transcript show: value; cr].
```

14.15 Collecting results (collect:)

If you want to apply a function to the elements of a collection and get a new collection with the results, rather than using do:, you are probably better off using collect:, or one of the other iterator methods. Most of these can be found in the enumerating protocol of Collection and its subclasses.

Imagine that we want a collection containing the doubles of the elements in another collection. Using the method do: we must write the following:

```
| double |
double := OrderedCollection new.
#(1 2 3 4 5 6) do: [ :e | double add: 2 * e ].
double
>>> an OrderedCollection(2 4 6 8 10 12)
```

14.15 Collecting results (collect:)

The message `collect:` executes its argument block for each element and returns a new collection containing the results. Using `collect:` instead, the code is much simpler:

```
#(1 2 3 4 5 6) collect: [ :e | 2 * e ]
>>> #(2 4 6 8 10 12)
```

The advantages of `collect:` over `do:` are even more important in the following example, where we take a collection of integers and generate as a result a collection of absolute values of these integers:

```
aCol :=  #( 2 -3 4 -35 4 -11).
result := aCol species new: aCol size.
1 to: aCol size do: [ :each |
  result at: each put: (aCol at: each) abs ].
result
>>> #(2 3 4 35 4 11)
```

Contrast the above with the much simpler following expression:

```
#( 2 -3 4 -35 4 -11) collect: [ :each | each abs ]
>>> #(2 3 4 35 4 11)
```

A further advantage of the second solution is that it will also work for sets and bags. Generally you should avoid using `do:`, unless you want to send messages to each of the elements of a collection.

Note that sending the message `collect:` returns the same kind of collection as the receiver. For this reason the following code fails. (A `String` cannot hold integer values.)

```
'abc' collect: [ :ea | ea asciiValue ]
>>> "error!"
```

Instead we must first convert the string to an `Array` or an `OrderedCollection`:

```
'abc' asArray collect: [ :ea | ea asciiValue ]
>>> #(97 98 99)
```

Actually `collect:` is not guaranteed to return a collection of exactly the same class as the receiver, but only the same *species*. In the case of an `Interval`, the species is an `Array`!

```
(1 to: 5) collect: [ :ea | ea * 2 ]
>>> #(2 4 6 8 10)
```

14.16 Selecting and rejecting elements

The message `select:` returns the elements of the receiver that satisfy a particular condition:

```
(2 to: 20) select: [ :each | each isPrime ]
>>> #(2 3 5 7 11 13 17 19)
```

The message `reject:` does the opposite:

```
(2 to: 20) reject: [ :each | each isPrime ]
>>> #(4 6 8 9 10 12 14 15 16 18 20)
```

Identifying an element with detect:

The message `detect:` returns the first element of the receiver that matches block argument.

```
'through' detect: [ :each | each isVowel ]
>>> $o
```

The message `detect:ifNone:` is a variant of the method `detect:`. Its second block is evaluated when there is no element matching the block.

```
Smalltalk globals allClasses
    detect: [:each | '*cobol*' match: each asString]
    ifNone: [ nil ]
>>> nil
```

Accumulating results with inject:into:

Functional programming languages often provide a higher-order function called *fold* or *reduce* to accumulate a result by applying some binary operator iteratively over all elements of a collection. In Pharo this is done by Collection>>inject:into:.

The first argument is an initial value, and the second argument is a two-argument block which is applied to the result this far, and each element in turn.

A trivial application of `inject:into:` is to produce the sum of a collection of numbers. In Pharo we could write this expression to sum the first 100 integers:

```
(1 to: 100) inject: 0 into: [ :sum :each | sum + each ]
>>> 5050
```

Another example is the following one-argument block which computes factorials:

```
factorial := [ :n |
   (1 to: n)
     inject: 1
     into: [ :product :each | product * each ] ].
factorial value: 10
>>> 3628800
```

14.17 Other high-order messages

There are many other iterator messages. You can check the Collection class. Here is a selection.

count: The message count: returns the number of elements satisfying a condition. The condition is represented as a boolean block.

```
Smalltalk globals allClasses
    count: [ :each | 'Collection*' match: each asString ]
>>> 10
```

includes: The message includes: checks whether the argument is contained in the collection.

```
| colors |
colors := {Color white . Color yellow .  Color blue . Color orange}.
colors includes: Color blue.
>>> true
```

anySatisfy: The message anySatisfy: answers true if at least one element of the collection satisfies the condition represented by the argument.

```
colors anySatisfy: [ :c | c red > 0.5 ]
>>> true
```

14.18 A common mistake: using add: result

The following error is one of the most frequent Smalltalk mistakes.

```
| collection |
collection := OrderedCollection new add: 1; add: 2.
collection
>>> 2
```

Here the variable collection does not hold the newly created collection but rather the last number added. This is because the method add: returns the element added and not the receiver.

The following code yields the expected result:

```
| collection |
collection := OrderedCollection new.
collection add: 1; add: 2.
collection
>>> an OrderedCollection(1 2)
```

You can also use the message `yourself` to return the receiver of a cascade of messages:

```
| collection |
collection := OrderedCollection new add: 1; add: 2; yourself
>>> an OrderedCollection(1 2)
```

14.19 A common mistake: Removing an element while iterating

Another mistake you may make is to remove an element from a collection you are currently iterating over. The bugs created but such mistakes can be really difficult to spot because the iterating order may be change depending on the storage strategy of the collection.

```
| range |
range := (2 to: 20) asOrderedCollection.
range do: [ :aNumber | aNumber isPrime
                        ifFalse: [ range remove: aNumber ] ].
range
>>> "error!"
```

The solution is to copy the collection before going over it.

```
| range |
range := (2 to: 20) asOrderedCollection.
range copy do: [ :aNumber | aNumber isPrime
                        ifFalse: [ range remove: aNumber ] ].
range
>>> an OrderedCollection(2 3 5 7 11 13 17 19)
```

14.20 A common mitaske: Redefining = but not hash

A difficult error to spot is when you redefine = but not hash. The symptoms are that you will lose elements that you put in sets or other strange behaviour. One solution proposed by Kent Beck is to use bitXor: to redefine hash. Suppose that we want two books to be considered equal if their titles and authors are the same. Then we would redefine not only = but also hash as follows:

Listing 14-3 Redefining = and hash.
```
Book >> = aBook
    self class = aBook class ifFalse: [ ^ false ].
    ^ title = aBook title and: [ authors = aBook authors ]

Book >> hash
    ^ title hash bitXor: authors hash
```

Another nasty problem arises if you use a mutable object, i.e., an object that can change its hash value over time, as an element of a Set or as a key to a Dictionary. Don't do this unless you love debugging!

14.21 Chapter summary

The collection hierarchy provides a common vocabulary for uniformly manipulating a variety of different kinds of collections.

- A key distinction is between SequenceableCollections, which maintain their elements in a given order, Dictionary and its subclasses, which maintain key-to-value associations, and Sets and Bags, which are unordered.

- You can convert most collections to another kind of collection by sending them the messages asArray, asOrderedCollection, etc...

- To sort a collection, send it the message asSortedCollection.

- #(...) creates arrays containing only literal objects (i.e., objects created without sending messages). { ... } creates dynamic arrays using a compact form.

- A Dictionary compares keys by equality. It is most useful when keys are instances of String. An IdentityDictionary instead uses object identity to compare keys. It is more suitable when Symbols are used as keys, or when mapping object references to values.

- Strings also understand the usual collection messages. In addition, a String supports a simple form of pattern-matching. For more advanced application, look instead at the RegEx package.

- The basic iteration message is do:. It is useful for imperative code, such as modifying each element of a collection, or sending each element a message.

- Instead of using do:, it is more common to use collect:, select:, reject:, includes:, inject:into: and other higher-level messages to process collections in a uniform way.

- Never remove an element from a collection you are iterating over. If you must modify it, iterate over a copy instead.
- If you override =, remember to override `hash` as well!

CHAPTER **15**

Streams

Streams are used to iterate over sequences of elements such as sequenced collections, files, and network streams. Streams may be either readable, or writeable, or both. Reading or writing is always relative to the current position in the stream. Streams can easily be converted to collections, and vice versa.

15.1 Two sequences of elements

A good metaphor to understand a stream is the following. A stream can be represented as two sequences of elements: a past element sequence and a future element sequence. The stream is positioned between the two sequences. Understanding this model is important, since all stream operations in Pharo rely on it. For this reason, most of the Stream classes are subclasses of PositionableStream. Figure 15-1 presents a stream which contains five characters. This stream is in its original position, i.e., there is no element in the past. You can go back to this position using the message reset defined in PositionableStream.

Reading an element conceptually means removing the first element of the fu-

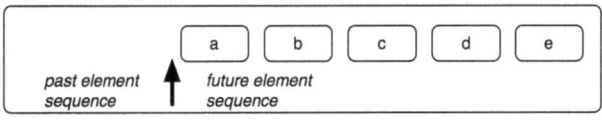

Figure 15-1 A stream positioned at its beginning.

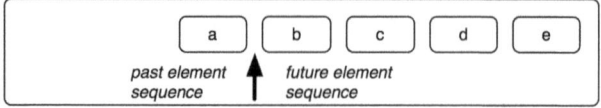

Figure 15-2 The same stream after the execution of the method next: the character a is *in the past* whereas b, c, d and e are *in the future*.

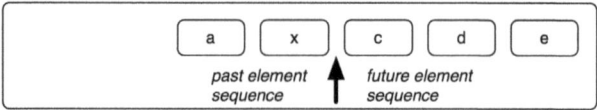

Figure 15-3 The same stream after having written an x.

ture element sequence and putting it after the last element in the past element sequence. After having read one element using the message next, the state of your stream is that shown in Figure 15-2.

Writing an element means replacing the first element of the future sequence by the new one and moving it to the past. Figure 15-3 shows the state of the same stream after having written an x using the message nextPut: anElement defined in Stream.

15.2 Streams vs. collections

The collection protocol supports the storage, removal and enumeration of the elements of a collection, but does not allow these operations to be intermingled. For example, if the elements of an OrderedCollection are processed by a do: method, it is not possible to add or remove elements from inside the do: block. Nor does the collection protocol offer ways to iterate over two collections at the same time, choosing which collection goes forward and which does not. Procedures like these require that a traversal index or position reference is maintained outside of the collection itself: this is exactly the role of ReadStream, WriteStream and ReadWriteStream.

These three classes are defined to *stream over* some collection. For example, the following snippet creates a stream on an interval, then it reads two elements.

```
| r |
r := ReadStream on: (1 to: 1000).
r next.
>>> 1
```

15.3 Reading collections

```
r next.
>>> 2
```

```
r atEnd.
>>> false
```

WriteStreams can write data to the collection:

```
| w |
w := WriteStream on: (String new: 5).
w nextPut: $a.
w nextPut: $b.
w contents.
>>>   'ab'
```

It is also possible to create ReadWriteStreams that support both the reading and writing protocols.

The following sections present the protocols in more depth.

Streams are really useful when dealing with collections of elements, and can be used for reading and writing those elements. We will now explore the stream features for collections.

15.3 Reading collections

Using a stream to read a collection essentially provides you a pointer into the collection. That pointer will move forward on reading, and you can place it wherever you want. The class ReadStream should be used to read elements from collections.

Messages next and next: defined in ReadStream are used to retrieve one or more elements from the collection.

```
| stream |
stream := ReadStream on: #(1 (a b c) false).
stream next.
>>>    1
```

```
stream next.
>>>    #(#a #b #c)
```

```
stream next.
>>>    false
```

```
| stream |
stream := ReadStream on: 'abcdef'.
stream next: 0.
>>>    ''
```

225

```
stream next: 1.
>>>     'a'
```
```
stream next: 3.
>>>     'bcd'
```
```
stream next: 2.
>>>     'ef'
```

15.4 Peek

The message peek defined in PositionableStream is used when you want to know what is the next element in the stream without going forward.

```
| stream negative number |
stream := ReadStream on: '-143'.
"look at the first element without consuming it."
negative := (stream peek = $-).
negative.
>>> true
```
```
"ignores the minus character"
negative ifTrue: [ stream next ].
number := stream upToEnd.
number.
>>> '143'
```

This code sets the boolean variable negative according to the sign of the number in the stream, and number to its absolute value. The message upToEnd defined in ReadStream returns everything from the current position to the end of the stream and sets the stream to its end. This code can be simplified using the message peekFor: defined in PositionableStream, which moves forward if the following element equals the parameter and doesn't move otherwise.

```
| stream |
stream := '-143' readStream.
(stream peekFor: $-).
>>> true
```
```
stream upToEnd
>>> '143'
```

peekFor: also returns a boolean indicating if the parameter equals the element.

You might have noticed a new way of constructing a stream in the above example: one can simply send the message readStream to a sequenceable collection (such as a String) to get a reading stream on that particular collection.

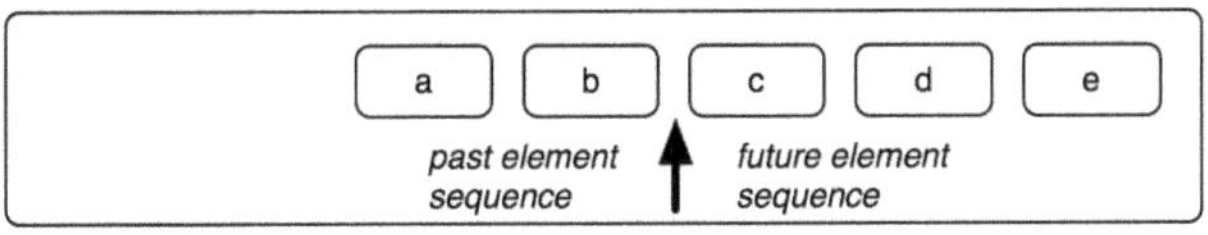

15.5 Positioning to an index

Figure 15-4 A stream at position 2.

15.5 Positioning to an index

There are messages to position the stream pointer. If you have the index, you can go directly to it using `position:` defined in `PositionableStream`. You can request the current position using `position`. Please remember that a stream is not positioned on an element, but between two elements. The index corresponding to the beginning of the stream is 0.

You can obtain the state of the stream depicted in 15-4 with the following code:

```
| stream |
stream := 'abcde' readStream.
stream position: 2.
stream peek
>>> $c
```

To position the stream at the beginning or the end, you can use the message `reset` or `setToEnd`.

15.6 Skipping elements

The messages `skip:` and `skipTo:` are used to go forward to a location relative to the current position: `skip:` accepts a number as argument and skips that number of elements whereas `skipTo:` skips all elements in the stream until it finds an element equal to its parameter. Note that it positions the stream after the matched element.

```
| stream |
stream := 'abcdef' readStream.
stream next
>>> $a
```

The stream is now positioned just after the $a.

```
stream skip: 3.
stream position
>>>   4
```

The stream is now after the $d.

```
stream skip: -2.
stream position
>>> 2
```

The stream is now after the $b.

```
stream reset.
stream position
>>> 0
```

```
stream skipTo: $e.
stream next.
>>> $f
```

Skipping up to an element positions the stream just after this element. Here the stream is just after the $e.

```
stream contents.
>>> 'abcdef'
```

The message contents always returns a copy of the entire stream.

15.7 Predicates

Some messages allow you to test the state of the current stream: atEnd returns true if and only if no more elements can be read, whereas isEmpty returns true if and only if there are no elements at all in the collection.

Here is a possible implementation of an algorithm using atEnd that takes two sorted collections as parameters and merges those collections into another sorted collection:

```
| stream1 stream2 result |
stream1 := #(1 4 9 11 12 13) readStream.
stream2 := #(1 2 3 4 5 10 13 14 15) readStream.

"The variable result will contain the sorted collection."
result := OrderedCollection new.
[ stream1 atEnd not & stream2 atEnd not ]
  whileTrue: [
    stream1 peek < stream2 peek
        "Remove the smallest element from either stream and add it to
    the result."
        ifTrue: [ result add: stream1 next ]
        ifFalse: [ result add: stream2 next ] ].

"One of the two streams might not be at its end. Copy whatever
    remains."
result
```

```
    addAll: stream1 upToEnd;
    addAll: stream2 upToEnd.
result.
>>>    an OrderedCollection(1 1 2 3 4 4 5 9 10 11 12 13 13 14 15)
```

15.8 Writing to collections

We have already seen how to read a collection by iterating over its elements using a ReadStream. We'll now learn how to create collections using WriteStreams.

WriteStreams are useful for appending a lot of data to a collection at various locations. They are often used to construct strings that are based on static and dynamic parts, as in this example:

```
| stream |
stream := String new writeStream.
stream
  nextPutAll: 'This image contains: ';
  print: Smalltalk globals allClasses size;
  nextPutAll: ' classes.';
  cr;
  nextPutAll: 'This is really a lot.'.

stream contents.
>>> 'This image contains: 9003 classes.
This is really a lot.'
```

This technique is used in the different implementations of the method printOn:, for example. There is a simpler and more efficient way of creating strings if you are only interested in the content of the stream:

```
| string |
string := String streamContents:
    [ :stream |
      stream
              print: #(1 2 3);
              space;
              nextPutAll: 'size';
              space;
              nextPut: $=;
              space;
              print: 3.  ].
string.
>>>   '#(1 2 3) size = 3'
```

The message streamContents: defined SequenceableCollection creates a collection and a stream on that collection for you. It then executes the block you gave passing the stream as a parameter. When the block ends, `stream-Contents:` returns the contents of the collection.

The following `WriteStream` methods are especially useful in this context:

`nextPut:` adds the parameter to the stream;

`nextPutAll:` adds each element of the collection, passed as a parameter, to the stream;

`print:` adds the textual representation of the parameter to the stream.

There are also convenient messages for printing useful characters to a stream, such as `space`, `tab` and `cr` (carriage return). Another useful method is `ensureASpace` which ensures that the last character in the stream is a space; if the last character isn't a space it adds one.

15.9 About string concatenation

Using `nextPut:` and `nextPutAll:` on a `WriteStream` is often the best way to concatenate characters. Using the comma concatenation operator (,) is far less efficient as shown by the two following performing the same task.

```
[| temp |
  temp := String new.
  (1 to: 100000)
    do: [:i | temp := temp, i asString, ' ' ] ] timeToRun
>>> 0:00:01:54.758
```

```
[| temp |
  temp := WriteStream on: String new.
  (1 to: 100000)
    do: [:i | temp nextPutAll: i asString; space ].
  temp contents ] timeToRun
>>> 0:00:00:00.024
```

Using a stream can be much more efficient than using a comma because the last one creates a new string containing the concatenation of the receiver and the argument, so it must copy both of them. When you repeatedly concatenate onto the same receiver, it gets longer and longer each time, so that the number of characters that must be copied goes up exponentially. Such concatenation of strings also creates a lot of garbage, which must be collected. Using a stream instead of string concatenation is a well-known optimization.

In fact, you can use the message `streamContents:` defined in `SequenceableCollection class` (mentioned earlier) to help you do this:

```
String streamContents: [ :tempStream |
  (1 to: 100000)
       do: [:i | tempStream nextPutAll: i asString; space ] ]
```

15.10 About printString

Let us take a moment to step back about stream usage in `printOn:` methods. Basically the `Object>>#printString` method creates a stream and passes this stream as argument of the `printOn:` method as shown below:

```
Object >> printString
  "Answer a String whose characters are a description of the receiver.
  If you want to print without a character limit, use fullPrintString."

  ^ self printStringLimitedTo: 50000
```
```
Object >> printStringLimitedTo: limit
  "Answer a String whose characters are a description of the receiver.
  If you want to print without a character limit, use fullPrintString."

  ^self printStringLimitedTo: limit using: [:s | self printOn: s]
```
```
Object >> printStringLimitedTo: limit using: printBlock
  "Answer a String whose characters are a description of the receiver
  produced by given printBlock. It ensures the result will be not
    bigger than given limit"

  | limitedString |
  limitedString := String streamContents: printBlock limitedTo: limit.
  limitedString size < limit ifTrue: [^ limitedString].
  ^ limitedString , '...etc...'
```

What you should see is that the method `printStringLimitedTo:using:` is creating a stream and passing it around.

When you redefine the method `printOn:` in your class, if you send the message `printString` on the instance variables of your object, you are in fact creating yet another stream and copying its contents in the first one. Here is an example:

```
MessageTally >> displayStringOn: aStream
  self displayIdentifierOn: aStream.
  aStream
    nextPutAll: ' (';
    nextPutAll: self tally printString;
    nextPutAll: ')'
```

Here the expression `self tally printString` invoked the same mechanism and create an extra stream instead of using the previous one. This is clearly counter productive. It is much better to send the message `print:` to the stream or `printOn:` to the instance variable it as follows:

```
MessageTally >> displayStringOn: aStream
  self displayIdentifierOn: aStream.
  aStream
    nextPutAll: ' (';
    print: self tally;
    nextPutAll: ')'
```

In this variant, the first created stream is used, there is no creation of an extra stream.

To understand what the method `print:`, here its definition:

```
Stream >> print: anObject
  "Have anObject print itself on the receiver."

  anObject printOn: self
```

Another example

This extra creation of stream is not limited to `printString` logic. Here is an example taken from Pharo that exhibits exactly the same problem.

```
printProtocol: protocol sourceCode: sourceCode

  ^ String streamContents: [ :stream |
    stream
      nextPutAll: '"protocol: ';
      nextPutAll: protocol printString;
      nextPut: $"; cr; cr;
      nextPutAll: sourceCode ]
```

What you should see is that a stream is created and then another stream is created and discarded with the expression `protocol printString`. A better implementation is the following one:

```
printProtocol: protocol sourceCode: sourceCode

  ^ String streamContents: [ :stream |
    stream
      nextPutAll: '"protocol: ';
      print: protocol;
      nextPut: $"; cr; cr;
      nextPutAll: sourceCode ]
```

15.11 Reading and writing at the same time

Figure 15-5 A new history is empty. Nothing is displayed in the web browser.

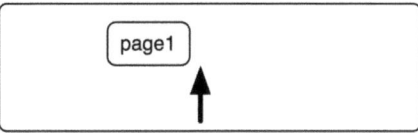

Figure 15-6 The user opens to page 1.

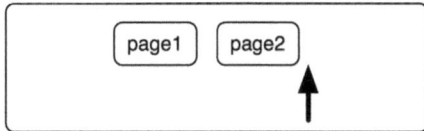

Figure 15-7 The user clicks on a link to page 2.

15.11 Reading and writing at the same time

It's possible to use a stream to access a collection for reading and writing at the same time. Imagine you want to create a `History` class which will manage backward and forward buttons in a web browser. A history reacts as in Figures 15-5 to 15-11.

This behaviour can be implemented using a `ReadWriteStream`.

```
Object subclass: #History
  instanceVariableNames: 'stream'
  classVariableNames: ''
  package: 'PBE-Streams'
```

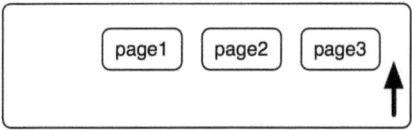

Figure 15-8 The user clicks on a link to page 3.

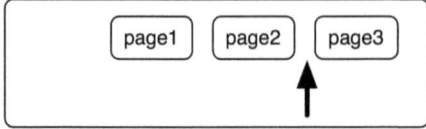

Figure 15-9 The user clicks on the Back button. They are now viewing page 2 again.

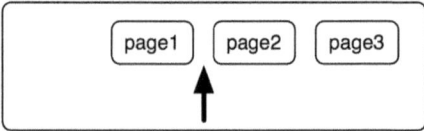

Figure 15-10 The user clicks again the back button. Page 1 is now displayed.

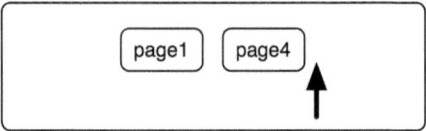

Figure 15-11 From page 1, the user clicks on a link to page 4. The history forgets pages 2 and 3.

```
History >> initialize
    super initialize.
    stream := ReadWriteStream on: Array new
```

Nothing really difficult here, we define a new class which contains a stream. The stream is created during the `initialize` method.

We need methods to go backward and forward:

```
History >> goBackward
  self canGoBackward
    ifFalse: [ self error: 'Already on the first element' ].
  stream skip: -2.
  ^ stream next.

History >> goForward
  self canGoForward
    ifFalse: [ self error: 'Already on the last element' ].
  ^ stream next
```

15.11 Reading and writing at the same time

Up to this point, the code is pretty straightforward. Next, we have to deal with the goTo: method which should be activated when the user clicks on a link. A possible implementation is:

```
History >> goTo: aPage
    stream nextPut: aPage
```

This version is incomplete however. This is because when the user clicks on the link, there should be no more future pages to go to, *i.e.*, the forward button must be deactivated. To do this, the simplest solution is to write nil just after, to indicate that history is at the end:

```
History >> goTo: anObject
   stream nextPut: anObject.
   stream nextPut: nil.
   stream back
```

Now, only methods canGoBackward and canGoForward remain to be implemented.

A stream is always positioned between two elements. To go backward, there must be two pages before the current position: one page is the current page, and the other one is the page we want to go to.

```
History >> canGoBackward
    ^ stream position > 1

History >> canGoForward
    ^ stream atEnd not and: [stream peek notNil ]
```

Let us add a method to peek at the contents of the stream:

```
History >> contents
    ^ stream contents
```

And the history works as advertised:

```
History new
   goTo: #page1;
   goTo: #page2;
   goTo: #page3;
   goBackward;
   goBackward;
   goTo: #page4;
   contents
>>> #(#page1 #page4 nil nil)
```

15.12 Chapter summary

Compared to collections, streams offer a better way to incrementally read and write a sequence of elements. There are easy ways to convert back and forth between streams and collections.

- Streams may be either readable, writeable or both readable and writeable.
- To convert a collection to a stream, define a stream *on* a collection, *e.g.*, `ReadStream on: (1 to: 1000)`, or send the messages `readStream`, etc. to the collection.
- To convert a stream to a collection, send the message `contents`.
- To concatenate large collections, instead of using the comma operator, it is more efficient to create a stream, append the collections to the stream with `nextPutAll:`, and extract the result by sending `contents`.

CHAPTER **16**

Morphic

Morphic is the name given to Pharo's graphical interface. Morphic supports two main aspects: on one hand Morphic defines all the low-level graphical entities and related infrastructure (events, drawing,...) and on the other hand Morphic defines all the widgets available in Pharo. Morphic is written in Pharo, so it is fully portable between operating systems. As a consequence, Pharo looks exactly the same on Unix, MacOS and Windows. What distinguishes Morphic from most other user interface toolkits is that it does not have separate modes for *composing* and *running* the interface: all the graphical elements can be assembled and disassembled by the user, at any time. We thank Hilaire Fernandes for permission to base this chapter on his original article in French.

16.1 The history of Morphic

Morphic was developed by John Maloney and Randy Smith for the Self programming language, starting around 1993. Maloney later wrote a new version of Morphic for Squeak, but the basic ideas behind the Self version are still alive and well in Pharo Morphic: *directness* and *liveness*. Directness means that the shapes on the screen are objects that can be examined or changed directly, that is, by clicking on them using a mouse. Liveness means that the user interface is always able to respond to user actions: information on the screen is continuously updated as the world that it describes changes. A simple example of this is that you can detach a menu item and keep it as a button.

Bring up the World Menu and Option-Command-Shift click once on it to bring up its morphic halo, then repeat the operation again on a menu item you want to detach, to bring up that item's halo (see Figure 16-1).

Morphic

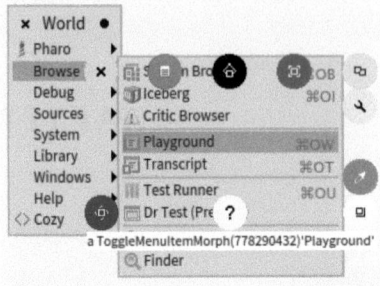

Figure 16-1 Detaching a morph, here the Playground menu item, to make it an independent button.

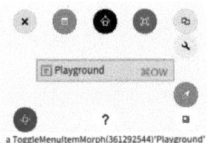

Figure 16-2 Dropping the menu item on the desktop, here the Playground menu item is now an independent button.

Now duplicate that item elsewhere on the screen by grabbing the green handle as shown in Figure 16-1.

Once dropped the menu item stays detached from the menu and you can interact with it as if it would be in the menu (see Figure 16-2).

This example illustrates what we mean by *directness* and *liveness*. This gives a lot of power when developing alternate user interface and prototyping alternate interactions.

Morphic is a bit showing its age, and the Pharo community is working since several years on a possible replacement. Replacing Morphic means to have both a new low-level infrastructure and a new widget sets. The project is called Bloc and got several iterations. Bloc is about the infrastructure and Brick is a set of widgets built on top. But let us have fun with Morphic.

16.2 Morphs

All of the objects that you see on the screen when you run Pharo are *Morphs*, that is, they are instances of subclasses of class Morph. The class Morph itself is

16.2 Morphs

Listing 16-3 Creation of a String Morph

```
'Morph' asMorph openInWorld
```

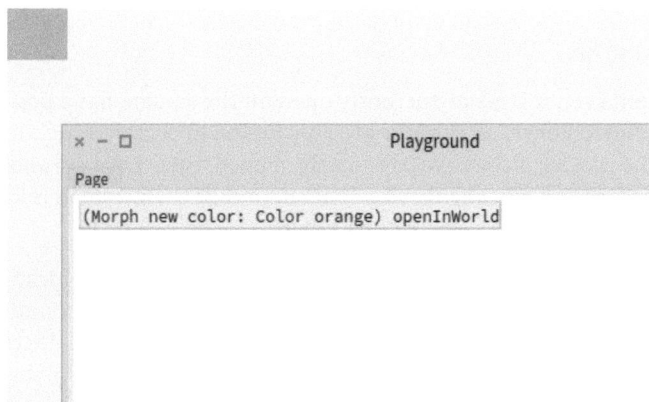

Figure 16-4 (Morph new color: Color orange) openInWorld.

a large class with many methods; this makes it possible for subclasses to implement interesting behaviour with little code.

To create a morph to represent a string object, execute the following code in a Playground.

This creates a Morph to represent the string 'Morph', and then opens it (that is, displays it) in the *world*, which is the name that Pharo gives to the screen. You should obtain a graphical element (a Morph), which you can manipulate by meta-clicking.

Of course, it is possible to define morphs that are more interesting graphical representations than the one that you have just seen. The method asMorph has a default implementation in class Object class that just creates a String-Morph. So, for example, Color tan asMorph returns a StringMorph labeled with the result of Color tan printString. Let's change this so that we get a coloured rectangle instead.

Now execute (Morph new colors: Color orange) openInWorld in a Playground. Instead of the string-like morph, you get an orange rectangle (see Figure 16-4)! You get the same executing (Morph new color: Color orange) openInWorld

16.3 Manipulating morphs

Morphs are objects, so we can manipulate them like any other object in Pharo: by sending messages, we can change their properties, create new subclasses of Morph, and so on.

Every morph, even if it is not currently open on the screen, has a position and a size. For convenience, all morphs are considered to occupy a rectangular region of the screen; if they are irregularly shaped, their position and size are those of the smallest rectangular *box* that surrounds them, which is known as the morph's bounding box, or just its *bounds*.

- The position method returns a Point that describes the location of the morph's upper left corner (or the upper left corner of its bounding box). The origin of the coordinate system is the screen's upper left corner, with y coordinates increasing *down* the screen and x coordinates increasing to the right.
- The extent method also returns a point, but this point specifies the width and height of the morph rather than a location.

Type the following code into a playground and Do it:

```
joe := Morph new color: Color blue.
joe openInWorld.
bill := Morph new color: Color red.
bill openInWorld.
```

Then type joe position and then Print it. To move joe, execute joe position: (joe position + (10@3)) repeatedly (see Figure 16-5).

It is possible to do a similar thing with size. joe extent answers joe's size; to have joe grow, execute joe extent: (joe extent * 1.1). To change the color of a morph, send it the color: message with the desired Color object as argument, for instance, joe color: Color orange. To add transparency, try joe color: (Color orange alpha: 0.5).

To make bill follow joe, you can repeatedly execute this code:

```
bill position: (joe position + (100@0))
```

If you move joe using the mouse and then execute this code, bill will move so that it is 100 pixels to the right of joe. You can see the result on Figure 16-6. Nothing suprising.

Note that you can delete the morphs you created by

- sending them the message delete
- selecting the cross in halos that you can bring using Meta-Option click.

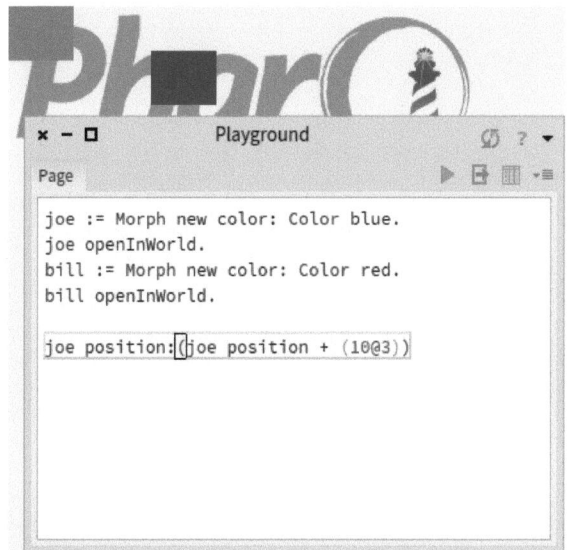

Figure 16-5 Bill and Joe after 10 moves.

16.4 Composing morphs

One way of creating new graphical representations is by placing one morph inside another. This is called *composition*; morphs can be composed to any depth. You can place a morph inside another by sending the message addMorph: to the container morph.

Try adding a morph to another one as follows:

```
balloon := BalloonMorph new color: Color yellow.
joe addMorph: balloon.
balloon position: joe position.
```

The last line positions the balloon at the same coordinates as joe. Notice that the coordinates of the contained morph are still relative to the screen, not to the containing morph. This absolute way of positioning morph is not really good and it makes programming morphs feels a bit odd. But there are many methods available to position a morph; browse the geometry protocol of class Morph to see for yourself. For example, to center the balloon inside joe, execute balloon center: joe center.

If you now try to grab the balloon with the mouse, you will find that you actually grab joe, and the two morphs move together: the balloon is *embedded* inside joe. It is possible to embed more morphs inside joe. In addition to doing this programmatically, you can also embed morphs by direct manipulation.

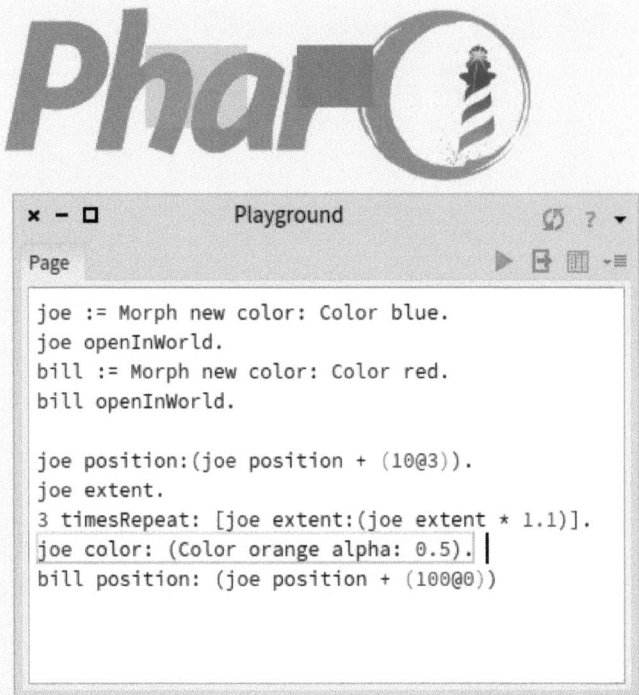

Figure 16-6 Bill follows Joe.

Figure 16-7 The balloon is contained inside joe, the translucent orange morph.

16.5 Creating and drawing your own morphs

While it is possible to make many interesting and useful graphical representations by composing morphs, sometimes you will need to create something completely different.

To do this you define a subclass of Morph and override the drawOn: method to change its appearance.

The morphic framework sends the message drawOn: to a morph when it needs to redisplay the morph on the screen. The parameter to drawOn: is a kind of Canvas; the expected behaviour is that the morph will draw itself on that

16.5 Creating and drawing your own morphs

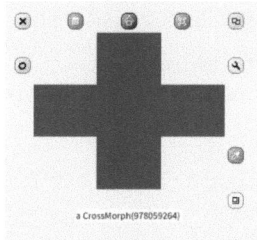

Figure 16-8 A `CrossMorph` with its halo; you can resize it as you wish.

canvas, inside its bounds. Let's use this knowledge to create a cross-shaped morph.

Using the browser, define a new class `CrossMorph` inheriting from `Morph`:

```
Morph subclass: #CrossMorph
    instanceVariableNames: ''
    classVariableNames: ''
    package: 'PBE-Morphic'
```

We can define the `drawOn:` method like this:

```
CrossMorph >> drawOn: aCanvas
    | crossHeight crossWidth horizontalBar verticalBar |
    crossHeight := self height / 3.
    crossWidth := self width / 3.
    horizontalBar := self bounds insetBy: 0 @ crossHeight.
    verticalBar := self bounds insetBy: crossWidth @ 0.
    aCanvas fillRectangle: horizontalBar color: self color.
    aCanvas fillRectangle: verticalBar color: self color
```

Sending the `bounds` message to a morph answers its bounding box, which is an instance of `Rectangle`. Rectangles understand many messages that create other rectangles of related geometry. Here, we use the `insetBy:` message with a point as its argument to create first a rectangle with reduced height, and then another rectangle with reduced width.

To test your new morph, execute `CrossMorph new openInWorld`.

The result should look something like Figure 16-8. However, you will notice that the sensitive zone — where you can click to grab the morph — is still the whole bounding box. Let's fix this.

When the Morphic framework needs to find out which Morphs lie under the cursor, it sends the message `containsPoint:` to all the morphs whose bounding boxes lie under the mouse pointer. So, to limit the sensitive zone of the morph to the cross shape, we need to override the `containsPoint:` method.

243

Define the following method in class `CrossMorph`:

```
CrossMorph >> containsPoint: aPoint
    | crossHeight crossWidth horizontalBar verticalBar |
    crossHeight := self height / 3.
    crossWidth := self width / 3.
    horizontalBar := self bounds insetBy: 0 @ crossHeight.
    verticalBar := self bounds insetBy: crossWidth @ 0.
    ^ (horizontalBar containsPoint: aPoint) or: [ verticalBar
        containsPoint: aPoint ]
```

This method uses the same logic as `drawOn:`, so we can be confident that the points for which `containsPoint:` answers `true` are the same ones that will be colored in by `drawOn:`. Notice how we leverage the `containsPoint:` method in class `Rectangle` to do the hard work.

There are two problems with the code in the two methods above.

The most obvious is that we have duplicated code. This is a cardinal error: if we find that we need to change the way that `horizontalBar` or `verticalBar` are calculated, we are quite likely to forget to change one of the two occurrences. The solution is to factor out these calculations into two new methods, which we put in the `private` protocol:

```
CrossMorph >> horizontalBar
    | crossHeight |
    crossHeight := self height / 3.
    ^ self bounds insetBy: 0 @ crossHeight
```

```
CrossMorph >> verticalBar
    | crossWidth |
    crossWidth := self width / 3.
    ^ self bounds insetBy: crossWidth @ 0
```

We can then define both `drawOn:` and `containsPoint:` using these methods:

```
CrossMorph >> drawOn: aCanvas
    aCanvas fillRectangle: self horizontalBar color: self color.
    aCanvas fillRectangle: self verticalBar color: self color
```

```
CrossMorph >> containsPoint: aPoint
    ^ (self horizontalBar containsPoint: aPoint) or: [ self verticalBar
        containsPoint: aPoint ]
```

This code is much simpler to understand, largely because we have given meaningful names to the private methods. In fact, it is so simple that you may have noticed the second problem: the area in the center of the cross, which is under both the horizontal and the vertical bars, is drawn twice. This doesn't matter when we fill the cross with an opaque colour, but the bug becomes apparent immediately if we draw a semi-transparent cross, as shown in Figure 16-9.

16.5 Creating and drawing your own morphs

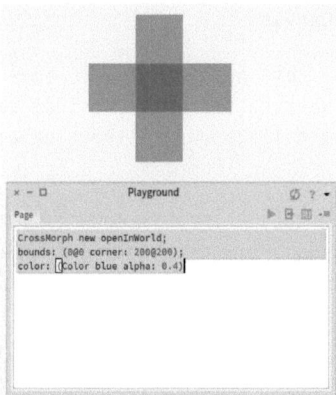

Figure 16-9 The center of the cross is filled twice with the color.

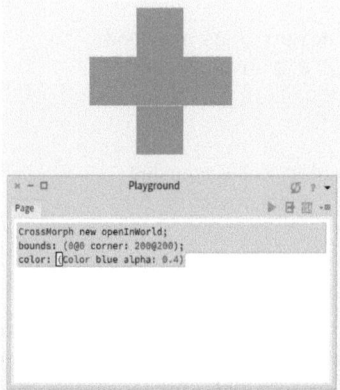

Figure 16-10 The cross-shaped morph, showing a row of unfilled pixels.

Execute the following code in a playground:

```
CrossMorph new openInWorld;
    bounds: (0@0 corner: 200@200);
    color: (Color blue alpha: 0.4)
```

The fix is to divide the vertical bar into three pieces, and to fill only the top and bottom. Once again we find a method in class Rectangle that does the hard work for us: r1 areasOutside: r2 answers an array of rectangles comprising the parts of r1 outside r2. Here is the revised code:

245

```
CrossMorph >> drawOn: aCanvas
  | topAndBottom |
  aCanvas fillRectangle: self horizontalBar color: self color.
  topAndBottom := self verticalBar areasOutside: self horizontalBar.
  topAndBottom do: [ :each | aCanvas fillRectangle: each color: self
    color ]
```

This code seems to work, but if you try it on some crosses and resize them, you may notice that at some sizes, a one-pixel wide line separates the bottom of the cross from the remainder, as shown in Figure 16-10. This is due to rounding: when the size of the rectangle to be filled is not an integer, `fillRectangle: color:` seems to round inconsistently, leaving one row of pixels unfilled.

We can work around this by rounding explicitly when we calculate the sizes of the bars as shown hereafter:

```
CrossMorph >> horizontalBar
  | crossHeight |
  crossHeight := (self height / 3) rounded.
  ^ self bounds insetBy: 0 @ crossHeight
```

```
CrossMorph >> verticalBar
  | crossWidth |
  crossWidth := (self width / 3) rounded.
  ^ self bounds insetBy: crossWidth @ 0
```

16.6 Mouse events for interaction

To build live user interfaces using morphs, we need to be able to interact with them using the mouse and keyboard. Moreover, the morphs need to be able respond to user input by changing their appearance and position — that is, by animating themselves.

When a mouse button is pressed, Morphic sends each morph under the mouse pointer the message `handlesMouseDown:`. If a morph answers `true`, then Morphic immediately sends it the `mouseDown:` message; it also sends the `mouseUp:` message when the user releases the mouse button. If all morphs answer `false`, then Morphic initiates a drag-and-drop operation. As we will discuss below, the `mouseDown:` and `mouseUp:` messages are sent with an argument — a `MouseEvent` object — that encodes the details of the mouse action.

Let's extend `CrossMorph` to handle mouse events. We start by ensuring that all crossMorphs answer `true` to the `handlesMouseDown:` message. Add the method to `CrossMorph` defined as follows:

```
CrossMorph >> handlesMouseDown: anEvent
  ^ true
```

Suppose that when we click on the cross, we want to change the color of the cross to red, and when we action-click on it, we want to change the color to yellow. We define the `mouseDown:` method as follows:

```
CrossMorph >> mouseDown: anEvent
    anEvent redButtonPressed
        ifTrue: [ self color: Color red ].    "click"
    anEvent yellowButtonPressed
        ifTrue: [ self color: Color yellow ]. "action-click"
    self changed
```

Notice that in addition to changing the color of the morph, this method also sends `self changed`. This makes sure that morphic sends `drawOn:` in a timely fashion.

Note also that once the morph handles mouse events, you can no longer grab it with the mouse and move it. Instead you have to use the halo: Option-Command-Shift click on the morph to make the halo appear and grab either the brown move handle or the black pickup handle at the top of the morph.

The `anEvent` argument of `mouseDown:` is an instance of `MouseEvent`, which is a subclass of `MorphicEvent`. `MouseEvent` defines the `redButtonPressed` and `yellowButtonPressed` methods. Browse this class to see what other methods it provides to interrogate the mouse event.

16.7 Keyboard events

To catch keyboard events, we need to take three steps.

1. Give the *keyboard focus* to a specific morph. For instance, we can give focus to our morph when the mouse is over it.
2. Handle the keyboard event itself with the `keyDown:` method. This message is sent to the morph that has keyboard focus when the user presses a key.
3. Release the keyboard focus when the mouse is no longer over our morph.

Let's extend `CrossMorph` so that it reacts to keystrokes. First, we need to arrange to be notified when the mouse is over the morph. This will happen if our morph answers `true` to the `handlesMouseOver:` message.

```
CrossMorph >> handlesMouseOver: anEvent
    ^ true
```

This message is the equivalent of `handlesMouseDown:` for the mouse position. When the mouse pointer enters or leaves the morph, the `mouseEnter:` and `mouseLeave:` messages are sent to it.

Define two methods so that `CrossMorph` catches and releases the keyboard focus, a third method to be notified when a key is pressed, and a fourth method to actually handle the key down event.

```
CrossMorph >> mouseEnter: anEvent
    anEvent hand newKeyboardFocus: self
```

```
CrossMorph >> mouseLeave: anEvent
    anEvent hand releaseKeyboardFocus: self
```

```
CrossMorph >> handlesKeyDown: anEvent
    ^ true
```

```
CrossMorph >> keyDown: anEvent
    | key |
    key := anEvent key.
    key = KeyboardKey up ifTrue: [ self position: self position - (0 @
        10) ].
    key = KeyboardKey down ifTrue: [ self position: self position + (0 @
        10) ].
    key = KeyboardKey right ifTrue: [ self position: self position + (10
        @ 0) ].
    key = KeyboardKey left ifTrue: [ self position: self position - (10
        @ 0) ].
```

We have written this method so that you can move the morph using the arrow keys. To discover the key values, you can open a Transcript window and add `Transcript show: anEvent keyValue` to the `handleKeystroke:` method.

The `anEvent` argument of `handleKeystroke:` is an instance of `KeyboardEvent`, another subclass of `MorphicEvent`. Browse this class to learn more about keyboard events.

If you want to move your morph with `Ctrl-` like shortcut, you could use code like:

```
anEvent controlKeyPressed ifTrue: [
    anEvent keyCharacter == $d ifTrue: [
        self position: self position + (0 @ 10) ] ]
```

16.8 Morphic animations

Morphic provides a simple animation system with two main methods: `step` is sent to a morph at regular intervals of time, while `stepTime` specifies the time in milliseconds between `step`s. `stepTime` is actually the *minimum* time between `step`s. If you ask for a `stepTime` of 1 ms, don't be surprised if Pharo is too busy to step your morph that often. In addition, `startStepping` turns on the stepping mechanism, while `stopStepping` turns it off again. `isStepping` can be used to find out whether a morph is currently being stepped.

Make `CrossMorph` blink by defining these methods as follows:

```
CrossMorph >> stepTime
    ^ 100
```

```
CrossMorph >> step
    (self color diff: Color black) < 0.1
        ifTrue: [ self color: Color red ]
        ifFalse: [ self color: self color darker ]
```

To start things off, you can open an inspector on a `CrossMorph` using the debug handle which look like a wrench in the morphic halo, type `self startStepping` in the small pane at the bottom, and `Do it`.

You can also redefine the `initialize` method as follows:

```
CrossMorph >> initialize
    super initialize.
    self startStepping
```

Alternatively, you can handle `key stroke` so that you can use the + and - keys to start and stop stepping.

Typically text is managed using the KeyStroke events while shortcuts are managed in KeyUp and KeyDown events.

To handle key stroke, we need a method to be notified when a key is pressed, and a second method to actually handle the key stroke event.

```
CrossMorph >> handlesKeyStroke: anEvent
    ^ true
```

```
CrossMorph >> keyStroke: anEvent
    | keyValue |
    keyValue := anEvent keyCharacter.
    keyValue == $+ ifTrue: [ self startStepping ].
    keyValue == $- ifTrue: [ self stopStepping ]
```

16.9 Interactors

To prompt the user for input, the `UIManager` class provides a large number of ready to use dialog boxes. For instance, the `request:initialAnswer:` method returns the string entered by the user (Figure 16-11).

```
UIManager default
    request: 'What''s your name?'
    initialAnswer: 'no name'
```

To display a popup menu, use one of the various `chooseFrom:` methods (Figure 16-12):

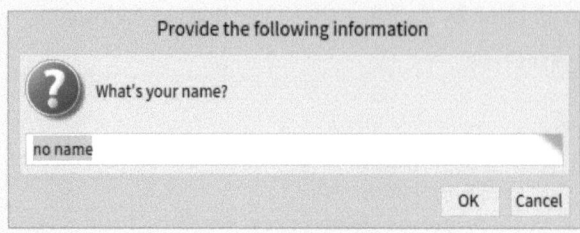

Figure 16-11 An input dialog.

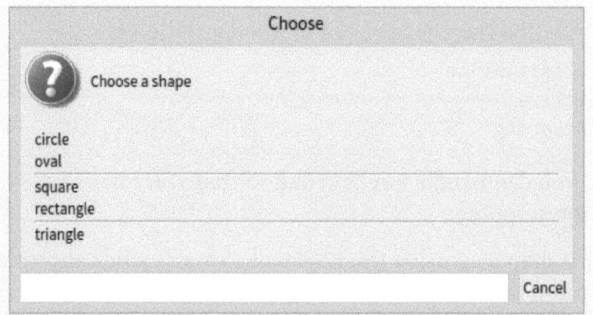

Figure 16-12 Pop-up menu.

```
UIManager default
  chooseFrom: #('circle' 'oval' 'square' 'rectangle' 'triangle')
  lines: #(2 4) message: 'Choose a shape'
```

Browse the UIManager class and try out some of the interaction methods offered.

16.10 Drag-and-drop

Morphic also supports drag-and-drop. Let's examine a simple example with two morphs, a receiver morph and a dropped morph. The receiver will accept a morph only if the dropped morph matches a given condition: in our example, the morph should be blue. If it is rejected, the dropped morph decides what to do.

Let's first define the receiver morph:

16.10 Drag-and-drop

```
Morph subclass: #ReceiverMorph
    instanceVariableNames: ''
    classVariableNames: ''
    package: 'PBE-Morphic'
```

Now define the initialization method in the usual way:

```
ReceiverMorph >> initialize
    super initialize.
    color := Color red.
    bounds := 0 @ 0 extent: 200 @ 200
```

How do we decide if the receiver morph will accept or reject the dropped morph? In general, both of the morphs will have to agree to the interaction. The receiver does this by responding to wantsDroppedMorph:event:. Its first argument is the dropped morph, and the second the mouse event, so that the receiver can, for example, see if any modifier keys were held down at the time of the drop. The dropped morph is also given the opportunity to check and see if it likes the morph onto which it is being dropped, by responding to the message wantsToBeDroppedInto:. The default implementation of this method (in class Morph) answers true.

```
ReceiverMorph >> wantsDroppedMorph: aMorph event: anEvent
    ^ aMorph color = Color blue
```

What happens to the dropped morph if the receiving morph doesn't want it? The default behaviour is for it to do nothing, that is, to sit on top of the receiving morph, but without interacting with it. A more intuitive behavior is for the dropped morph to go back to its original position. This can be achieved by the receiver answering true to the message repelsMorph:event: when it doesn't want the dropped morph:

```
ReceiverMorph >> repelsMorph: aMorph event: anEvent
    ^ (self wantsDroppedMorph: aMorph event: anEvent) not
```

That's all we need as far as the receiver is concerned.

Create instances of ReceiverMorph and EllipseMorph in a playground:

```
ReceiverMorph new openInWorld;
    bounds: (100@100 corner: 200@200).
EllipseMorph new openInWorld.
```

Try to drag and drop the yellow EllipseMorph onto the receiver. It will be rejected and sent back to its initial position.

To change this behaviour, change the color of the ellipse morph to the color blue (by sending it the message color: Color blue; right after new). Blue morphs should be accepted by the ReceiverMorph.

Morphic

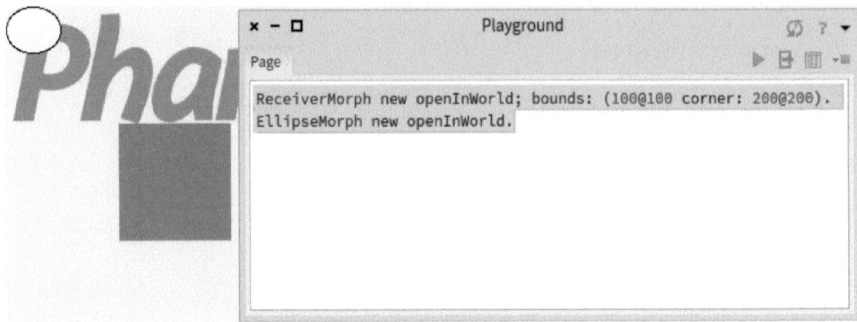

Figure 16-13 A `ReceiverMorph` and an `EllipseMorph`.

Let's create a specific subclass of `Morph`, named `DroppedMorph`, so we can experiment a bit more. Let us define a new kind of morph called `DroppedMorph`.

```
Morph subclass: #DroppedMorph
    instanceVariableNames: ''
    classVariableNames: ''
    package: 'PBE-Morphic'
```

```
DroppedMorph >> initialize
    super initialize.
    color := Color blue.
    self position: 250 @ 100
```

Now we can specify what the dropped morph should do when it is rejected by the receiver; here it will stay attached to the mouse pointer:

```
DroppedMorph >> rejectDropMorphEvent: anEvent
    | h |
    h := anEvent hand.
    WorldState addDeferredUIMessage: [ h grabMorph: self ].
    anEvent wasHandled: true
```

Sending the hand message to an event answers the *hand*, an instance of `HandMorph` that represents the mouse pointer and whatever it holds. Here we tell the `World` that the hand should grab `self`, the rejected morph.

Create two instances of `DroppedMorph` of different colors, and then drag and drop them onto the receiver.

```
ReceiverMorph new openInWorld.
morph := (DroppedMorph new color: Color blue) openInWorld.
morph position: (morph position + (70@0)).
(DroppedMorph new color: Color green) openInWorld.
```

The green morph is rejected and therefore stays attached to the mouse pointer.

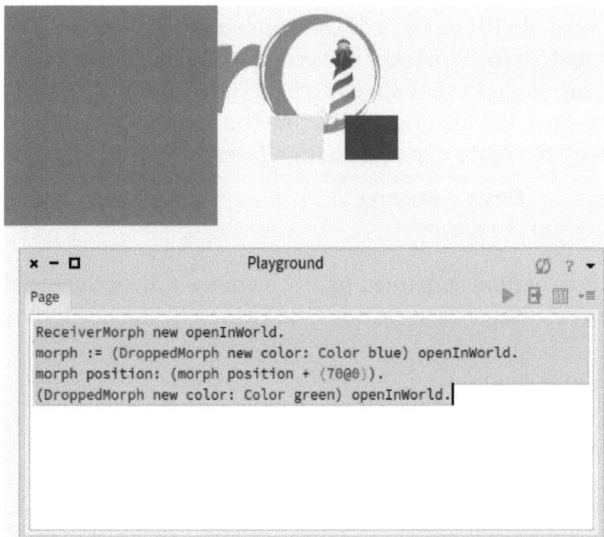

Figure 16-14 Creation of DroppedMorph and ReceiverMorph.

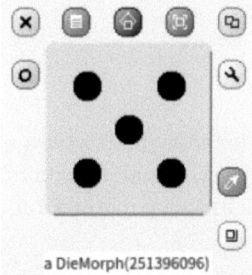

Figure 16-15 The die in Morphic.

16.11 A complete example

Let's design a morph to roll a die. Clicking on it will display the values of all sides of the die in a quick loop, and another click will stop the animation.

Define the die as a subclass of BorderedMorph instead of Morph, because we will make use of the border.

```
BorderedMorph subclass: #DieMorph
  instanceVariableNames: 'faces dieValue isStopped'
  classVariableNames: ''
  package: 'PBE-Morphic'
```

The instance variable `faces` records the number of faces on the die; we allow dice with up to 9 faces! `dieValue` records the value of the face that is currently displayed, and `isStopped` is true if the die animation has stopped running. To create a die instance, we define the `faces: n` method on the *class* side of `DieMorph` to create a new die with n faces.

```
DieMorph class >> faces: aNumber
  ^ self new faces: aNumber
```

The `initialize` method is defined on the instance side in the usual way; remember that `new` automatically sends `initialize` to the newly-created instance.

```
DieMorph >> initialize
  super initialize.
  self extent: 50 @ 50.
  self
    useGradientFill;
    borderWidth: 2;
    useRoundedCorners.
  self setBorderStyle: #complexRaised.
  self fillStyle direction: self extent.
  self color: Color green.
  dieValue := 1.
  faces := 6.
  isStopped := false
```

We use a few methods of `BorderedMorph` to give a nice appearance to the die: a thick border with a raised effect, rounded corners, and a color gradient on the visible face. We define the instance method `faces:` to check for a valid parameter as follows:

```
DieMorph >> faces: aNumber
  "Set the number of faces"

  ((aNumber isInteger and: [ aNumber > 0 ]) and: [ aNumber <= 9 ])
    ifTrue: [ faces := aNumber ]
```

It may be good to review the order in which the messages are sent when a die is created. For instance, if we start by evaluating `DieMorph faces: 9`:

- The class method `DieMorph class >> faces:` sends new to `DieMorph class`.
- The method for `new` (inherited by `DieMorph class` from `Behavior`) creates the new instance and sends it the `initialize` message.
- The `initialize` method in `DieMorph` sets `faces` to an initial value of 6.

16.11 A complete example

- `DieMorph class >> new` returns to the class method `DieMorph class >> faces:`, which then sends the message `faces: 9` to the new instance.
- The instance method `DieMorph >> faces:` now executes, setting the `faces` instance variable to 9.

Before defining `drawOn:`, we need a few methods to place the dots on the displayed face:

```
DieMorph >> face1
    ^ {(0.5 @ 0.5)}
```

```
DieMorph >> face2
    ^{0.25@0.25 . 0.75@0.75}
```

```
DieMorph >> face3
    ^{0.25@0.25 . 0.75@0.75 . 0.5@0.5}
```

```
DieMorph >> face4
    ^{0.25@0.25 . 0.75@0.25 . 0.75@0.75 . 0.25@0.75}
```

```
DieMorph >> face5
    ^{0.25@0.25 . 0.75@0.25 . 0.75@0.75 . 0.25@0.75 . 0.5@0.5}
```

```
DieMorph >> face6
    ^{0.25@0.25 . 0.75@0.25 . 0.75@0.75 . 0.25@0.75 . 0.25@0.5 .
      0.75@0.5}
```

```
DieMorph >> face7
    ^{0.25@0.25 . 0.75@0.25 . 0.75@0.75 . 0.25@0.75 . 0.25@0.5 .
      0.75@0.5 . 0.5@0.5}
```

```
DieMorph >> face8
    ^{0.25@0.25 . 0.75@0.25 . 0.75@0.75 . 0.25@0.75 . 0.25@0.5 .
      0.75@0.5 . 0.5@0.5 . 0.5@0.25}
```

```
DieMorph >> face9
    ^{0.25@0.25 . 0.75@0.25 . 0.75@0.75 . 0.25@0.75 . 0.25@0.5 .
      0.75@0.5 . 0.5@0.5 . 0.5@0.25 . 0.5@0.75}
```

These methods define collections of the coordinates of dots for each face. The coordinates are in a square of size 1x1; we will simply need to scale them to place the actual dots.

The `drawOn:` method does two things: it draws the die background with the super-send, and then draws the dots as follows:

```
DieMorph >> drawOn: aCanvas
    super drawOn: aCanvas.
    (self perform: ('face', dieValue asString) asSymbol)
        do: [ :aPoint | self drawDotOn: aCanvas at: aPoint ]
```

Listing 16-16 Create a Die 6

```
[(DieMorph faces: 6) openInWorld.
```

Figure 16-17 A new die 6 with (DieMorph faces: 6) openInWorld

The second part of this method uses the reflective capacities of Pharo. Drawing the dots of a face is a simple matter of iterating over the collection given by the faceX method for that face, sending the drawDotOn:at: message for each coordinate. To call the correct faceX method, we use the perform: method which sends a message built from a string, ('face', dieValue asString) asSymbol.

```
DieMorph >> drawDotOn: aCanvas at: aPoint
  aCanvas
    fillOval: (Rectangle
      center: self position + (self extent * aPoint)
      extent: self extent / 6)
    color: Color black
```

Since the coordinates are normalized to the [0:1] interval, we scale them to the dimensions of our die: self extent * aPoint. We can already create a die instance from a playground (see result on Figure 16-17):

To change the displayed face, we create an accessor that we can use as myDie dieValue: 5:

```
DieMorph >> dieValue: aNumber
  ((aNumber isInteger and: [ aNumber > 0 ]) and: [ aNumber <= faces ])
    ifTrue: [
      dieValue := aNumber.
      self changed ]
```

Now we will use the animation system to show quickly all the faces:

```
DieMorph >> stepTime
  ^ 100
```

```
DieMorph >> step
  isStopped ifFalse: [self dieValue: (1 to: faces) atRandom]
```

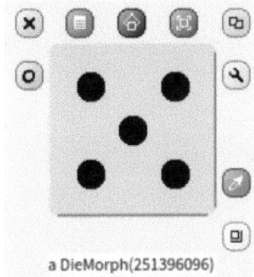

Figure 16-18 Result of `(DieMorph faces: 6) openInWorld; dieValue: 5.`

Now the die is rolling!

To start or stop the animation by clicking, we will use what we learned previously about mouse events. First, activate the reception of mouse events:

```
DieMorph >> handlesMouseDown: anEvent
    ^ true
```

Second, we will stop and start alternatively a roll on mouse click.

```
DieMorph >> mouseDown: anEvent
    anEvent redButtonPressed
        ifTrue: [isStopped := isStopped not]
```

Now the die will roll or stop rolling when we click on it.

16.12 More about the canvas

The `drawOn:` method has an instance of `Canvas` as its sole argument; the canvas is the area on which the morph draws itself. By using the graphics methods of the canvas you are free to give the appearance you want to a morph. If you browse the inheritance hierarchy of the `Canvas` class, you will see that it has several variants. The default variant of `Canvas` is `FormCanvas`, and you will find the key graphics methods in `Canvas` and `FormCanvas`. These methods can draw points, lines, polygons, rectangles, ellipses, text, and images with rotation and scaling.

It is also possible to use other kinds of canvas, for example to obtain transparent morphs, more graphics methods, antialiasing, and so on. To use these features you will need an `AlphaBlendingCanvas` or a `BalloonCanvas`. But how can you obtain such a canvas in a `drawOn:` method, when `drawOn:` receives an instance of `FormCanvas` as its argument? Fortunately, you can transform one kind of canvas into another.

Figure 16-19 The die displayed with alpha-transparency

To use a canvas with a 0.5 alpha-transparency in DieMorph, redefine drawOn: like this:

```
DieMorph >> drawOn: aCanvas
  | theCanvas |
  theCanvas := aCanvas asAlphaBlendingCanvas: 0.5.
  super drawOn: theCanvas.
  (self perform: ('face', dieValue asString) asSymbol)
    do: [:aPoint | self drawDotOn: theCanvas at: aPoint]
```

That's all you need to do!

16.13 Chapter summary

Morphic is a graphical framework in which graphical interface elements can be dynamically composed.

- You can convert an object into a morph and display that morph on the screen by sending it the messages asMorph openInWorld.
- You can manipulate a morph using Command-Option+Shift click on it and using the handles that appear. (Handles have help balloons that explain what they do.)
- You can compose morphs by embedding one onto another, either by drag and drop or by sending the message addMorph:.
- You can subclass an existing morph class and redefine key methods, such as initialize and drawOn:.
- You can control how a morph reacts to mouse and keyboard events by redefining the methods handlesMouseDown:, handlesMouseOver:, etc.
- You can animate a morph by defining the methods step (what to do) and stepTime (the number of milliseconds between steps).

CHAPTER **17**

Classes and metaclasses

In Pharo, everything is an object, and every object is an instance of a class. Classes are no exception: classes are objects, and class objects are instances of other classes. This model is lean, simple, elegant, and uniform. It fully captures the essence of object-oriented programming. However, the implications of this uniformity may confuse newcomers.

Note that you do not need to fully understand the implications of this uniformity to program fluently in Pharo. Nevertheless, the goal of this chapter is twofold: (1) go as deep as possible and (2) show that there is nothing complex, *magic* or special here: just simple rules applied uniformly. By following these rules, you can always understand why the situation is the way that it is.

17.1 Rules for classes

The Pharo object model is based on a limited number of concepts applied uniformly. To refresh your memory, here are the rules of the object model that we explored in Chapter : The Pharo Object Model.

Rule 1 Everything is an object.

Rule 2 Every object is an instance of a class.

Rule 3 Every class has a superclass.

Rule 4 Everything happens by sending messages.

Rule 5 Method lookup follows the inheritance chain.

Rule 6 Classes are objects too and follow exactly the same rules.

A consequence of Rule 1 is that *classes are objects too,* so Rule 2 tells us that classes must also be instances of classes. The class of a class is called a *metaclass*.

17.2 Metaclasses

A metaclass is created automatically for you whenever you create a class. Most of the time you do not need to care or think about metaclasses. However, every time that you use the browser to browse the *class side* of a class, it is helpful to recall that you are actually browsing a different class. A class and its metaclass are two separate classes. Indeed a point is different from the class Point and this is the same for a class and its metaclass.

To properly explain classes and metaclasses, we need to extend the rules from Chapter : The Pharo Object Model with the following additional rules.

Rule 7 Every class is an instance of a metaclass.

Rule 8 The metaclass hierarchy parallels the class hierarchy.

Rule 9 Every metaclass inherits from Class and Behavior.

Rule 10 Every metaclass is an instance of Metaclass.

Rule 11 The metaclass of Metaclass is an instance of Metaclass.

Together, these 11 simple rules complete Pharo's object model.

We will first briefly revisit the 5 rules from Chapter : The Pharo Object Model with a small example. Then we will take a closer look at the new rules, using the same example.

17.3 Revisiting the Pharo object model

Rule 1. Since everything is an object, an ordered collection in Pharo is also an object.

```
OrderedCollection withAll: #(4 5 6 1 2 3)
>>> an OrderedCollection(4 5 6 1 2 3)
```

Rule 2. Every object is an instance of a class. An ordered collection is instance of the class OrderedCollection:

```
(OrderedCollection withAll: #(4 5 6 1 2 3)) class
>>> OrderedCollection
```

Rule 3. Every class has a superclass. The superclass of OrderedCollection is SequenceableCollection and the superclass of SequenceableCollection is Collection:

17.4 Every class is an instance of a metaclass

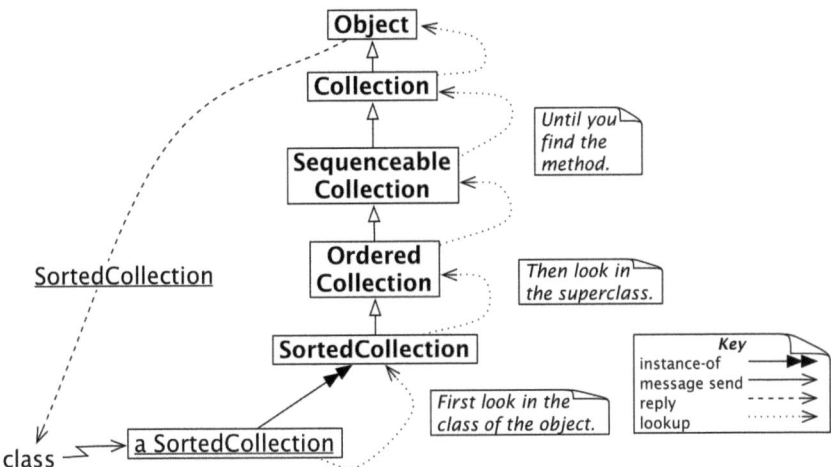

Figure 17-1 Sending the message class to a sorted collection

```
OrderedCollection superclass
>>> SequenceableCollection
```

```
SequenceableCollection superclass
>>> Collection
```

```
Collection superclass
>>> Object
```

Rule 4. Everything happens by sending messages, so we can deduce that with-All: is a message sent to OrderedCollection and class are messages sent to the ordered collection instance, and superclass is a message sent to the class OrderedCollection and SequenceableCollection, and Collection. The receiver in each case is an object, since everything is an object, but some of these objects are also classes.

Rule 5. Method lookup follows the inheritance chain, so when we send the message class to the result of (OrderedCollection withAll: #(4 5 6 1 2 3)) asSortedCollection, the message is handled when the corresponding method is found in the class Object, as shown in Figure 17-1.

17.4 Every class is an instance of a metaclass

As we mentioned earlier in Section 17.2, classes whose instances are themselves classes are *called* metaclasses. This is to make sure that we can precisely refer to the class Point and the class of the class Point.

Classes and metaclasses

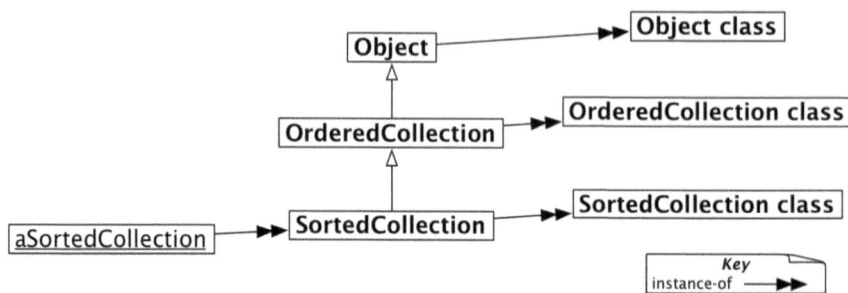

Figure 17-2 The metaclasses of SortedCollection and its superclasses (elided).

Metaclasses are implicit

Metaclasses are automatically created when you define a class. We say that they are *implicit* since as a programmer you never have to worry about them. An implicit metaclass is created for each class you create, so each metaclass has only a single instance.

Whereas ordinary classes are named, metaclasses are anonymous. However, we can always refer to them through the class that is their instance. The class of SortedCollection is SortedCollection class, and the class of Object is Object class:

```
SortedCollection class
>>> SortedCollection class
```

```
Object class
>>> Object class
```

In fact metaclasses are not truly anonymous, their name is deduced from the one of their single instance.

```
SortedCollection class name
>>> 'SortedCollection class'
```

```
Object class name
>>> 'Object class'
```

Figure 17-2 shows how each class is an instance of its metaclass. Note that we only skip SequenceableCollection and Collection from the figure and explanation due to space constraints. Their absence does not change the overall meaning.

262

17.5 Querying Metaclasses

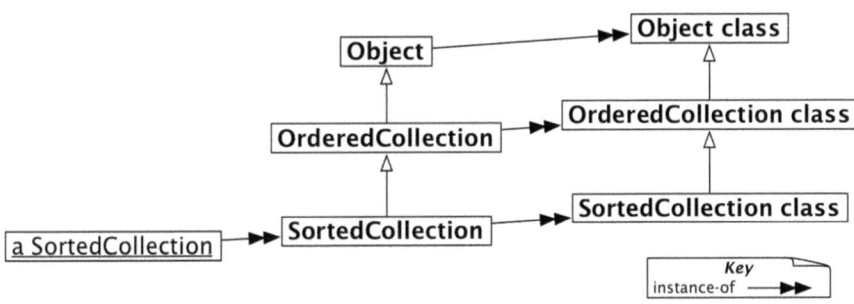

Figure 17-3 The metaclass hierarchy parallels the class hierarchy (elided).

17.5 Querying Metaclasses

The fact that classes are also objects makes it easy for us to query them by sending messages. Let's have a look:

```
OrderedCollection subclasses
>>> {SortedCollection . ObjectFinalizerCollection .
    WeakOrderedCollection . OCLiteralList . GLMMultiValue}
```

```
SortedCollection subclasses
>>> #()
```

```
SortedCollection allSuperclasses
>>> an OrderedCollection(OrderedCollection SequenceableCollection
    Collection Object ProtoObject)
```

```
SortedCollection instVarNames
>>> #(#sortBlock)
```

```
SortedCollection allInstVarNames
>>> #(#array #firstIndex #lastIndex #sortBlock)
```

```
SortedCollection selectors
>>>  #(#sortBlock: #add: #groupedBy: #defaultSort:to: #addAll:
    #at:put: #copyEmpty #, #collect: #indexForInserting:
    #insert:before: #reSort #addFirst: #join: #median #flatCollect:
    #sort: #sort:to: #= #sortBlock)
```

17.6 The metaclass hierarchy parallels the class hierarchy

Rule 7 says that the superclass of a metaclass cannot be an arbitrary class: it is constrained to be the metaclass of the superclass of the metaclass's unique

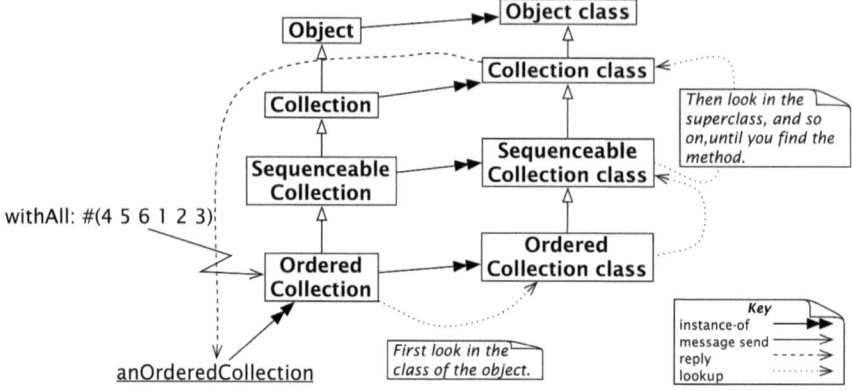

Figure 17-4 Message lookup for classes is the same as for ordinary objects.

instance: the metaclass of SortedCollection inherits from the metaclass of OrderedCollection (the superclass of SortedCollection).

```
SortedCollection class superclass
>>> OrderedCollection class
```

```
SortedCollection superclass class
>>> OrderedCollection class
```

This is what we mean by the metaclass hierarchy being parallel to the class hierarchy. Figure 17-3 shows how this works in the SortedCollection hierarchy.

```
SortedCollection class
>>> SortedCollection class
```

```
SortedCollection class superclass
>>> OrderedCollection class
```

```
SortedCollection class superclass superclass
>>> SequenceableCollection class
```

```
SortedCollection class superclass superclass superclass superclass
>>> Object class
```

17.7 Uniformity between Classes and Objects

It is interesting to step back a moment and realize that there is no difference between sending a message to an object and to a class. In both cases the lookup for the corresponding method starts in the *class of the receiver*, and *proceeds up the inheritance chain*.

17.7 Uniformity between Classes and Objects

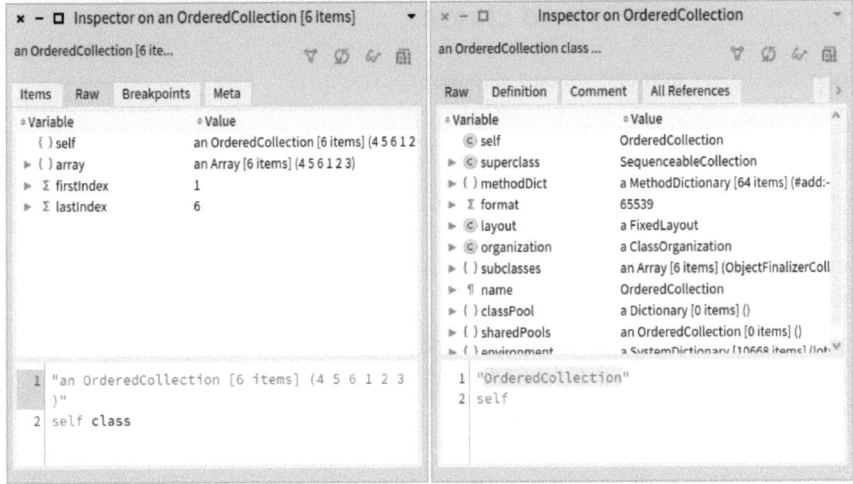

Figure 17-5 Classes are objects too.

Thus, messages sent to classes follow the metaclass inheritance chain. Consider, for example, the method `withAll:`, which is implemented on the class side of `Collection`. When we send the message `withAll:` to the class `OrderedCollection`, then it is looked up the same way as any other message. The lookup starts in `OrderedCollection class` (since it starts in the class of the receiver and the receiver is `OrderedCollection`), and proceeds up the metaclass hierarchy until it is found in `Collection class` (see Figure 17-4). It returns a new instance of `OrderedCollection`.

```
OrderedCollection withAll: #(4 5 6 1 2 3)
>>> an OrderedCollection (4 5 6 1 2 3)
```

Only one method lookup

There is only one uniform kind of method lookup in Pharo. Classes are just objects, and behave like any other objects. Classes have the power to create new instances only because classes happen to respond to the message `new`, and because the `new` method knows how to create new instances.

Normally, non-class objects do not understand this message, but if you have a good reason to do so, there is nothing stopping you from adding a `new` method to a non-metaclass.

17.8 Inspecting objects and classes

Since classes are objects, we can also inspect them.

Inspect `OrderedCollection withAll: #(4 5 6 1 2 3)` and `OrderedCollection`.

Notice that in one case you are inspecting an instance of `OrderedCollection` and in the other case the `OrderedCollection` class itself. This can be a bit confusing, because the title bar of the inspector names the *class* of the object being inspected.

The inspector on `OrderedCollection` allows you to see the superclass, instance variables, method dictionary, and so on, of the `OrderedCollection` class, as shown in Figure 17-5.

17.9 Every metaclass inherits from Class and Behavior

Every metaclass is a kind of a class (a class with a single instance), hence inherits from `Class`. `Class` in turn inherits from its superclasses, `ClassDescription` and `Behavior`. Since everything in Pharo is an object, these classes all inherit eventually from `Object`. We can see the complete picture in Figure 17-6.

Where is new defined?

To understand the importance of the fact that metaclasses inherit from `Class` and `Behavior`, it helps to ask where `new` is defined and how it is found.

When the message `new` is sent to a class, it is looked up in its metaclass chain and ultimately in its superclasses `Class`, `ClassDescription` and `Behavior` as shown in Figure 17-7.

When we send `new` to the class `SortedCollection`, the message is looked up in the metaclass `SortedCollection class` and follows the inheritance chain. Remember it is the same lookup process than for any objects.

The question *Where is new defined?* is crucial. `new` is first defined in the class `Behavior`, and it can be redefined in its subclasses, including any of the metaclass of the classes we define, when this is necessary.

Now when a message `new` is sent to a class it is looked up, as usual, in the metaclass of this class, continuing up the superclass chain right up to the class `Behavior`, if it has not been redefined along the way.

Note that the result of sending `SortedCollection new` is an instance of `SortedCollection` and *not* of `Behavior`, even though the method is looked up in the class `Behavior`!

17.9 Every metaclass inherits from Class and Behavior

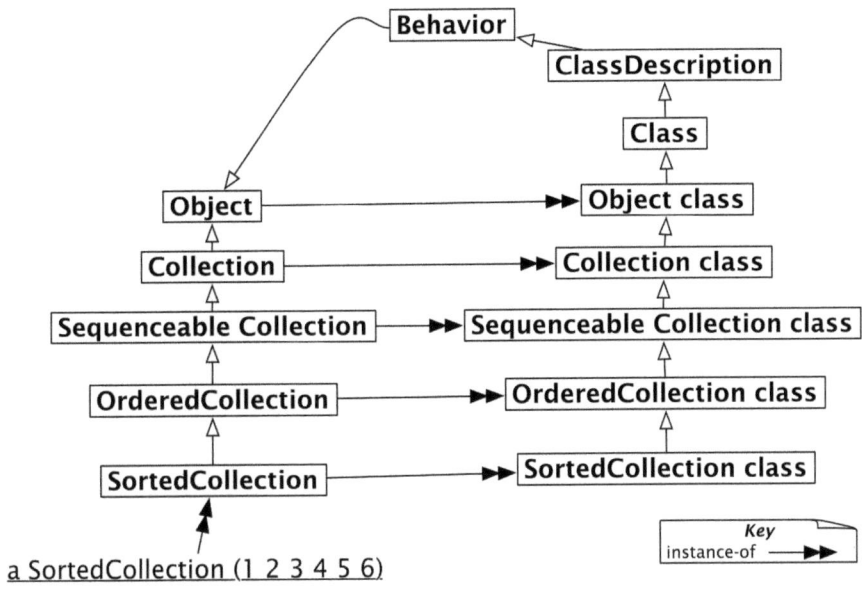

Figure 17-6 Metaclasses inherit from Class and Behavior.

The method new always returns an instance of self, the class that receives the message, even if it is implemented in another class.

```
SortedCollection new class
>>> SortedCollection     "not Behavior!"
```

A common mistake

A common mistake is to look for new in the superclass of the receiving class. The same holds for new:, the standard message to create an object of a given size. For example, Array new: 4 creates an array of 4 elements. You will not find this method defined in Array or any of its superclasses. Instead you should look in Array class and its superclasses, since that is where the lookup will start (See Figure 17-7).

The method new and new: are defined in metaclasses, because they are executed in response to messages sent to classes.

In addition since a class is an object it can also be the receiver of messages whose methods are defined on Object. When we send the message class or error: to the class Point, the method lookup will go over the metaclass chain (looking in Point class, Object class....) up to Object.

Classes and metaclasses

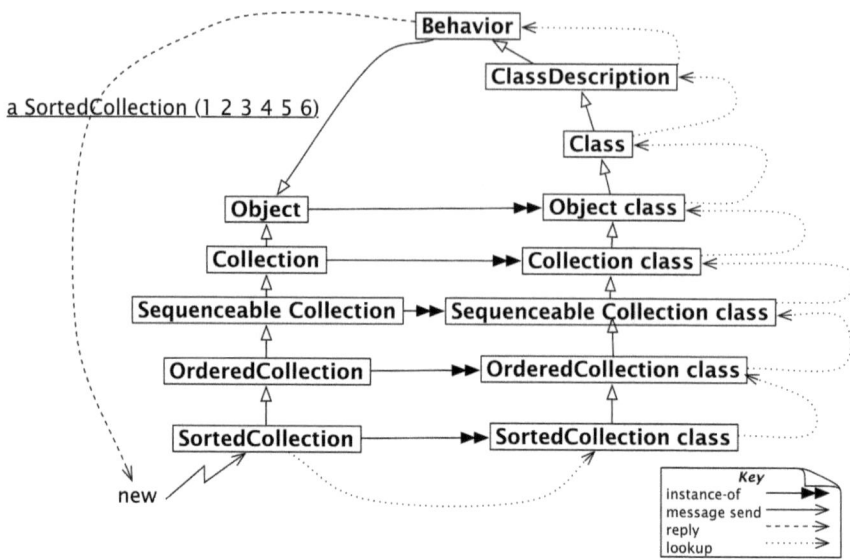

Figure 17-7 `new` is an ordinary message looked up in the metaclass chain.

17.10 Responsibilities of `Behavior`, `ClassDescription`, and `Class`

Behavior

`Behavior` provides the minimum state necessary for objects that have instances, which includes a superclass link, a method dictionary and the class format. The class format is an integer that encodes the pointer/non-pointer distinction, compact/non-compact class distinction, and basic size of instances. `Behavior` inherits from `Object`, so it, and all of its subclasses, can behave like objects.

`Behavior` is also the basic interface to the compiler. It provides methods for creating a method dictionary, compiling methods, creating instances (i.e., `new`, `basicNew`, `new:`, and `basicNew:`), manipulating the class hierarchy (i.e., `superclass:`, `addSubclass:`), accessing methods (i.e., `selectors`, `allSelectors`, `compiledMethodAt:`), accessing instances and variables (i.e., `allInstances`, `instVarNames`...), accessing the class hierarchy (i.e., `superclass`, `subclasses`) and querying (i.e., `hasMethods`, `includesSelector`, `canUnderstand:`, `inheritsFrom:`, `isVariable`).

ClassDescription

`ClassDescription` is an abstract class that provides facilities needed by its two direct subclasses, `Class` and `Metaclass`. `ClassDescription` adds a number of facilities to the base provided by `Behavior`: named instance variables, the categorization of methods into protocols, the maintenance of change sets and the logging of changes, and most of the mechanisms needed for filing out changes.

Class

`Class` represents the common behaviour of all classes. It provides a class name, compilation methods, method storage, and instance variables. It provides a concrete representation for class variable names and shared pool variables (`addClassVarName:`, `addSharedPool:`, `initialize`). Since a metaclass is a class for its sole instance (*i.e.*, the non-meta class), all metaclasses ultimately inherit from `Class` (as shown by Figure 17-9).

17.11 Every metaclass is an instance of `Metaclass`

The next question is since metaclasses are objects too, they should be instances of another class, but which one? Metaclasses are objects too; they are instances of the class `Metaclass` as shown in Figure 17-8. The instances of class `Metaclass` are the anonymous metaclasses, each of which has exactly one instance, which is a class.

`Metaclass` represents common metaclass behaviour. It provides methods for instance creation (`subclassOf:`), creating initialized instances of the metaclass's sole instance, initialization of class variables, metaclass instance, method compilation, and class information (inheritance links, instance variables, ...).

17.12 The metaclass of `Metaclass` is an instance of `Metaclass`

The final question to be answered is: what is the class of `Metaclass class`?

The answer is simple: it is a metaclass, so it must be an instance of `Metaclass`, just like all the other metaclasses in the system (see Figure 17-9).

Figure 17-9 shows how all metaclasses are instances of `Metaclass`, including the metaclass of `Metaclass` itself. If you compare Figures 17-8 and 17-9 you will see how the metaclass hierarchy perfectly mirrors the class hierarchy, all the way up to `Object class`.

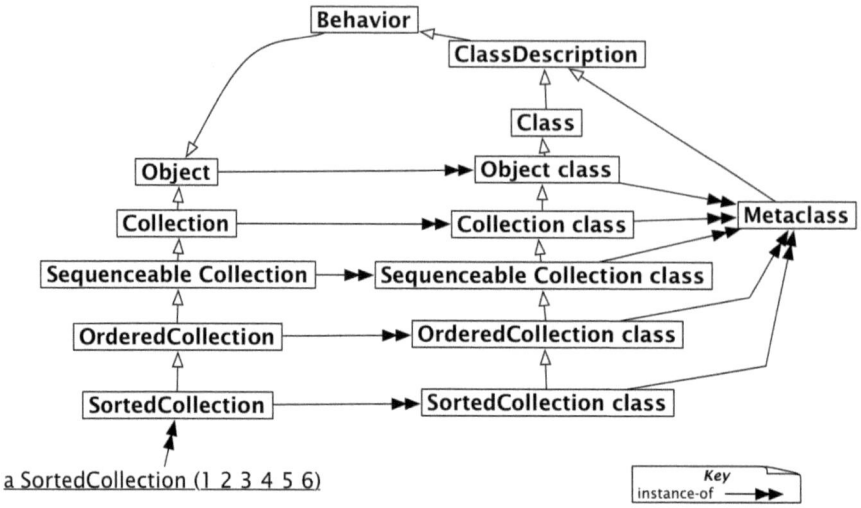

Figure 17-8 Every metaclass is a `Metaclass`.

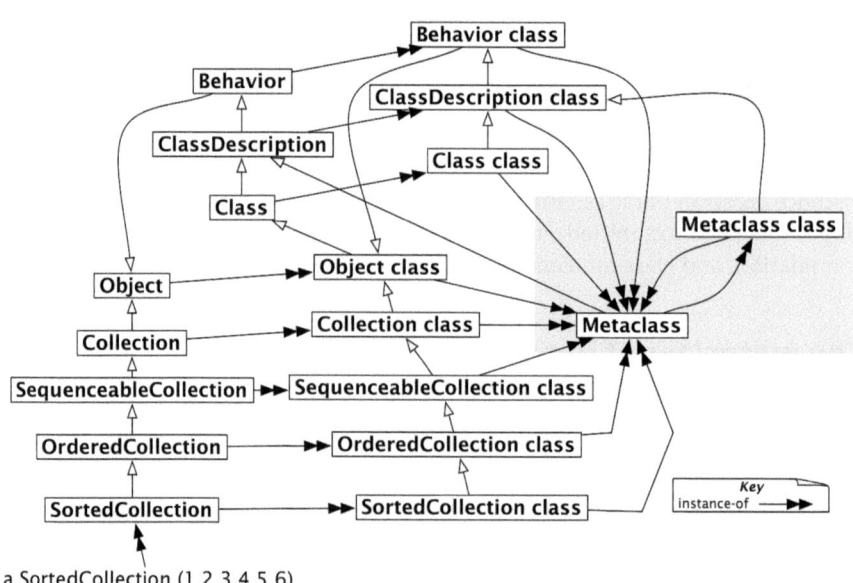

Figure 17-9 All metaclasses are instances of the class `Metaclass`, even the metaclass of `Metaclass`.

The following examples show us how we can query the class hierarchy to demonstrate that Figure 17-9 is correct. (Actually, you will see that we told a white lie — `Object class superclass --> ProtoObject class`, not `Class`. In Pharo, we must go one superclass higher to reach `Class`.)

```
Collection superclass
>>> Object
```

```
Collection class superclass
>>> Object class
```

```
Object class superclass superclass
>>> Class
```

```
Class superclass
>>> ClassDescription
```

```
ClassDescription superclass
>>> Behavior
```

```
Behavior superclass
>>> Object
```

```
"The class of a metaclass is the class Metaclass"
Collection class class
>>> Metaclass
```

```
  "The class of a metaclass is the class Metaclass"
Object class class
>>> Metaclass
```

```
"The class of a metaclass is the class Metaclass"
Behavior class class
>>> Metaclass
```

```
"The class of a metaclass is the class Metaclass"
Metaclass class class
>>> Metaclass
```

```
"Metaclass is a special kind of class"
Metaclass superclass
>>> ClassDescription
```

17.13 Chapter summary

This chapter gave an in-depth look into the uniform object model of Pharo, and a more thorough explanation of how classes are organized. If you get lost or confused, you should always remember that message passing is the key: *you look for the method in the class of the receiver*. This works on *any* receiver. If the method is not found in the class of the receiver, it is looked up in its superclasses.

- Every class is an instance of a metaclass. Metaclasses are implicit. A metaclass is created automatically when you create the class that is its sole instance. A metaclass is simply a class whose unique instance is a class.

- The metaclass hierarchy parallels the class hierarchy. Method lookup for classes parallels method lookup for ordinary objects, and follows the metaclass's superclass chain.

- Every metaclass inherits from `Class` and `Behavior`. Every class *is a* `Class`. Since metaclasses are classes too, they must also inherit from `Class`. `Behavior` provides behavior common to all entities that have instances.

- Every metaclass is an instance of `Metaclass`. `ClassDescription` provides everything that is common to `Class` and `Metaclass`.

- The metaclass of `Metaclass` is an instance of `Metaclass`. The *instance-of* relation forms a closed loop, so `Metaclass class class` is `Metaclass`.

CHAPTER **18**

Reflection

Pharo is a reflective programming language. Reflection is both being able to query various aspects of the system own execution and modifying it. The query capabilities are often called *introspection* and the possibility called *intercession*. In this chapter we present several aspects around the introspection capabilities of Pharo: how to access and modify instance variable value, how to navigate the system, or how to perform cross references. Then we present some aspects of behavioral reflection, i.e., how to modify the system and extend it.

18.1 Reflection in a nutshell

Reflection supports the idea that programs are able to *reflect* on their own execution and structure. With reflection the internal mechanisms that support the execution of a program (class, methods, but also stack) are accessible to the developer using the same way than their normal programs. In Pharo it means that such internal mechanisms are described as objects and that the developer will send them messages. We often call the objects that support program execution *metaobjects* to express the fact that they are at another level than plain objects.

More technically, *metaobjects* of the runtime system are *reified* as ordinary objects, which can be queried and inspected. The metaobjects in Pharo are classes, metaclasses, method dictionaries, compiled methods, but also the runtime stack, processes, and so on. This form of reflection is also called *introspection*, and nowadays it is supported by many modern programming languages (it was heavily promoted by Smalltalk-80 the ancestor of Pharo).

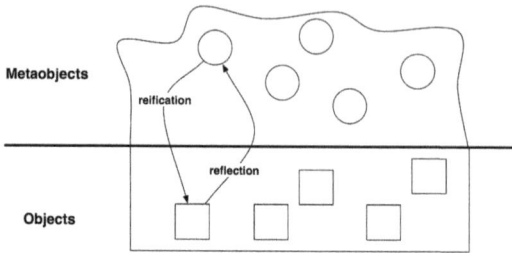

Figure 18-1 Reification and reflection.

Conversely, it is possible in Pharo to modify reified metaobjects and *reflect* these changes back to the runtime system (see Figure 18-1). This is also called *intercession*, and is supported mainly by dynamic programming languages, and only to a very limited degree by static languages. So pay attention when people say that Java is a reflective language, it is an introspective one not a reflective one.

A program that manipulates other programs (or even itself) is a *metaprogram*. For a programming language to be reflective, it should support both introspection and intercession. Introspection is the ability to *examine* the data structures that define the language, such as objects, classes, methods and the execution stack. Intercession is the ability to *modify* these structures, in other words to change the language semantics and the behavior of a program from within the program itself. *Structural reflection* is about examining and modifying the structures of the runtime, and *behavioural reflection* is about modifying the interpretation of these structures.

In this chapter we will focus mainly on structural reflection. We will explore many practical examples illustrating how Pharo supports introspection and metaprogramming.

18.2 Introspection

Using the inspector, you can look at an object, change the values of its instance variables, and even send messages to it.

Evaluate the following code in a playground:

```
w := StPlayground open.
w inspect
```

This will open a second playground and an inspector. The inspector shows the internal state of this new playground, listing its instance variables on the left

18.3 Accessing instance variables

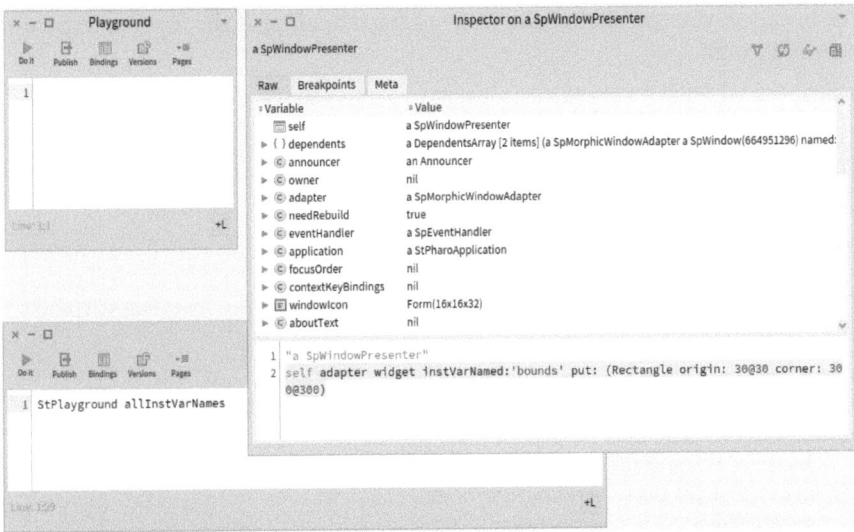

Figure 18-2 Inspecting a StPlayground.

(announcer, owner, ...) and the value of the selected instance variable on the right.

Now choose the inspector and click the playground area of the inspector which has a comment on top and type self bounds: (Rectangle origin: 10@10 corner: 300@300) in it as shown in Figure 18-2 and then *Do It* like you do with a code of a Playground.

Immediately you will see the Playground that we created will change and resize itself.

18.3 Accessing instance variables

How does the inspector work? In Pharo, all instance variables are protected. In theory, it is impossible to access them from another object if the class doesn't define any accessor. In practice, the inspector can access instance variables without needing accessors, because it uses the reflective abilities of Pharo. Classes define instance variables either by name or by numeric indices. The inspector uses methods defined by the Object class to access them: instVarAt: index and instVarNamed: aString can be used to get the value of the instance variable at position index or identified by aString, respectively. Similarly, to assign new values to these instance variables, it uses instVarAt:put: and instVarNamed:put:.

For instance, you can change the value of the w binding of the first workspace by evaluating:

```
w adapter widget instVarNamed:'bounds' put: (Rectangle origin: 30@30
    corner: 300@300)
```

Click on it to raise a refresh and see the result.

Instance variables

The method `allInstVarNames` returns all the names of the instance variables of a given class.

```
StPlayground allInstVarNames
>>>
#(#dependents #announcer #owner #adapter #needRebuild #eventHandler
    #application #focusOrder
 #contextKeyBindings #windowIcon #aboutText #askOkToClose #titleHolder
    #additionalSubpresentersMap
 #layout #visible #extent #styles #millerList #model
    #lastPageSelectedTabName #withHeaderBar)
```

The following code snippet shows how to display the values of the instance variables of an arbitrary instance (w) of class `StPlayground`.

```
w := StPlayground someInstance.
w class allInstVarNames collect: [:each | each -> (w instVarNamed:
    each)]
```

In the same spirit, it is possible to gather instances that have specific properties iterating over instances of a class using an iterator such as `select:`. For instance, to get all objects who are directly included in the world morph (the main root of the graphical displayed elements), try this expression:

```
Morph allSubInstances
  select: [ :each |
      | own |
      own := (each instVarNamed: 'owner').
      own isNotNil and: [ own  isWorldMorph ]]
```

18.4 About reflective behavior

Such expressions are handy for debugging or for building development tools, using them to develop conventional applications is a bad idea: these reflective methods break the encapsulation boundary of your objects. They break the tool navigation. They will make your code much harder to understand and maintain. A nice quote to remember is: 'With super powers come super responsibility'. So this is not because you can do something that you should.

18.5 About primitives

Both `instVarAt:` and `instVarAt:put:` are primitive methods, meaning that they are implemented as primitive operations of the Pharo virtual machine. If you consult the code of these methods, you will see the pragma `<primitive: N>` where N is an integer. This tags the method to be treated differently.

```
Object >> instVarAt: index
  "Primitive. Answer a fixed variable in an object. ..."

  <primitive: 173 error: ec>
  self primitiveFailed
```

Any Pharo code after the primitive declaration is executed only if the primitive fails. In this specific case, there is no way to implement this method, so the whole method just fails.

Other methods are implemented on the VM for faster execution. For example some arithmetic operations on SmallInteger:

```
* aNumber
  "Primitive. Multiply the receiver by the argument and answer with the
  result if it is a SmallInteger. Fail if the argument or the result
    is not a
  SmallInteger. Essential. No Lookup. See Object documentation
    whatIsAPrimitive."

  <primitive: 9>
  ^ super * aNumber
```

If this primitive fails, for example if the VM does not handle the type of the argument, the Pharo code is executed. Although it is possible to modify the code of primitive methods, beware that this can be risky business for the stability of your Pharo system.

18.6 Querying classes and interfaces

The development tools in Pharo (system browser, debugger, inspector...) all use the reflective features we have seen so far.

Here are a few other messages that might be useful to build development tools:

The message `isKindOf:` aClass returns true if the receiver is instance of aClass or of one of its subclasses. For instance:

```
1.5 class
>>> SmallFloat64
```

```
1.5 isKindOf: Float
>>> true
```

```
1.5 isKindOf: Number
>>> true
```

```
1.5 isKindOf: Integer
>>> false
```

The message `respondsTo: aSymbol` returns true if the receiver has a method whose selector is aSymbol. For instance:

```
1.5 respondsTo: #floor
>>> true     "since Number implements floor"
```

```
1.5 floor
>>> 1
```

```
Exception respondsTo: #,
>>> true     "exception classes can be grouped"
```

Watch out!

Although these features are especially useful for implementing development tools, they are normally not appropriate for typical applications. Asking an object for its class, or querying it to discover which messages it understands, are typical signs of design problems, since they violate the principle of encapsulation. Development tools, however, are not normal applications, since their domain is that of software itself. As such these tools have a right to dig deep into the internal details of code.

18.7 Simple code metrics

Let's see how we can use Pharo's introspection features to quickly extract some code metrics. Code metrics measure aspects such as the depth of the inheritance hierarchy, the number of direct or indirect subclasses, the number of methods or instance variables in each class, or the number of locally defined methods or instance variables. Here are a few metrics for the class Morph, which is the superclass of all graphical objects in Pharo, revealing that it is a huge class, and that it is at the root of a huge hierarchy. This shows that it needs some refactoring!

```
"inheritance depth"
Morph allSuperclasses size.
>>> 2
```

```
"number of methods"
Morph allSelectors size.
>>> 1442
```

```
"number of instance variables"
Morph allInstVarNames size.
>>> 6
```

```
"number of new methods"
Morph selectors size.
>>> 931
```

```
"number of new variables"
Morph instVarNames size.
>>> 6
```

```
"direct subclasses"
Morph subclasses size.
>>> 73
```

```
"total subclasses"
Morph allSubclasses size.
>>>   445
```

```
"total lines of code!"
Morph linesOfCode.
>>> 5088
```

One of the most interesting metrics in the domain of object-oriented languages is the number of methods that extend methods inherited from the superclass. This informs us about the relation between the class and its superclasses. In the next sections we will see how to exploit our knowledge of the runtime structure to answer such questions.

18.8 Browsing instances

In Pharo, everything is an object. In particular, classes are objects that provide useful features for navigating through their instances. Most of the messages we will look at now are implemented in `Behavior`, so they are understood by all classes.

For example, you can obtain a random instance of a given class by sending it the message `someInstance`.

```
Point someInstance
>>> (-1@-1)
```

You can also gather all the instances with `allInstances`, or the number of active instances in memory with `instanceCount`.

```
ByteString allInstances
>>> #('collection' 'position'  ...)
```

```
ByteString instanceCount
>>> 58514
```

```
String allSubInstances size
>>>    138962
```

Such methods access the instances that are stored inside methods. And since Pharo has around 130 000 methods. Such numbers are not totally crazy.

18.9 From methods to instance variables

These features can be very useful when debugging an application, because you can ask a class to enumerate those of its methods exhibiting specific properties. Here are some more interesting and useful methods for code discovery through reflection.

whichSelectorsAccess: returns the list of all selectors of methods that read or write the instance variable named by the argument

whichSelectorsStoreInto: returns the selectors of methods that modify the value of an instance variable

whichSelectorsReferTo: returns the selectors of methods that send a given message

```
Point whichSelectorsAccess: 'x'
>>> #(#octantOf: #roundDownTo: #+ #asIntegerPoint #transposed ...)
```

```
Point whichSelectorsStoreInto: 'x'
>>> #(#fromSton: #setX:setY: #setR:degrees: #bitShiftPoint:)
```

```
Point whichSelectorsReferTo: #+
>>> #(#+)
```

The following messages take inheritance into account:

whichClassIncludesSelector: returns the superclass that implements the given message

unreferencedInstanceVariables returns the list of instance variables that are neither used in the receiver class nor any of its subclasses

```
Rectangle whichClassIncludesSelector: #inspect
>>> Object
```

```
Rectangle unreferencedInstanceVariables
>>> #()
```

18.10 About SystemNavigation

SystemNavigation is a facade that supports various useful methods for querying and browsing the source code of the system. SystemNavigation default returns an instance you can use to navigate the system. For example:

```
SystemNavigation default allClassesImplementing: #yourself
>>> an OrderedCollection(Object)
```

The following messages should also be self-explanatory:

```
SystemNavigation default allSentMessages size
>>>43985
```

```
(SystemNavigation default allUnsentMessagesIn: Object selectors) size
>>> 37
```

```
SystemNavigation default allUnimplementedCalls size
>>> 335
```

Note that messages implemented but not sent are not necessarily useless, since they may be sent implicitly (*e.g.*, using perform:). Messages sent but not implemented, however, are more problematic, because the methods sending these messages will fail at execution. They may be a sign of unfinished implementation, obsolete APIs, or missing libraries. They are also frequent in tests about implementation of tools.

Point allCallsOn returns all messages sent explicitly to Point as a receiver.

All these features are integrated into the programming environment of Pharo, in particular the code browsers. As we mentioned before, there are convenient keyboard shortcuts for browsing all implementors (CMD-m) and browsing senders (CMD-n) of a given message. What is perhaps not so well known is that there are many such pre-packaged queries implemented as methods of the SystemNavigation class in the query protocol. For example, you can programmatically browse all implementors of the message ifTrue: by evaluating:

```
SystemNavigation default browseAllImplementorsOf: #ifTrue:
```

Particularly useful are the methods browseAllSelect: and browseMethodsWithSourceString:matchCase:. Here are two different ways to browse all methods in the system that perform super sends (the first way is rather brute force, the second way is better and eliminates some false positives):

```
SystemNavigation default
  browseMethodsWithSourceString: 'super'
  matchCase: true
```

Reflection

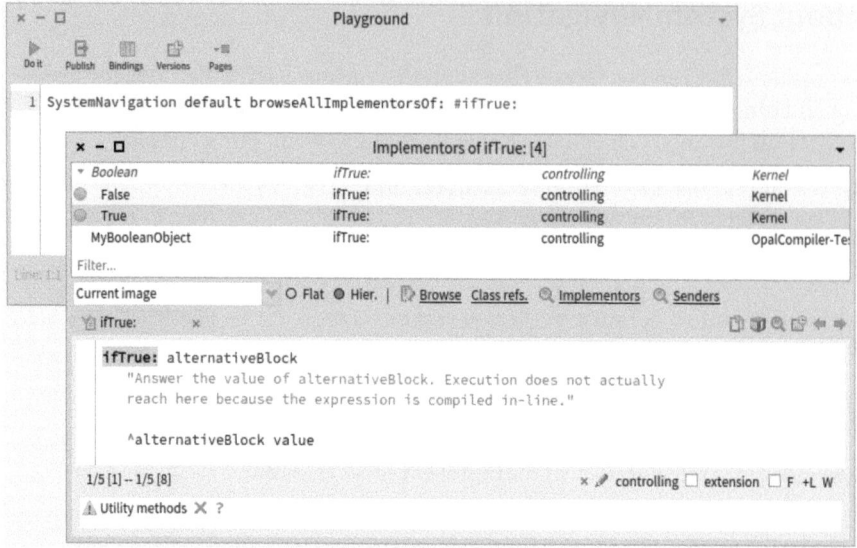

Figure 18-3 Browse all implementations of `ifTrue:`.

```
SystemNavigation default
    browseAllSelect: [:method | method sendsToSuper ]
```

18.11 Classes, method dictionaries, and methods

Since classes are objects, we can inspect or explore them just like any other object.

Evaluate `Point inspect`. In Figure 18-4, the inspector shows the structure of class `Point`. You can see that the class stores its methods in a dictionary, indexing them by their selector. The selector `#*` points to the decompiled bytecode of `Point>>*`.

Let us consider the relationship between classes and methods. In Figure 18-5 we see that classes and metaclasses have the common superclass `Behavior`. This is where `new` is defined, amongst other key methods for classes. Every class has a method dictionary, which maps method selectors to compiled methods. Each compiled method knows the class in which it is installed. In Figure 18-4 we can even see the decompiled bytecodes of the method.

We can exploit the relationships between classes and methods to pose queries about the system. For example, to discover which methods that do not over-

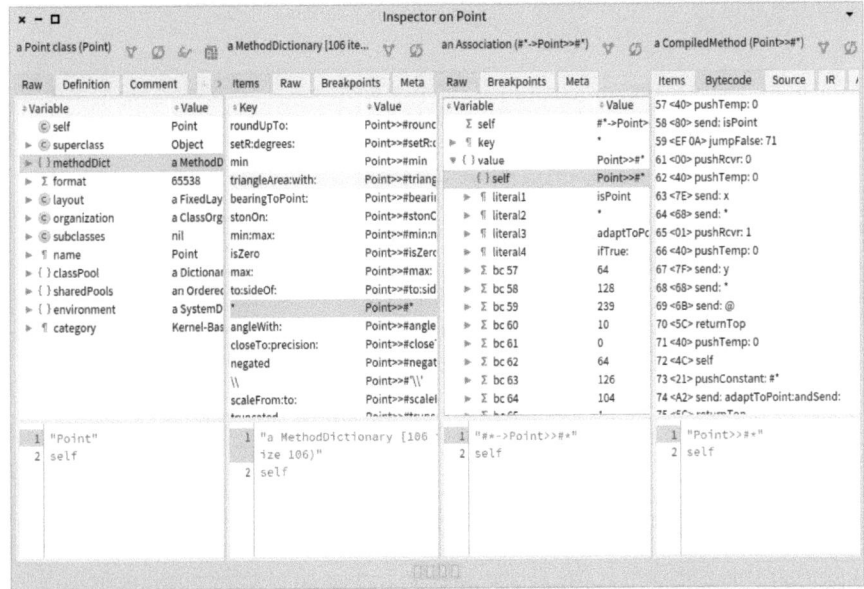

Figure 18-4 Inspector on class Point and the bytecode of its #* method.

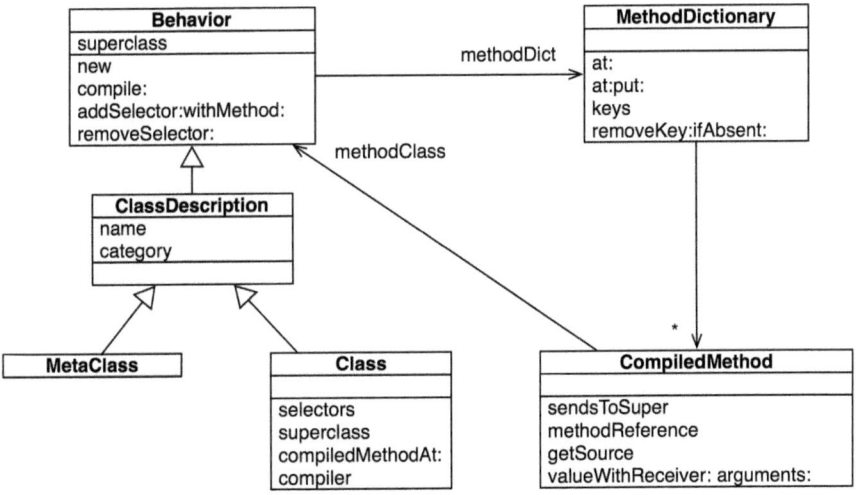

Figure 18-5 Classes, method dictionaries, and compiled methods

ride superclass methods, we can navigate from the class to the method dictionary as follows:

```
| aClass |
aClass := SmallInteger.
aClass methodDict keys select: [ :aMethod |
  (aClass superclass canUnderstand: aMethod) not ]
>>> an IdentitySet(#threeDigitName #printStringBase:nDigits: ...)
```

A compiled method does not simply store the bytecode of a method. It is also an object that provides numerous useful methods for querying the system. One such method is isAbstract (which tells if the method sends subclassResponsibility). We can use it to identify all the abstract methods of a class.

```
| aClass |
aClass := Number.
aClass methodDict keys select: [ :aMethod |
  (aClass>>aMethod) isAbstract ]
>>>   #(#* #asFloat #storeOn:base: #printOn:base: #+ #round: #/ #-
    #adaptToInteger:andSend: #nthRoot: #sqrt #adaptToFraction:andSend: )
```

Note that this code sends the >> message to a class to obtain the compiled method for a given selector.

To browse the super-sends within a given hierarchy, for example within the Collections hierarchy, we can pose a more sophisticated query:

```
class := Collection.
SystemNavigation default
  browseMessageList: (class withAllSubclasses gather: [ :each |
    each methodDict associations
      select: [:assoc | assoc value sendsToSuper ]
      thenCollect: [:assoc | RGMethodDefinition realClass: each
    selector: assoc key]])
  name: 'Supersends of ', class name, ' and its subclasses'
```

Note how we navigate from classes to method dictionaries to compiled methods to identify the methods we are interested in. A RGMethodDefinition is a lightweight proxy for a compiled method that is used by many tools. There is a convenience method CompiledMethod>>methodReference to return the method reference for a compiled method.

```
(Object>>#=) methodReference selector
>>> #=
```

18.12 **Browsing environments**

Although `SystemNavigation` offers some useful ways to programmatically query and browse system code, there are more ways. The Browser, which is integrated into Pharo, allows us to restrict the environment in which a search is to perform.

Suppose we are interested to discover which classes refer to the class `Point` but only in its own package.

Open a browser on the class `Point`. Click on the top level package `Kernel` in the package pane and select `Scoped View` radio button. Browser now shows only the package `Kernel` and all classes within this package (and some classes which have extension methods from this package). Now, in this browser, select again the class `Point`, Action-click on the class name and select `Class refs`. This will show all methods that have references to the class `Point` but only those from the package `Kernel`. Compare this result with the search from a Browser without restricted scope.

This scope is what we call a *Browsing Environment* (class `RBBrowserEnvironment`). All other searches, like *senders of a method* or *implementors of a method* from within this browser are restricted to this environments too.

Browser environments can also be created programmatically. Here, for example, we create a new `RBBrowserEnvironment` for `Collection` and its subclasses, select the super-sending methods, and browse the resulting environment.

```
((RBBrowserEnvironment new forClasses: (Collection withAllSubclasses))
    selectMethods: [:method | method sendsToSuper])
    browse.
```

Note how this is considerably more compact than the earlier, equivalent example using `SystemNavigation`.

Finally, we can find just those methods that send a different super message programmatically as follows:

```
((RBBrowserEnvironment new forClasses: (Collection withAllSubclasses))
    selectMethods: [:method |
        method sendsToSuper
        and: [(method parseTree superMessages includes: method selector)
        not]])
```

Here we ask each compiled method for its (Refactoring Browser) parse tree, to find out whether the super messages differ from the method's selector. Have a look at the `querying` protocol of the class `RBProgramNode` to see some the things we can ask of parse trees.

Reflection

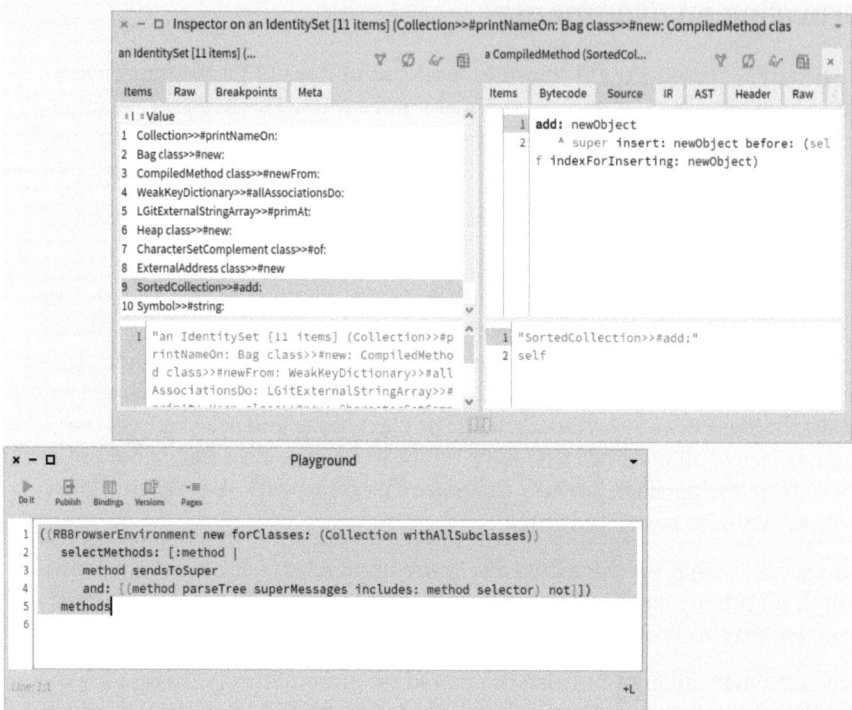

Figure 18-6 Finding methods that send a different super message.

In Figure 18-6 we can see that 10 of such methods have been found within the Collection hierarchy, including Collection>>printNameOn:, which sends super printOn:. Of course, we could also display the results using a message browser but this is another story.

18.13 Pragmas: method annotation

A *pragma* is a method annotation that specifies data about a program, but is not involved in the execution of the program. Pragmas have no direct effect on the operation of the method they annotate. Pragmas have a number of uses, among them:

Information for the compiler: pragmas can be used by the compiler to make a method call a primitive function. This function has to be defined by the virtual machine or by an external plug-in.

Runtime processing: Some pragmas are available to be examined at runtime.

18.13 Pragmas: method annotation

A method may declare one or more pragmas, and the pragmas have to be declared prior any Pharo statement. Internally a pragma is a static message send with literal arguments.

We briefly saw pragmas when we introduced primitives earlier in this chapter. A primitive is nothing more than a pragma declaration. Consider the expression <primitive: 173 error:ec> defined in the Object>>#instVarAt: method. The pragma's selector is primitive:error: and its arguments is an immediate literal value, 173. The variable ec is an error code, filled by the VM in case the execution of the implementation on the VM side failed.

The compiler is probably the bigger user of pragmas. SUnit is another tool that makes use of annotations. SUnit is able to estimate the coverage of an application from a test unit. One may want to exclude some methods from the coverage. This is the case of the documentation method in SplitJointTest class:

```
SplitJointTest class >> documentation
  <ignoreForCoverage>
  "self showDocumentation"

  ^ 'This package provides function.... '
```

By simply annotating a method with the pragma <ignoreForCoverage> one can control the scope of the coverage.

Pragmas are first class objects instances of the class Pragma. A compiled method answers to the message pragmas by returning an array of pragmas.

```
(SplitJoinTest class >> #documentation) pragmas.
>>> an Array(<ignoreForCoverage>)
```

```
(SmallFloat64>>#+) pragmas
>>> an Array(<primitive: 541>)
```

Sending the message allNamed:in: to the class Pragma, we can identify the methods defining a particular pragma. In the following example, the class side of SplitJoinTest contains some methods annotated with <ignoreForCoverage>:

```
Pragma allNamed: #ignoreForCoverage in: SplitJoinTest class
>>> an Array(<ignoreForCoverage> <ignoreForCoverage>)
```

A pragma knows in which method it is defined (using method), the name of the method (selector), the class that contains the method (methodClass), its number of arguments (numArgs), about the literals the pragma has for arguments (hasLiteral: and hasLiteralSuchThat:).

18.14 Accessing the run-time context

We have seen how Pharo's introspective capabilities let us query and explore objects, classes and methods. But what about the run-time environment?

Method contexts

In fact, the run-time context of an executing method is in the virtual machine — it is not in the image at all! On the other hand, the debugger obviously has access to this information, and we can happily explore the run-time context, just like any other object. How is this possible?

Actually, there is nothing magical about the debugger. The secret is the pseudo-variable thisContext, which we have encountered only in passing before. Whenever thisContext is referred to in a running method, the entire run-time context of that method is reified and made available to the image as a series of chained Context objects.

We can easily experiment with this mechanism ourselves.

Change the definition of Integer>>slowFactorial by inserting the expression thisContext inspect. self halt. as shown below:

```
Integer >> slowFactorial
    "Answer the factorial of the receiver."
    self = 0 ifTrue: [thisContext inspect. self halt. ^ 1].
    self > 0 ifTrue: [^ self * (self - 1) slowFactorial].
    self error: 'Not valid for negative integers'
```

Now evaluate 3 slowFactorial in a workspace. You should obtain both a debugger window and an inspector, as shown in Figure 18-7.

Inspecting thisContext gives you full access to the current execution context, the stack, the local temporaries and arguments, the senders chain and the receiver. Welcome to the poor man's debugger! If you now browse the class of the explored object (*i.e.*, by evaluating self browse in the bottom pane of the inspector) you will discover that it is an instance of the class Context, as is each sender in the chain.

thisContext is not intended to be used for day-to-day programming, but it is essential for implementing tools like debuggers, and for accessing information about the call stack. You can evaluate the following expression to discover which methods make use of thisContext:

```
SystemNavigation default browseMethodsWithSourceString: 'thisContext'
    matchCase: true
```

As it turns out, one of the most common applications is to discover the sender of a message. A typical application consists of providing better information to

18.15 Intelligent contextual breakpoints

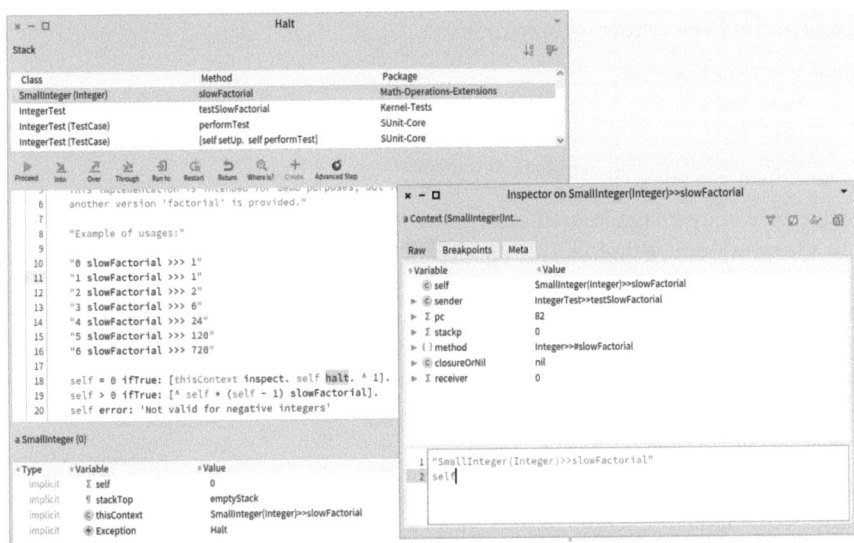

Figure 18-7 Inspecting `thisContext`.

the developer. Let us take an example, by convention, methods that send `self subclassResponsibility` are considered to be abstract. But how does `Object>>subclassResponsibility` provide a useful error message indicating which abstract method has been invoked? Very simply, by asking `thisContext` for the sender.

```
subclassResponsibility
  "This message sets up a framework for the behavior of the class'
    subclasses.
  Announce that the subclass should have implemented this message."

  SubclassResponsibility signalFor: thisContext sender selector
```

18.15 Intelligent contextual breakpoints

The Pharo way to set a breakpoint is to evaluate `self halt` at an interesting point in a method. This will cause `thisContext` to be reified, and a debugger window will open at the breakpoint. Unfortunately this poses problems for methods that are intensively used in the system.

Suppose, for instance, that we want to explore the execution of `Morph>>openInWorld`. Setting a breakpoint in this method is problematic.

Pay attention the following experiment will break everything! Take a *fresh* image and set the following breakpoint:

```
Morph >> openInWorld
    "Add this morph to the world."
    self halt.
    self openInWorld: self currentWorld
```

Notice how your image immediately freezes as soon as you try to open any new Morph (Menu/Window/...)! We do not even get a debugger window. The problem is clear once we understand that 1) `Morph>>openInWorld` is used by many parts of the system, so the breakpoint is triggered very soon after we interact with the user interface, but 2) *the debugger itself* sends `openInWorld` as soon as it opens a window, preventing the debugger from opening! What we need is a way to *conditionally halt* only if we are in a context of interest. This is exactly what `Object>>haltIf:` offers.

Suppose now that we only want to halt if `openInWorld` is sent from, say, the context of `MorphTest>>testOpenInWorld`.

Fire up a fresh image again, and set the following breakpoint:

```
Morph >> openInWorld
    "Add this morph to the world."
    self haltIf: #testOpenInWorld.
    self openInWorld: self currentWorld
```

This time the image does not freeze. Try running the `MorphTest`. It will halt and open a debugger.

```
MorphTest run: #testOpenInWorld.
```

How does this work? Let's have a look at `Object>>haltIf:`. It first calls `if:` with the condition to the `Exception` class `Halt`. This method itself checks if the condition is a symbol, which is true and calls `haltIf-CallChain:contains:`

```
Object >> haltIf: condition
  <debuggerCompleteToSender>
  Halt if: condition.
```

```
Halt class >> haltIfCallChain: haltSenderContext contains: aSelector
  | cntxt |
  cntxt := haltSenderContext.
  [ cntxt isNil ] whileFalse: [
    cntxt selector = aSelector ifTrue: [ self signalIn:
    haltSenderContext ].
    cntxt := cntxt sender ]
```

Starting from `thisContext`, `haltIfCallChainContains:` goes up through the execution stack, checking if the name of the calling method is the same as the one passed as parameter. If this is the case, then it signals itself, the exception which, by default, summons the debugger.

It is also possible to supply a boolean or a boolean block as an argument to `haltIf:`, but these cases are straightforward and do not make use of `thisContext`.

18.16 Intercepting not understood messages

So far we have used Pharo's reflective features mainly to query and explore objects, classes, methods and the run-time stack. Now we will look at how to use our knowledge of its system structure to intercept messages and modify behaviour at run time.

When an object receives a message, it first looks in the method dictionary of its class for a corresponding method to respond to the message. If no such method exists, it will continue looking up the class hierarchy, until it reaches `Object`. If still no method is found for that message, the object will *send itself* the message `doesNotUnderstand:` with the message selector as its argument. The process then starts all over again, until `Object>>doesNotUnderstand:` is found, and the debugger is launched.

But what if `doesNotUnderstand:` is overridden by one of the subclasses of `Object` in the lookup path? As it turns out, this is a convenient way of realizing certain kinds of very dynamic behaviour. An object that does not understand a message can, by overriding `doesNotUnderstand:`, fall back to an alternative strategy for responding to that message.

Two very common applications of this technique are 1) to implement lightweight proxies for objects, and 2) to dynamically compile or load missing code. This is what we will describe in the following sections.

18.17 Lightweight proxies

To implement lightweight proxies, we introduce a *minimal object* to act as a proxy for an existing object. Since the proxy will implement virtually no methods of its own, any message sent to it will be trapped by `doesNotUnderstand:`. By implementing this message, the proxy can then take special action before delegating the message to the real subject it is the proxy for.

Let us have a look at how this may be implemented. We define a `LoggingProxy` as follows:

```
ProtoObject subclass: #LoggingProxy
  instanceVariableNames: 'subject invocationCount'
  classVariableNames: ''
  package: 'PBE-Reflection'
```

Note that we subclass `ProtoObject` rather than `Object` because we do not want our proxy to inherit around 450 methods (!) from `Object`.

```
Object methodDict size
>>> 479
```

Our proxy has two instance variables: the `subject` it is a proxy for, and a count of the number of messages it has intercepted. We initialize the two instance variables and we provide an accessor for the message count. Initially the `subject` variable points to the proxy object itself.

```
LoggingProxy >> initialize
  invocationCount := 0.
  subject := self.
```

```
LoggingProxy >> invocationCount
  ^ invocationCount
```

We simply intercept all messages not understood, print them to the Transcript, update the message count, and forward the message to the real subject.

```
LoggingProxy >> doesNotUnderstand: aMessage
  Transcript show: 'performing ', aMessage printString; cr.
  invocationCount := invocationCount + 1.
  ^ aMessage sendTo: subject
```

Here comes a bit of magic. We create a new `Point` object and a new `LoggingProxy` object, and then we tell the proxy to `become:` the point object:

```
point := 1@2.
LoggingProxy new become: point.
```

This expression has the effect of swapping all the references to the object pointed by the variable `point` to the proxy instance and (vice versa). Most importantly, the proxy's `subject` instance variable will now refer to the point!

```
point invocationCount
>>> 0
```

```
point + (3@4)
>>> 4@6
```

```
point invocationCount
>>> 1
```

18.17 Lightweight proxies

This works nicely in most cases, but there are some shortcomings:

```
point class
>>> LoggingProxy
```

Actually the method class is implemented in ProtoObject, but even if it were implemented in Object, which LoggingProxy does not inherit from, it isn't actually send to the LoggingProxy or its subject. The message is directly answered by the virtual machine. yourself is also never truly sent.

Other messages that may be directly interpreted by the VM, depending on the receiver, include:

```
+ - < > <= >= = ~= * / \\ =\=
@ bitShift: // bitAnd: bitOr:
at: at:put: size
next nextPut: atEnd
blockCopy: value value: do: new new: x y
```

Selectors that are never sent, because they are inlined by the compiler and transformed to comparison and jump bytecodes:

```
ifTrue: ifFalse: ifTrue:ifFalse: ifFalse:ifTrue:
and: or:
whileFalse: whileTrue: whileFalse whileTrue
to:do: to:by:do:
caseOf: caseOf:otherwise:
ifNil: ifNotNil:  ifNil:ifNotNil: ifNotNil:ifNil:
```

Attempts to send these messages to non-boolean normally results in an exception from the VM as it can not use the inlined dispatching for non-boolean receivers. You can intercept this and define the proper behavior by overriding mustBeBoolean in the receiver or by catching the NonBooleanReceiver exception.

Even if we can ignore such special message sends, there is another fundamental problem which cannot be overcome by this approach: self-sends cannot be intercepted:

```
point := 1@2.
LoggingProxy new become: point.
point invocationCount
>>> 0
```

```
point rectangle: (3@4)
>>> 1@2 corner: 3@4
```

```
point invocationCount
>>> 1
```

Our proxy has been cheated out of two self-sends in the rectangle: method:

293

```
Point >> rectangle: aPoint
  "Answer a Rectangle that encompasses the receiver and aPoint.
  This is the most general infix way to create a rectangle."

  ^ Rectangle
      point: self
      point: aPoint
```

Although messages can be intercepted by proxies using this technique, one should be aware of the inherent limitations of using a proxy. In Section 18.19 we will see another, more general approach for intercepting messages.

18.18 Generating missing methods

The other most common application of intercepting not understood messages is to dynamically load or generate missing methods. Consider a very large library of classes with many methods. Instead of loading the entire library, we could load a stub for each class in the library. The stubs know where to find the source code of all their methods. The stubs simply trap all messages not understood, and dynamically creates the missing methods on demand. At some point, this behaviour can be deactivated, and the loaded code can be saved as the minimal necessary subset for the client application.

Let us look at a simple variant of this technique where we have a class that automatically adds accessors for its instance variables on demand. Here is the logic: Any message not understood will be trapped. If an instance variable with the same name as the message sent exists, then we ask our class to compile an accessor for that instance variables and we re-send the message.

```
Object subclass: #DynamicAccessors
  instanceVariableNames: 'x'
  classVariableNames: ''
  package: 'PBE-Reflection'
```

```
DynamicAcccessors >> doesNotUnderstand: aMessage
  | messageName |
  messageName := aMessage selector asString.
  (self class instVarNames includes: messageName)
    ifTrue: [
      self class compile: messageName, String cr, ' ^ ', messageName.
      ^ aMessage sendTo: self ].
  ^ super doesNotUnderstand: aMessage
```

Suppose the class DynamicAccessors has an instance variable x but no predefined accessor. Then the following will generate the accessor dynamically and retrieve the value:

18.18 Generating missing methods

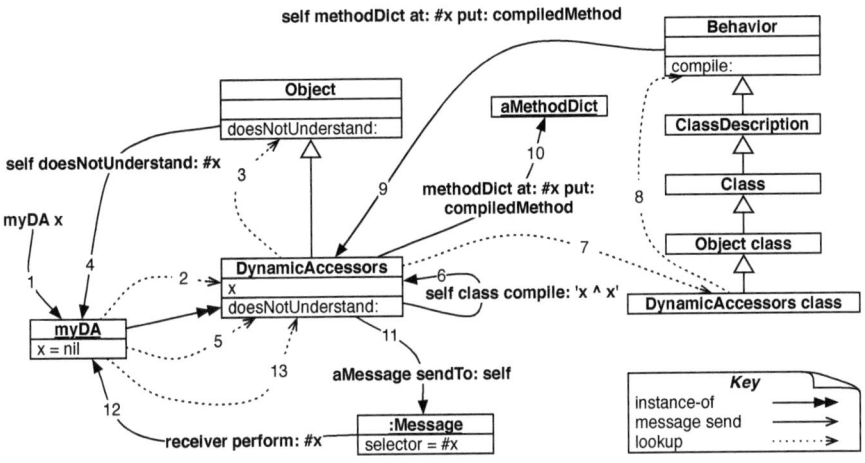

Figure 18-8 Dynamically creating accessors.

```
myDA := DynamicAccessors new.
myDA x
>>> nil
```

Let us step through what happens the first time the message x is sent to our object (see Figure 18-8).

(1) We send x to myDA, (2) the message is looked up in the class, and (3) not found in the class hierarchy. (4) This causes self doesNotUnderstand: #x to be sent back to the object, (5) triggering a new lookup. This time doesNotUnderstand: is found immediately in DynamicAccessors, (6) which asks its class to compile the string 'x ^ x'. The compile method is looked up (7), and (8) finally found in Behavior, which (9-10) adds the new compiled method to the method dictionary of DynamicAccessors. Finally, (11-13) the message is resent (using the message sendTo:), and this time it is found.

In case the original message sent does not correspond to and instance variables, the default behavior of doesNotUnderstand: is invoked using super.

The same technique can be used to generate setters for instance variables, or other kinds of boilerplate code, such as visiting methods for a Visitor.

About the message sendTo:.

The method sendTo: on the class Message is implemented as follows:

```
Message >> sendTo: receiver
  "answer the result of sending this message to receiver"

  ^ receiver perform: selector withArguments: args
```

The method `Object>>perform:` can be used to send messages that are composed at run-time:

```
5 perform: #factorial
>>> 120
```
```
6 perform: ('fac', 'torial') asSymbol
>>> 720
```
```
4 perform: #max: withArguments: (Array with: 6)
>>> 6
```

18.19 Objects as method wrappers

We have already seen that compiled methods are objects in Pharo, and they support a number of methods that allow the programmer to query the runtime system.

What is perhaps a bit more surprising, is that *any object* can play the role of a compiled method, and be placed inside a method dictionary. All such an object has to do is respond to the message `run:with:in:` and a few other important messages. Using this mechanism we can build other spying tools. Here is the principle: we create objects that refer to original method to execute them, but replace the methods in a method dictionary by such objects (called method wrappers). This way can log if a method has been executed and the number of times it was executed.

We will play with the principle of method wrappers. Pharo comes with a simple class named `ObjectsAsMethodsExample` to illustrate this principle.

Define an empty class `Demo`. Evaluate `Demo new answer42` and notice how the usual *Message Not Understood* error is raised.

```
Object subclass: #Demo
  instanceVariableNames: ''
  classVariableNames: ''
  package: 'PBE-Reflection'
```
```
Demo new answer42
```

Now we will install a plain object in the method dictionary of our `Demo` class.

```
Demo methodDict
  at: #answer42
  put: ObjectsAsMethodsExample new
```

Now try again to print the result of Demo new answer42. This time we get the answer 42.

```
Demo new answer42
>>> 42
```

If we take look at the class ObjectsAsMethodsExample we will find the following methods:

```
ObjectsAsMethodsExample >> run: oldSelector with: arguments in:
    aReceiver
  ^ self perform: oldSelector withArguments: arguments
```

```
ObjectsAsMethodsExample >> answer42
  ^ 42
```

When our Demo instance receives the message answer42, method lookup proceeds as usual, however the virtual machine will detect that in place of a compiled method, an ordinary Pharo object is trying to play this role. The VM will then send this object a new message run:with:in: with the original method selector, arguments and receiver as arguments. Since ObjectsAsMethodsExample implements this method, it intercepts the message and delegates it to itself.

We can remove the fake method as follows:

```
Demo methodDict removeKey: #answer42 ifAbsent: []
```

If we take a closer look at ObjectsAsMethodsExample, we will see that its superclass also implements some methods like flushcache, methodClass: and selector:, but they are all empty. These messages may be sent to a compiled method, so they need to be implemented by an object pretending to be a compiled method. flushcache is the most important method to be implemented; others may be required by some tools and depending on whether the method is installed using Behavior>>addSelector:withMethod: or directly using MethodDictionary>>at:put:.

Now for serious use of the idea presented in this section, we strongly suggest to use the library named MethodProxies and available on the http://github.com/pharo-contributions/MethodProxies since it is a lot more robust and safer.

18.20 Chapter summary

Reflection refers to the ability to query, examine and even modify the metaobjects of the runtime system as ordinary objects.

- The Inspector uses instVarAt: and related methods to view *private* instance variables of objects.

- The method `Behavior>>allInstances` query instances of a class.
- The messages `class`, `isKindOf:`, `respondsTo:` etc. are useful for gathering metrics or building development tools, but they should be avoided in regular applications: they violate the encapsulation of objects and make your code harder to understand and maintain.
- `SystemNavigation` is a utility class holding many useful queries for navigation and browsing the class hierarchy. For example, use `SystemNavigation default browseMethodsWithSourceString: 'pharo' matchCase:true.` to find and browse all methods with a given source string. (Slow, but thorough!)
- Every Pharo class points to an instance of `MethodDictionary` which maps selectors to instances of `CompiledMethod`. A compiled method knows its class, closing the loop.
- `RGMethodDefinition` is a lightweight proxy for a compiled method, providing additional convenience methods, and used by many Pharo tools.
- `RBBrowserEnvironment`, part of the Refactoring Browser infrastructure, offers a more refined interface than `SystemNavigation` for querying the system, since the result of a query can be used as a the scope of a new query. Both GUI and programmatic interfaces are available.
- `thisContext` is a pseudo-variable that reifies the runtime stack of the virtual machine. It is mainly used by the debugger to dynamically construct an interactive view of the stack. It is also especially useful for dynamically determining the sender of a message.
- Contextual breakpoints can be set using `haltIf:`, taking a method selector as its argument. `haltIf:` halts only if the named method occurs as a sender in the run-time stack.
- A common way to intercept messages sent to a given target is to use a *minimal object* as a proxy for that target. The proxy implements as few methods as possible, and traps all message sends by implementing `doesNotUnderstand:`. It can then perform some additional action and then forward the message to the original target.
- Send `become:` to swap the references of two objects, such as a proxy and its target.
- Beware, some messages, like `class` and `yourself` are never really sent, but are interpreted by the VM. Others, like `+`, `-` and `ifTrue:` may be directly interpreted or inlined by the VM depending on the receiver.

18.20 Chapter summary

- Another typical use for overriding `doesNotUnderstand:` is to lazily load or compile missing methods. `doesNotUnderstand:` cannot trap self-sends.